SECRETS

OF

COOKING

ARMENIAN / LEBANESE / PERSIAN

SECRETS
OF
COOKING

ARMENIAN / LEBANESE / PERSIAN

Photographs by Rene Chirinian
Designed by Ryuichi Minakawa

LIONHART INC. / PUBLISHERS CONNECTICUT

To my husband Rene,
and my sons Richard and Alfred
who appreciate good eating

Published by Lionhart Inc./ Publishers
440 Canoe Hill Road, New Canaan, Connecticut

Manufactured in Japan
Typeset in United States of America by Voskedar

Library of Congress Cataloging in Publication Data

Secrets of Cooking
Armenian/Lebanese/Persian

Linda Chirinian

Includes index.

ISBN   0-9617033-0-X

10 9 8 7 6 5 4 3 2
Second Edition

Symbols

Armenian

Lebanese

Persian

Contents

6

7

Introduction

SECOND EDITION

"Cookery is become an art,
a noble science;
cooks are gentlemen".
     Robert Burton, 1577-1640

The publication of Secrets of Cooking has been a stimulating experience for me. With thousands of cook books already on the booksellers' shelves, I was apprehensive about expecting anything more than a casual interest when I decided to go ahead with the project. But, I am delighted that *Secrets of Cooking* had an overwelming reception not only in the U.S. and Canada, but also overseas, even in the far corners of the world like Kashmir, Singapore, and Japan.

With the initial printing already exhausted, the continuing demand for the book clearly indicated the need for a second printing, which gave me the opportunity to make a few revisions based on the suggestions of my readers. Remembering the popular adage "if it ain't broke, don't fix it," the contents and design remain intact, except for certain minor changes.

Keeping up with the demands of the inquisitive *Secrets of Cooking* continues to be as much of a challenge as writing it. Despite my twenty years of watching and learning experience in the setting where most of these dishes were originated, I continue to discover new, alluring, and exciting recipes.

For the cautious and the conservative cook, the Armenian, Lebanese and Persian meals may, on the outset, seem time-consuming and difficult to prepare. They shouldn't be. *Secrets of Cooking* was inspired by and designed for people who were discouraged from preparing these tasteful, authentic dishes who needed a simple, step by step approach to creating original meals without disappointment. It pleases me to know that *Secrets of Cooking* has proven valuable for those who took the initiative to follow the exact instructions to end up with delicious results. The only time these recipes will call for personal judgement is in applying spices and flavorings, which of course depend on individual taste. The measurements I have given are mere guidelines.

In selecting the recipes for *Secrets of Cooking*, special attention was given to the benefits of eating simple, basic, naturally healthy foods, as well as keeping in mind on-going dietary changes by recommending fresh and natural ingredients readily available everywhere. When applicable, I have used the revolutionary food processor as a practical time-saving device.

The three countries represented here -Armenia, Lebanon, and Iran- belong to the world's most ancient civilization. They are part of a dozen or so countries in the Middle East, a term that should probably be redefined for the 1990s. The majority of the countries in the area belong to the Arab World which excludes Israel, Iran, Turkey, and Cyprus. While they all share environmental and physical characteristics, and comparable social and cultural lifestyles, each offers a distinct culinary adventure. The history of the region dates back three or four centuries before Christ, during which the prolonged periods of social and cultural interactivity has made it impossible to appropriately trace the origin of each dish.

Armenia does not fall in the Middle East territory, but the pogroms of 1915 forced thousands of Armenians to flee their homeland and find shelter in the region, eventually becoming a significant element of local communities. As English historian Arnold J. Toynbee points out, the Armenians are perhaps the oldest established civilized race in Western Asia. They emerged as a nation in the sixth century, B.C., and they are still going strong while most of their contemporaries have disappeared. Armenians were the first in the world to adopt Christianity as their national religion. They are also credited for forging bronze, inventing the wheel, and cultivating grapes. Identified as Indo-Europeans, they migrated from Europe by way of Asia Minor and settled in a land inhabited by Urartuians, a highly civilized society whose scientific successes in agriculture, metallurgy, horticulture, and animal husbandry have impacted their character.

Today, over half of the world's approximately seven million Armenians live in Armenia, which is only a fraction of the historic territory that reached from the Caspian and Black sea to the Mediterranean. When the first edition of *Secrets of Cooking* appeared, Armenia was one of the 15 republics of the former Soviet Union, now restructured as the Commonwealth of Independent States. Armenia declared independence at the end of 1991 and was renamed the Republic of Armenia. Its language, a branch of the Indo-European family, is recognized for its pure and extremely precise diction. The artistic, educational, scientific and technological contributions of Armenians far outweigh their current geo-political status. The Armenian church, with its religious center in Etchmiadzin, near the capital of Armenia, enjoys considerable power and influence on its people in the homeland as well as in the diaspora. Many of the colorful cuisines of *Secrets of Cooking* originated and matured in Constantinople (Istanbul), where Armenians had a viable community life with their own churches and schools during the Byzantine period.

Lebanon, that small mountainous land of milk and honey, is blessed with the magical touch of the Mediterranean sea. During the civil war, lasting over 15 years, the country was off-limits for those who have regularly enjoyed its gentle climate and hospitality. The new Lebanon is on the mend and no doubt it will regain its old stature as the hub of the Middle East. Most Lebanese preferred living on the coast and the immediate foothills in the midst of the historical sites ranging from Neolithic, Phoenician, Greco-Roman, to early Arab, Crusador, and Ottoman.

Unlike the rest of the population in the Arab world, the Lebanese claim equal representation of Moslems and Christians governing the country. It is significant that within this tiny land there are at least 17 recognized sects, each with its own code of family and personal law. The essence of the political and social life of the country is its religious diversity. The Constitution clearly specifies the distribution of seats in the Parliament by representatives of each recognized sect.

Lebanon has diversified and sophisticated agricultural products. Orchards, fruit and vegetable crops, olive groves, peaches, apples, and pear plantations are found everywhere. Almost every type of vegetable is grown in Bekaa Valley which is also famous for its onions, carrots, melons, chick-peas, and a variety of beans.

For thousands of years, Lebanon as well as Syria have played a crucial role in shaping the history of the Middle East. The rich and fertile soil has given them an abundant supply of ingredients to prepare unique dishes with exquisite flavors. The famous tabouleh, a combination of parsley and bulgur (cracked wheat) salad, the kibbehs, a mixture of bulgur with lamb, are characteristic dishes with unique tastes. Moreover, the gracious hospitality of the native provides ideal combination for sumptuous eating.

Iran until 1935 was known as Persia; the two names are synonymous. The people of Iran (meaning the homeland of the Aryans) moved into the region from the steppes of Central Asia around 900 B.C. They are Moslems and relatively few minority groups live in the country, which is slightly larger than the state of Alaska. The official language is Farsi (Persian).

The high mountain ranges of Iran leave very little land area for cultivation. Despite the scanty rainfall, however, it still produces fruits of exceptional flavor- i.e., apricots, plums, cherries, peaches, apples, and kumquats. Iranians love bread. Flat, round loaves are standard, but bakers often specialize in elaborate shapes. The well known breads of Iran are Barbari, Taftoon, and Sangak.

The Persian New Year, No Rooz, is one of the most joyous occasions celebrating the first day of Spring, March 21. It signifies the beginning of a new life, for which preparations begin well in advance. Each household plants seeds of wheat or lentils in a shallow bowl, which grow a cluster of fresh grass shoot in time for the festivities. It continues for 13 days, and the last day is spent on picnic grounds around the majestic mountains and parks, feasting on food prepared for the occasion.

The last Wednesday of the old year is called Chahr Shambeh Suri, a day for a special festival. Each family gathers bundles of dry wood or desert thorn for a bonfire and festivities, after which the ashes are scattered at a crossroad.

Iran's geographical position as the crossroads of trade and migration routes has contributed to its cuisine. A famous Iranian meal is chelo kabob, a simple dish, yet its preparation requires special care. Another popular dish is Persian khoresht (stew), a combination of meat or poultry with herbs, spices, vegetables or fruits; it is always served with rice. Fish, an important source of protein, is especially popular in coastal regions.

The 17th century English clergyman and scholar Robert Burton, whose quotation appears at the beginning, considered cooking a form of art, a thought that has not changed much over the centuries. Craig Claiborne, a contemporary author of cookbooks, raised the same thoughts when he wrote, "Most people who write seriously about food seem to do it with genuine passion. This feeling comes not from gluttony but from an appreciation of the preparation and consumption of food as an art form."

I find cooking exciting, and hope you will too.

New Canaan, Conn.

CHAPTER ONE

Mezas

Meza is the Arabic word used to describe hors d'oeuvres or appetizers. A meza consists of delicious tidbits served before the main course. They may be presented hot or cold in large or small quantities, depending on the occasion. In the summer months a meza can be a main meal when it's too hot to eat anything heavy. There are many ways a Meza can be presented. It can be passed on trays as a finger food, placed attractively on a cocktail table for casual entertaining or elaborately served on a buffet table. Arak, an anise flavored liquor made from grapes, is traditionally served to help prepare the palate for the courses to follow.

An interesting assortment of mezas consists of very simple dishes such as roasted pumpkin, sunflower or watermelon seeds, cucumbers peeled and sliced lengthwise, sunripened tomatoes, cut in wedges sprinkled with oregano, mint and salt, and assortment of cheeses and spiced olives.

There is an Arabic saying when planning your dinner light mezas should be followed by a heavy meal and heavy mezas should be followed by a light meal.

13

A very unusual looking and tasting appetizer specially when served on crunchy cucumber slices. The important ingredients in this recipe are red pepper paste, cumin, and walnuts. They provide and exotic taste that is very popular in Syria and Lebanon.

Red Pepper and Walnut Spread

Red Pepper and Walnut Spread
MOUHAMARA

PREPARATION TIME: 15 MINUTES

> 2 cups chopped walnuts
> 1/3 cup fresh bread crumbs
> 1/2 cup olive oil
> 2 tablespoons finely chopped onion
> 1 tablespoon pomegranate molasses *
> 1 to 1 1/2 teaspoons cumin
> 4 to 5 tablespoons Red

> Pepper Paste, (page 256)*
> 1/4 teaspoon sugar
> Salt to taste
> Cayenne to taste
> 1 tablespoon pine nuts to garnish (optional)
> Cucumber slices, cocktail bread, crackers, or crudites to serve.

1. Place walnuts, bread crumbs, olive oil, onion, pomegranate molasses, cumin, red pepper paste, sugar, salt, and cayenne in container of food processor. Turn on-off to mix well (do not puree mixture, it should have coarse texture).

2. Spread on serving dish and garnish with pine nuts. Sprinkle lightly with extra oil, if desired. Serve with crunchy cucumber slices, bread, crackers, or crudites.

MAKES 2 CUPS

* *Red pepper paste and pomegranate molasses are available in Middle Eastern speciality stores.*

Fool is a Middle Eastern peasant dish and each country has its own variation. This is the Lebanese version, Egyptians add quartered hard-cooked eggs to the mixture and omit chick-peas. They call it Ful Medamis, and cook it very slowly in a special pot, and serve it at any meal. Fava beans are high in protein and inexpensive as well.

Simmered Fava Bean
FOOL

PREPARATION TIME: 15 MINUTES (plus soaking of beans)
COOKING TIME: 1 1/2 HOURS

Simmered Fava Bean

1 cup small dry fava beans, picked over
1/3 cup dry chick-peas, picked over
1/4 to 1/2 cup lemon juice
1/4 cup olive oil
3 cloves garlic, crushed
1/2 teaspoon cumin

1/2 teaspoon allspice
1/4 teaspoon paprika
Dash cayenne
Salt and freshly ground pepper to taste
Pita bread, cheese, olives, and chopped tomatoes to serve

1. Place fava beans and chick-peas in large saucepan. Cover with enough water to come 3-inches above beans. Bring to a boil, cover, reduce heat, and simmer 1 1/2 hours, or until beans are tender. Add additional water if necessary.

2. Strain cooking liquid into bowl and set aside. Place beans in large bowl. Add lemon juice, olive oil, garlic, cumin, allspice, paprika, cayenne, salt and pepper. Stir gently. Add about 1/2 cup reserved cooking liquid, mix, and adjust seasoning. Spoon into bowls and serve.

SERVES 4 TO 6

SERVING SUGGESTION: Make a beautiful arrangement of chopped parsley, green and red peppers, scallions or onions, fresh sprigs of mint and extra lemon juice, olive oil, and cayenne to surround the fool. These garnishes can be added to the mixture or eaten as an accompaniment.

ALTERNATIVE COOKING METHOD: Place fava beans and chick-peas in pressure cooker. Cover with enough water to come 2-inches above beans. Cook over high heat until whistles. Reduce heat to low and cook 40 minutes. Proceed as directed above.

A very popular, easy to make, delicious spread served throughout the Middle East. It can be served as a dip with wedges of pita bread or crudites, and goes well with broiled or grilled meat or chicken kabobs.

Chick-Pea Sesame Seed Puree
HUMMUS BI TAHINI

PREPARATION TIME: 15 MINUTES

2 to 3 cloves garlic, peeled and hard tip removed
2 cups cooked chick-peas
1/3 cup tahini (sesame seed paste)
1 teaspoon salt, or to taste
3 tablespoons olive oil (preferably virgin)

1/3 cup lemon juice
Paprika and freshly chopped parsley to garnish
Pita bread and crudites to serve

1. Place steel blade in work bowl of food processor. Turn motor on and drop garlic cloves, one at a time, through feed tube. Stop motor and remove cover. Set aside 9 chick-peas for decoration. Add remaining chick-peas, tahini, and salt. Cover and process a few seconds. Add oil and lemon juice through feed tube with motor running. Process until smooth, scraping down sides of bowl as needed. Adjust seasoning.

2. Spread on serving platter. Place 3 reserved chick-peas in center of platter and 3 on each side of platter. Sprinkle with paprika and garnish with chopped parsley. Additional olive oil can be poured over Hummus when served, if desired. Serve with pita bread (khoubis) or crudites.

MAKES 2 CUPS

HINTS: If Hummus is too thick, add a few tablespoons of water and blend thoroughly. Add a dash of sour salt (citric acid) with lemon juice to make it more tart. Mix tahini thoroughly before using to incorporate oil that separates during storage. If desired, cover Hummus and store in refrigerator up to 1 week.

Chick-Pea Sesame Seed Puree

T hese spicy, meat-balls are thinly sliced after cooking and serv-ed as an appetizer or "meza."

Beef Rounds
MORTADEL

PREPARATION TIME: 20 MINUTES
COOKING TIME: 40 MINUTES

2 pounds boneless sirloin or
  top round of beef
1 teaspoon crushed garlic
3/4 teaspoon allspice
1/2 teaspoon freshly ground
  pepper
1/4 teaspoon cayenne or to
  taste
1 teaspoon cinnamon

1 teaspoon salt or to taste
6 hard-cooked eggs, or 1/4
  cup whole pine nuts and
  1/4 cup pistachios, or
  twelve 3-inch long,
  cooked carrot sticks for
  filling
2 tablespoons vegetable oil
1/2 cup red wine vinegar
  Parsley leaves to garnish

1. Cut meat into small pieces and place in container of food processer. Process until almost the consistency of paste. Add garlic, 1/2 teaspoon allspice, 1/4 teaspoon pepper, cayenne, cinnamon, and salt. Process just until well mixed.

2. Shape mixture into 6 equal-size balls. Place hard-cooked egg, or pine nuts, and pistachios, or carrot sticks in center of each meatball. Reshape into cylinders and set aside.

3. Heat oil in skillet over medium-heat. Cook mortadel about 15 minutes, or until browned on all sides, turning often.

4. Sprinkle with remaining 1/4 teaspoon allspice and 1/4 teaspoon pepper. Add vinegar, cover, and cook over low heat 20 minutes. Set aside until completely cooled.

5. Slice and arrange on platter in overlapping pattern. Garnish with parsley leaves. Serve with drinks or as a first course with pickles, radishes, and olives.

SERVES 10 TO 12

HINTS: Cool, wrap in aluminum foil, and refrigerate or freeze. Do not freeze egg stuffed Mortadels because the hard-cooked eggs will pull away from the meatball and crumbles when sliced. Raw Mortadels can be brushed with lightly beaten egg white before cooking to give a slight shine.

Beef Rounds

Yogurt Cheese

L abni is made by draining yogurt and can be substituted for sour cream. If it is drained for 1 to 2 days, it will resemble cream cheese and can be used interchangeably. It is simple to make, low in fat content, and delicious. A favorite in Lebanon and is used in many recipes. Serve it for breakfast with olives on pita or toasted bread.

Yogurt Cheese
LABNI

PREPARATION TIME: 10 HOURS

2 *containers (16 ounces each) plain yogurt*	*Dried crushed mint and olive oil to garnish*
1/4 *teaspoon salt or to taste*	*Pita bread to serve*

1. Mix yogurt and salt. Line colander with a new handiwipe. Spoon yogurt onto cloth and place colander over large bowl.

2. Refrigerate, uncovered, 10 hours. Drain bowl at least once. During the refrigeration scrape down sides of yogurt with spatula, and stir mixture once or twice.

3. Spoon into bowl, cover, and store in refrigerator.

4. To serve, spread yogurt cheese onto shallow serving dish, sprinkle top with mint, and drizzle with olive oil. Serve with pita bread. It's delicious spread on toast with jam or served as a dip with crudites.

MAKES 2 1/2 CUPS

VARIATION: CHEESE BALLS IN OIL: (Labni Makbous): Drain Labni 13 hours until very thick. Add 1 teaspoon salt and mix well. Place several thicknesses of paper towel on large dish to absorb moisture. Place mixture on paper towels by teaspoonfulls and place in refrigerator until firm, 10 to 12 hours. Shape into round balls and place in glass jar. Fill jar with olive oil. Cover and store at room temperature up to 1 week, or refrigerate up to 1 month. To serve, spoon into serving dish and top with oil. Serve with toast or crackers.

Another variation is to mix 1 teaspoon crushed mint or thyme into mixture before shaping balls. Alternatively, roll balls in dried mint or thyme before adding oil to jar.

Stuffed Grape Leaves
TZITAYOUGHOV DEREVI PATOOG

PREPARATION TIME: 1 HOUR
COOKING TIME: 1 HOUR

1 jar (16 ounces) grape leaves

FILLING:
- 1 1/2 cups short-grain rice
- 2 1/2 cups chopped onions
- 2 tomatoes, seeded and chopped
- 1 large green pepper, seeded and chopped
- 2 cups freshly chopped parsley, stems reserved
- 1 cup freshly chopped mint or 2 1/2 tablespoons dried crushed mint
- 2 tablespoons tomato paste
- 1/4 teaspoon cayenne or to taste
- 1 tablespoon allspice
  Salt and freshly ground pepper to taste
- 3/4 to 1 cup lemon juice
- 1/2 cup olive oil
- 1/4 cup pine nuts

TO COOK:
- 1/2 cup lemon juice
- 1/4 cup olive oil
  lemon slices to garnish

This pungent recipe was given to me by my mother-in-law. The combined aroma of tangy lemon, grape leaves, and spices are mouth watering. This is a large recipe, but it can be cut in half, if desired.

1. Drain grape leaves, rinse, and taste for saltiness. If leaves are too salty, soak in warm water 15 minutes, changing water twice. Drain.

2. Place all filling ingredients, in large bowl and mix well. Set aside.

3. Spread 10 grape leaves at a time with shiny side down, on work surface. Cut off stems with scissors. Make all leaves about the same size. Trim any leaves that are unusually large.

4. Place 1 tablespoon filling in center of each leaf. Fold sides over filling. Roll from stem end to tip. Do not roll tightly because rice needs room to expand.

5. Line bottom of 4-quart saucepan (preferably non-stick) with parsley stems or extra pieces of grape leaves. Place rolls, seam side down in row around edge of saucepan. Place remaining rolls in center.

6. Mix 2 cups water, 1/2 cup lemon juice, and 1/4 cup olive oil. Pour over rolls. Invert and place a plate over rolls to hold them in place while cooking.

7. Bring to a boil over medium heat. Reduce heat to low, cover, and simmer 1 hour. Cool completely in liquid. Remove cover, hold plate in place over rolls, and gently drain off liquid. Remove plate. Place large platter over pan and invert rolls onto platter. Lift pan off slowly to keep rolls in place.

8. Chill if desired. Garnish with lemon slices. Keeps, well covered, in refrigerator.

ABOUT 55 TO 60 ROLLS

VARIATION: Substitute a mix of small eggplants and green peppers for grape leaves. Hollow out vegetables, and season inside lightly with salt and pepper. Fill and cook as directed above, or until tender. Remove carefully to platter with a slotted spoon. Serve cold or at room temperature. A recipe for meat and rice stuffing for grape leaves can be found on (page 150), under Stuffed Cabbage Leaves.

HINTS: Extra grape leaves can be wrapped in foil and frozen.

Stuffed Grape Leaves

T his recipe was given to me by my Aunt. A zesty accent with any dish, especially with Vosbov Kufta (page 196).

Cabbage and Cauliflower Pickles
KARNAVADS TUTVASH

PREPARATION TIME: 20 MINUTES
COOKING TIME: 10 MINUTES

> 1 *small head cabbage*
> 1 *small cauliflower, cut*
>   *into flowerets*
> 1 1/2 *cups vinegar*
> 1/3 *cup sea salt*
> 1 *teaspoon sugar*
> 4 *cloves garlic*
> 2 *hot chili peppers, slit*
>   *down center*

1. Discard wilted outer leaves of cabbage and remove core. Bring 8 cups water to a boil in large saucepan. Add cabbage and cook 2 minutes. Seperate leaves, remove with slotted spoon and place in bowl of cold water to stop cooking. Drain well and set aside.

2. Bring 6 cups water to a boil and cook cauliflowerets 3 minutes. Place in cold water, drain, and set aside as above.

3. Place vinegar, 1 1/2 cups water, sea salt, and sugar, in saucepan, stirring to mix well. Bring to a boil and cook 2 minutes.

4. Sterilize two 1-quart jars. Place 2 cloves garlic and 1 chili pepper in each jar. Fill jars with cauliflowerets and cabbage leaves. Cover with vinegar mixture, and seal. Set aside in cool place 1 week. Refrigerate after opening.

MAKES 2 QUARTS

VARIATION: For pinkish colored pickles, add 1 small raw beet peeled and sliced.

Cabbage and Cauliflower Pickles
Pickled Beets

A pungent tasting pickle.

Pickled Beets
JAGUNTEGHI   TUTVASH

PREPARATION TIME: 25 MINUTES

       2 *pounds cooked sliced*
           beets
       3 *whole cloves*
       5 *whole allspice*
       5 *black peppercorns*
   1/4 *-inch long stick of*
           cinnamon
       1 *cup wine vinegar*
       3 *tablespoons sugar*
       1 *tablespoon salt*

1. Place sliced beets, cloves, allspice, peppercorns, and cinnamon stick in a sterilized 1-quart mason jar. Boil vinegar and sugar for 1 minute. Add salt, stir and pour over beets.

2. Cover and store in cool place one week.

3. Refrigerate after opening. Serve with roasts, casseroles and pastas.

MAKES   1-QUART MASON JAR

These pickles are a favorite Middle Eastern delicacy. Raw beets turn the turnips a beautiful soft or sharp pink color, depending on the number of beets used.

Turnip Pickles
KABIS EL LIFT

PREPARATION TIME: 2 1/2 HOURS

> 2 *pounds small firm white turnips*
> 1/2 *cup sea salt*
> 1 1/2 *cups vinegar*
> 1 *teaspoon sugar*
> 1 *teaspoon dry mustard (optional)*
>
> 1 *or 2 hot chili peppers, slit down centers*
> 4 *cloves garlic*
> 1 *large raw beet, peeled and sliced*

1. Wash turnips and cut root and stem ends off. Cut into quarters or slice and place in bowl. Sprinkle with 3 tablespoons sea salt and toss to coat. Set aside 2 hours to sweat, stirring at least 4 times.

2. Pour vinegar, 1 1/2 cups water, and remainder of sea salt in saucepan. Bring to a boil, add sugar and mustard, and stir to combine. Set aside.

3. Drain turnips, rinse well, and pat dry with paper towels. Place in 1-quart sterilized jar. Add chili peppers, garlic, and beets. Pour in vinegar mixture and seal jar. Set aside in cool place 1 week. Refrigerate after opening.

MAKES 1 QUART MASON JAR

VARIATION: For more intense color, drain liquid from 8 ounce sliced can of beets. Add 1/2 of beets to jar. Measure liquid and add enough water to make the 1 1/2 cups needed in recipe above. Continue as directed. (Use remainder of beets in salad.)

Turnip Pickles
Eggplant Pickles

Eggplant Pickles
SUMPOOGI TUTVASH

PREPARATION TIME: 10 MINUTES
COOKING TIME: 20 MINUTES

1 pound small Italian eggplants (about 8)
3 cups cider vinegar
1 tablespoon sugar
2 tablespoons salt
5 whole allspice
6 black peppercorns

2 large cloves garlic, sliced
1 hot chili pepper, slit down center
4 sprigs of parsley
2 sprigs mint or 1 1/2 teaspoons dried crushed mint

1. Trim around stalk of eggplant, cutting pointed tips of collar, leaving stems intact. Rinse and put in a medium-size saucepan.

2. Pour vinegar over eggplants. Add sugar and salt, bring to a boil. Reduce to medium-low and cook 15 to 20 minutes or till eggplants are easily pierced with prongs of a fork.

3. Transfer to a sterilized 1-quart mason jar. Add rest of ingredients, pour vinegar on top, cover and keep in a cool place for 10 days. Refrigerate after opening.

MAKES 1-QUART MASON JAR

baba ghanoush is a national dish of Lebanon and Syria, and is often served with raw or blanched vegetables. The combined flavors of eggplant, garlic, and lemon juice are very Mediterranean. For a smokey flavor, grill eggplant over hot charcoal instead of baking in the oven. This is one of my favorite dips. It goes exceptionally well with Kibbeh Bil Sineya (Layered Meat with Bulgur (page 195).

Eggplant Appetizer
BABA GHANOUSH

PREPARATION TIME: 15 MINUTES
COOKING TIME: 35 TO 45 MINUTES

2 *eggplants, about 1 1/2 pounds*
1/4 *cup lemon juice*
1/4 *cup tahini (seesame seed paste)*
2 *cloves garlic, crushed*

Salt to taste
Olive oil
Freshley chopped parsley, paprika or pomegranate seeds to garnish
Pita bread and crudites to serve

1. Preheat oven to 400° F. Cover baking sheet with foil. Wipe eggplant and pierce with point of sharp knife. Place on prepared baking sheet and bake in preheated oven 35 to 45 minutes. When cool enough to handle, peel eggplants and remove seeds. Place in container of food processor and sprinkle with lemon juice to keep from browning.

2. Add tahini, garlic, and salt. Process until smooth.

3. Spread onto serving platter and pour small amount of olive oil over top. Garnish with chopped parsley, paprika, or pomegranate seeds. Serve with warmed pita bread and crudites. Cover and store in refrigerator.

MAKES 2 CUPS

VARIATION: In Greece, olive oil is used instead of tahini. In Syria yogurt is added for a lighter tasting dish. In Turkey it is called Hunkar Begendi, tahini and garlic are omitted and 1 cup white sauce and 1/3 cup grated cheese are mixed into the egglplant and heated before serving.

Eggplant Appetizer

Lebanese Sausage
MAANI

PREPARATION TIME: 1 HOUR (plus refrigeration)
COOKING TIME: 10 MINUTES

4 pounds bonless beef or
  lamb shoulder, cubed
1 pound suet
1 cup dry white wine
1/4 cup white vinegar
1/2 cup pine nuts
1/4 cup crushed coriander seeds
2 tablespoons cinnamon

1/4 teaspoon ground cloves
2 tablespoons salt or to
  taste
2 tablespoons freshly
  ground pepper
24 feet thin sausage casing
  Butter
  Lemon juice to serve

1. Put meat and suet through meat grinder, fitted with coarse disk, twice. Add wine, vinegar, pine nuts, coriander seed, cinnamon, cloves, salt and pepper. Place in glass bowl, cover, and refrigerate 24 hours.

2. If using salted intestines for casing, wash and soak intestines in cold water 6 to 8 hours, changing water several times. Cut casings into 4-foot lenghts. Clean inside of casing.

3. Place sausage attachment on meat grinder. Place 1 end of casing on nozzle and make knot at opposite end. Push meat mixture through grinder and ease off sausage when casing is loosely filled. Knot other end. Alternatively, push meat filling with spoon through large funnel into casing.

4. Twist loosely filled sausages into 1 1/2 to 2-inch lenghts, or tie with kitchen string to retain shape of sausage.

5. Place in refrigerator 24 hours to dry out, turning sausages over twice to dry evenly. Broil or saute sausages in butter. Sprinkle lightly with lemon juice and serve hot with bread and pickles as an appetizer. Goes very well with drinks. Freeze uncooked up to 6 months.

MAKES 5 POUNDS

VARIATION: Make one-fourth of sausage mix. Do not put in casing. Shape into 1 1/2-inch cylinders and saute in a little butter. Sprinkle lightly with lemon juice and serve immediately with pita bread or as finger food with toothpicks.

This is the Lebanese version of Syrian sausage called Sarcijio. Coriander seed and pine nuts give these small spicy sausages an interesting flavor. They are usually served in small earthenware bowls, bubbling in oil and lemon juice. You can serve them with warm pita bread as finger food, or as a first course.

Lebanese Sausage

These easy-to-make cheese filled treats are a simplified version of small phyllo triangles or rolls called Boeregs. Layered phyllo leaves are brushed with butter and filled with cheese. Cooked meat, or spinach may also be used. Boeregs make a very attractive, and delicious appetizer, and can also be served as a main dish with salad.

Cheese Filled Phyllo
BANEEROV KHUMOREGHEN

PREPARATION TIME: 20 MINUTES
COOKING TIME: 45 MINUTES

1/2 pound butter, melted
1 pound feta cheese, rinsed and patted dry
1 pound cottage cheese
2 eggs, lightly beaten
Pinch of nutmeg

1/4 cup freshly chopped parsley or dill (optional)
1 package (16 ounces) phyllo leaves
Pickles, radishes, and cucumbers, to serve

1. Preheat oven to 350° F. Brush bottom of a 13 x 9-inch baking dish with butter, and set aside.

2. Mix cheese, eggs, nutmeg, and parsley in bowl.

3. Place 1 phyllo leaf in prepared dish and brush with butter. Fold sides of pastry over to fit dish. Repeat with half of phyllo leaves. Cover with cheese mixture. Add remaining phyllo leaves, brushing butter over every leaf, tuck edges of last leaf under top leaf to make smooth top layer. Brush top with remaining butter.

4. Cut three-fourths of the way down in square or diamond shapes with sharp knife. Bake in preheated oven about 45 minutes, or until golden. Cut again to separate. Serve hot as a main dish with tossed mixed salad or as an appetizer.

SERVES 6 TO 8

VARIATION: Substitute for the cheeses a doubled recipe of meat filling (page 207).

Chick-Pea Appetizer
TOPIG

PREPARATION TIME: 1 1/2 HOURS (plus soaking time)
COOKING TIME: 1 HOUR

Traditionally this very old Armenian recipe is served during Lent.

SHELL:

1/2 pound dried chick-peas, picked over	3/4 cup tahini
1 medium potato, cooked and peeled	1/4 cup pine nuts
2 tablespoons tahini	1/4 cup currants
1 teaspoon salt or to taste	1 teaspoon cumin
	1 teaspoon cinnamon
	1 teaspoon allspice
	1/4 teaspoon freshly ground pepper

Lemon slices to garnish
Lemon juice and olive oil to serve

FILLING:

2 pounds onions, halved and sliced
1 tablespoon salt or to taste

1. To make shell, place chick-peas in cold water and set aside to soak 24 hours. Drain and place on dish towel. Cover with second towel. Roll rolling pin firmly over peas to loosen skins. Pop off skins if not already loosened. Repeat with rolling pin as necessary. Alternatively, after soaking, rub a handfull of peas in palms of hands at a time, return to liquid, stir gently, and set aside about 10 minutes. Skins should float to top of liquid.

2. Place chick-peas in large saucepan. Add 2 cups water, bring to a boil, reduce heat to medium, and cook, uncovered, 25 minutes or until peas are tender. Cool in liquid.

3. Mash chick-peas and cooked potato with coarse disk of food mill or grinder. Place in bowl and stir in tahini and 1 teaspoon salt. Form into ball, cover dish, and set aside.

4. To make filling, place onions in large saucepan. Add 1 tablespoon salt and stir well. Cook over moderate heat, stirring constantly, 10 minutes or until moisture has evaporated. Reduce heat to low, and cook 20 minutes, stirring often, until transparent, but not golden. Let cool. Place in bowl and mix thoroughly with tahini, pine nuts, currants, cumin, cinnamon, allspice, and pepper.

5. Divide chick-pea-potato mixture into 4-equal portions. Cut 4 pieces of cheesecloth into 12-inch squares. Dampen and spread on work surface. Place one-fouth of mixture in center of each piece of cloth. Flatten slightly with palm of hand. Cover with squares of plastic wrap. Roll out mixture to 10-inch round, rolling from center out toward edge and leaving about 5-inches in center slightly thicker than edges.

6. Remove plastic and spoon one-fourth of filling onto center of each shell.

7. Lift corners of cloth carefully to bring corners of shell over filling. Handle carefully to prevent bottom of shell from cracking. Tuck ends of cloth in over shell. Place on cookie sheet or platter and refrigerate until chilled about 24 hours. Remove cloth, place on serving dish and garnish with lemon slices. Serve as appetizer cut into wedges, with lemon juice and olive oil sprinkled on top.

MAKES 4 ROUNDS

Chick-Pea Appetizer

Bean Croquettes
FALAFEL

PREPARATION TIME: 30 MINUTES (plus soaking time for beans)
COOKING TIME: 1 MINUTE EACH

1 cup dried fava beans
1 cup dried chick-peas
1 medium onion, finely
    chopped
2 to 3 cloves garlic, crushed
1/2 cup freshly chopped
    parsley (optional)
1 tablespoon dried crushed
    mint (optional)
2 teaspoons cumin
2 teaspoons ground
    coriander

1/2 teaspoon allspice
1/2 teaspoon cinnamon
    Cayenne to taste
1 teaspoon baking soda
1 teaspoon salt or to taste
1/2 teaspoon freshly ground
    pepper
    Vegetable oil for deep frying
    Pita bread, Tarator Sauce
    (page 257), Turnip Pickles
    (page 24), sliced tomatoes,
    and mint or parsley
    sprigs to serve

1. Place fava beans in large saucepan with enough water to come 3-inches above beans. Soak 48 hours, changing water twice. (Soak only 12 to 15 hours if using skinned fava beans.)

2. Soak chick-peas 12 to 15 hours.

3. Skin fava beans if necessary (see note). Do not skin chick-peas. Place beans in container of food processor. Add onion, through to salt and pepper. Process until pureed. Remove to glass bowl, cover, and refrigerate 1 hour.

4. Shape mixture into 1 1/2-inch patties. Place about 4-inches oil in deep-fat fryer and heat to 375°F. Fry patties in hot oil 1/2 to 1 minute. (For crisper patties, fry 1 1/2 minutes.) Drain on paper towels.

5. Serve in warmed pita bread with tarator sauce, turnip pickles, sliced tomatoes, and mint or parsley sprigs.

MAKES 26 TO 28 CROQUETTES

HINTS: Skinned fava beans are available in Middle Eastern food stores. If using unskinned beans, squeeze firmly to pop. Alternatively, slit beans carefully with tip of sharp knife.

NOTE: Falafel mix is also available in Middle Eastern food stores.

F alafel as they are called in Lebanon and Israel, are popular throughout the Middle East. They are patties made of dried chick peas, fava beans, and spices, deep-fried in oil. The Egyptians call it Ta'amia, and consider it a national dish. They use white fave beans or broad beans instead of chick-peas. Recipes vary slightly in other countries.

Bean Croquettes

Olive and Onion Cheese Spread

Olive and Onion Cheese Spread
LABNI ZEITOUN WA BASSAL

PREPARATION TIME: 15 MINUTES (plus Labni)

> *1 cup labni (page 19)*
> *1/3 cup black olives pitted and chopped*
> *1/3 cup chopped scallions*
> *Salt and freshly ground pepper to taste*

> *1/4 teaspoon medium-hot cayenne or to taste*
> *1/2 teaspoon dried crushed mint*

1. Mix labni, black olives, scallions, salt and pepper, cayenne, and dried mint together.

2. Transfer into a small bowl or crock, cover and refrigerate till ready to serve. Keeps several days.

MAKES ABOUT 1 CUP

SERVING: Scoop out inside of cherry tomatoes, salt and pepper insides. Drain on paper towels for 10 minutes. Fill with yogurt cheese spread. Serve on a bed of parsley. Cut celery 1 1/2 to 2-inches long, fill with spread. Put cheese spread on crackers and sprinkle paprika or freshly chopped parsley, snipped chives or chopped walnuts on top.

Roasted Peppers

Roasted Peppers
KHOROVADZ BUGHBEGH

PREPARATION TIME: 10 MINUTES
COOKING TIME: 10 MINUTES

6 green, red, or yellow peppers

DRESSING:

1/4 cup olive oil (preferable virgin)

1 tablespoon red wine vinegar

1 tablespoon lemon juice salt and freshly ground pepper to taste

2 cloves garlic, minced Cocktail onions and capers to garnish

1. Cover baking sheet with aluminum foil. Place peppers on baking sheet and broil about 10 minutes or until skins blister, turning 3 times. Alternatively, bake in preheated 400° F. oven 40 minutes.

2. Peel off skins while still hot. Cut in half lenghtwise and remove seeds and any white membranes. Cut lenghtwise again into quarters and arrange in dish.

3. Mix dressing and sprinkle over peppers. Garnish with cocktail onions and capers.

SEVES 6

Spiced Olives
ZEITOUN MSABBAH

A mix of cracked green or whole black olives with cayenne and lemon juice. Keep on hand for serving as a "meza."

PREPARATION TIME: 10 MINUTES

2 cups cracked green olives (available in Middle Eastern speciality shops).

1 teaspoon cayenne or to taste

1/2 to 3/4 cup of freshly squeezed lemon juice.

1. Taste olives, rinse if too salty. Taste again, sometimes olives must be soaked for a few hours to remove salty taste.

2. Place olives in bowl and mix with pepper and lemon juice. Transfer to a jar, store at room temperature, turning bottle several times during one day. Store in refrigerator. Serve with Labni (page 19) and toast. Keeps for several weeks in refrigerator.

MAKES 2 CUPS

VARIATION: Place one clove of garlic on bottom of jar fill with olives and place another on top.

W hen I first sampled this
smooth sweet taste with
the oniony meat, I im-
mediately placed it on my list of
favorites.

Stuffed Prunes
LETZVATZ SALOR

PREPARATION TIME: 20 MINUTES
COOKING TIME: 30 MINUTES

> 2 *tablespoons corn oil*
> 1 *large onion, sliced*
> 1/2 *pound lean ground beef*
> 1 *egg. lightly beaten*
> 1/4 *cup coarsely chopped*
> *walnuts*
> 1 *small onion, finely*
> *chopped*
> 1 *package (12 ounces)*
> *pitted prunes*
> 1/4 *cup strained orange juice*
> *Parsley sprigs for garnish*

Stuffed Prunes

1. Preheat oven 350° F. Heat oil in small skillet and saute sliced onion until transparent. Spoon into 8 x 8-inch baking dish and set aside.

2. Combine ground meat, egg, walnuts, and chopped onion. Slit prunes if necessary to widen hole on one side and spoon stuffing into prunes.

3. Arrange prunes, stuffed side up, over sauted onions. Sprinkle prunes with orange juice, cover with foil, and bake in preheated oven 20 minutes.

4. Uncover and bake 10 minutes. Discard sliced onion. Serve warm or at room temperature on bed of parsley sprigs.

SERVES 10

VARIATION: Mix 1/2 pound lean ground beef, 1/4 cup coarsely chopped walnuts, 1/2 teaspoon finely grated orange rind, salt and freshly ground pepper to taste. Stuff prunes as above. Place in baking dish just large enough to hold stuffed prunes close together. Cover and bake in preheated 450° F. oven 15 minutes. Uncover bake 10 minutes longer, and serve hot or at room temperature.

Cheese and Caraway Spread

Serve this spread with fresh warm Persian bread (page 211), and freshly brewed chai (tea). Tea the most popular drink in Iran is served in small glasses with lumps of sugar on the side. To sweeten the tea a piece of sugar is held between teeth and the hot tea sipped through sugar. I never learned this technique, and would go through too many lumps of sugar.

Cheese and Caraway Spread
PANIR SEFID BA ADVIA

PREPARATION TIME: 10 MINUTES

1/2 pound Feta cheese	1 tablespoon caraway seeds
1 tablespoon nigella seeds	2 to 4 tablespoons milk
(black sesame seeds)	

1. Rinse cheese and pat dry with paper towels. Mash cheese with back of a fork. Add milk and mix.

2. Stir in seeds. Blend thoroughly and place in a crock, cover, and refrigerate. Keeps for several days.

MAKES 1/2 POUND

SUGGESTION: Use as a spread on wheat crackers and top with finely chopped or thin sliced tomatoes. As a sandwich, in pita bread, use spread sparingly, add tomato, watercress, and cucumber slices.

VARIATION: CARAWAY WITH MOZZARELLA: Use 1/2 pound mozzarella cut into cubes. Mix with 1 1/2 tablespoons caraway seed, 1 1/2 tablespoons cumin powder and 1/4 cup virgin olive oil, salt to taste. Serve with crackers or Kahke (page 214).

Armenian Sausage

S ujuk is homemade sausage made from a blend of spices and meat then cured by air drying. It is a favorite of those who like spicy hors d'oeuvres and is the highlight of my cocktail parties.

Armenian Sausage
SUJUK

PREPARATION TIME: 20 MINUTES (plus stuffing and refrigeration)
AIR DRIED: 7 TO 10 DAYS

4 pounds lean ground sirloin	3 1/2 tablespoons crushed fresh garlic
2 pounds (not too lean) ground chuck	2 tablespoons cayenne
2/3 cup cumin	2 1/2 tablespoons sweet paprika
5 1/2 tablespoons allspice	2 1/2 tablespoons salt
3 1/2 teaspoons garlic powder	

1. Place all ingredients in large glass bowl. Wear plastic gloves and mix all ingredients very thoroughly by hand. Cover with foil and refrigerate overnight to blend flavors.

2. Cut 6 rectangles of double-thick cheesecloth, each 5 x 15-inches. Sew on 3 sides and set aside.

3. Heat skillet. Remove meat from refrigerator and pinch off piece about the size of a walnut. Add to heated skillet, cook over medium heat, taste, and add more seasoning if needed.

4. Slip on plastic gloves. Divide meat into 6-equal portions. Divide each portion into 8 smaller portions and place the 8 small portions in each cheesecloth bag. Meat mixture should come to within 3-inches of top of bag. Tie bags with long pieces of kitchen string and flatten bags with rolling pin to smooth out filling.

5. Hang bags high with kitchen string in well ventilated cool place 7 to 10 days until meat is dried. Remove cheesecloth casings. Wrap in foil, and refrigerate 2 days or place in freezer.

6. When ready to serve, heat non-stick skillet. Thinly slice Sujuk and cook briefly on both sides. Serve hot with wedges of warm pita bread.

MAKES 6 SAUSAGES

SERVING SUGGESTIONS: Serve Sujuk for breakfast instead of bacon; use instead of pepperoni on pizza.

CHAPTER TWO

Soups

Soups are called shorbah in Arabic, Abour in Armenian and Ash in Persian. They are like stews bursting with flavor from the vegetables, rice, dried beans, herbs, spices, lemon juice, garlic and mint. The amount of water added depends on the number of people to be served. The Iranians make what is called Meat Water, the liquids of the soup are strained, the meat chunks and vegetables mashed and served as a side dish with the broth and then eaten with bread shaped into scoops. They all have a meatball soup, the Iranian style is very thick with yellow split peas or rice. Lebanese and Armenian version is with yogurt and thickened with eggwhites or corn starch, stirring the pot in one direction only.

Most of the soups in this chapter can be served as a main course. They are inexpensive to make and very nourishing. The ingredients can be adjusted to what is available and your personal tastes.

Meat Soup

This dish originally was cooked in an earthenware pot and baked slowly for several hours. The aroma that came from the food as it cooked was irresistible. A special bread called Sangag, is usually served with the soup. This bread cannot be made succesfully at home because it must be baked over hot pebbles. When more water and yellow split peas are added, this soup-stew is called Dizi. When meat and vegetables are separated from broth and pounded to a smooth mixture it is called Gushte Kubideh (see variation).

Meat Soup
AB GUSHT

PREPARATION TIME: 20 MINUTES
COOKING TIME: 2 1/2 HOURS

2 *tablespoons butter*
1 *tablespoon vegetable oil*
1 1/2 *pounds leg or shoulder of lamb, cut into 1-inch chunks or 3 to 4 lamb shanks, trimmed.*
1 *large onion, quartered*
1 *can (6 ounces) tomato paste*
1 *bay leaf*
1 1/2 *fresh limes, thickly sliced and seeded or 3 dried limes (Limoon Amoni), pierced*

1 *tablespoon bulgur*
2 *cups cooked chick-peas*
2 *cups cooked red kidney beans*
Cayenne to taste (optional)
Salt and freshly ground pepper to taste
1/8 *teaspoon cinnamon*
3 *medium potatoes, peeled and quartered*
1/4 *teaspoon turmeric*

1. Heat butter and oil in large saucepan. Saute meat and onion, stirring until meat is browned.

2. Mix tomato paste with 8 cups water and pour over meat. Add bay leaf, limes, and bulgur. Bring to a boil, reduce heat to medium-low, cover, and cook 1 1/2 to 2 hours or until meat is almost tender.

3. Add chick-peas, kidney beans, cayenne, salt and pepper, cinnamon, potatoes, and turmeric. Bring to a boil, reduce heat, and simmer 20 minutes. Discard bay leaf and bones if using lamb shanks. (Squeeze out dry lime to extract flavor and eat or discard).

SERVES 6 TO 8

VARIATION: GUSHTE KUBIDEH: Drain liquid through colander into large saucepan and keep warm. Puree meat and vegetables in food processor to consistency of thick mashed potatoes. If mixture is too thick, add some broth and mix well. Serve with thin Lavash or Barbari Bread (page 211), radishes, and onion slices. For extra flavor, add a few drops of hot pepper sauce to meat mixture.

NOTE: Dried limes and Lavash bread are available in Near or Middle Eastern specialty shops.

In October, when pomegranates are in season, this delicately flavored and unusual soup is often served. Iranians are very found of pomegranates. They serve them peeled and seeded or whole, squeezing them gently but firmly to release the juice. A small portion of the outer skin is bitten off and the pomegranate is sucked. A word of caution, they must be eaten carefully because the juice will stain. Many drinks are also made with fresh pomegranate juice.

Pomegranate Soup
ASHE ANAR

PREPARATION TIME: 20 MINUTES
COOKING TIME: 1 1/2 HOURS

2 *lamb shanks, cracked*	1 1/2 *cups freshly chopped*
1/3 *cup yellow split peas*	*spinach*
1 *medium onion, quartered*	1 1/2 *cups chopped beet leaves*
1/4 *cup rice*	1 *cup pomegranate juice or*
1 *medium beet, peeled and*	2 *tablespoons*
finely chopped	*pomegranate molasses**
1/3 *cup chopped scallions,*	1 *beef bouillon cube*
green tops included	1 *tablespoon dried crushed*
1/2 *cup freshly chopped*	*mint*
parsley	1/4 *teaspoon cinnamon*
1/4 *cup sugar*	1/4 *teaspoon freshly ground*
3 *tablespoons lime juice*	*pepper*

1. Bring 7 cups water to a boil in large saucepan. Add lamb shanks, split peas, and onion. Return to a boil, reduce heat, and skim surface. Cover and simmer 40 minutes. Add rice and beets and cook 25 minutes.

2. Remove lamb shanks, pull meat off bones, and chop meat, discarding bones. Return meat to saucepan. Add scallions, parsley, sugar, lime juice, spinach, beet leaves, and pomegranate juice. Dissolve bouillon cube in water and add, if desired. Cook just until heated through.

3. Sprinkle soup with mint, cinnamon, and pepper. Mix well and spoon into serving bowls.

SERVES 6 TO 8

VARIATION: Substitute 1 pound lean ground lamb or beef, shaped into 1/2-inch size meatballs, for lamb shanks. Cook split peas and rice 30 minutes, add meatballs and beet, and continue as above.

* *Pomegranate molasses is available in Middle Eastern speciality Stores.*

Hot Yogurt Soup
MADZOUNOV KUFTA ABOUR

PREPARATION TIME: 1 HOUR
COOKING TIME: 15 MINUTES

9   tablespoons butter
    Salt and freshly ground
    pepper to taste
1/2 recipe Kibbeh Mix
    (page 194)

4   cups chichen broth
1   container (32 ounces)
    plain yogurt)
1   egg, lightly beaten
3   tablespoons dried crushed
    mint

1. Form 6 tablespoons butter into 80 equal pieces. Flash freeze 10 minutes. Sprinkle with salt and pepper and return to freezer.

2. Form Kibbeh Mix into 80 equal-size balls. Stuff each meatball with 1 piece of seasoned frozen butter. Be careful to enclose butter completely so it won't ooze out during cooking. Dampen hands with cold water periodically to prevent meat from sticking to hands and to keep butter from getting warm.

3. Bring broth to a boil in large saucepan. Add meatballs, return to a boil, and lower heat to medium. Cook 5 minutes, remove meatballs with slotted spoon, and set broth aside.

4. Place yogurt and egg in large saucepan. Add salt to taste and beat over medium heat until mixture is hot, beating constantly. Add meatballs and stir gently. Add broth, stirring carefully, until mixture is heated throughout.

5. Melt remaining 3 tablespoons butter in small saucepan and stir in mint. Spoon soup into serving bowls and spoon mint sauce generously on top.

SERVES 4 TO 6

VARIATION: Use only 3 tablespoons butter to stuff meatballs and add 2 tablespoons coarsely chopped walnuts with butter. Add 2 poached chicken cutlets, cut into strips lengthwise, just before serving.

HINT: Remove leftover meatballs from liquid, store separately, covered in refrigerator. Reheat meatballs and liquid together over medium-low heat, stirring gently and often till heated throughout.

This hot soup is a hearty meal by itself. When I make the Kibbeh Meatballs used in this recipe I like to double the amount and freeze half of them to use next time I make the soup. If homemade yogurt is used, it should not be used immediately. The yogurt is better when it has been allowed to sit for a few days. Armenians brought this recipe with them when they fled from Turkey in 1915.

Hot Yogurt Soup

Tarragon Soup
BEKHOV ABOUR

PREPARATION TIME: 10 MINUTES
COOKING TIME: 1 1/2 TO 2 HOURS

      3/4 cup barley
        5 cups well flavored
           chicken or beef broth
      3/4 cup brown lentils, picked
           over and rinsed
        4 tablespoons fresh taragon
           leaves

    1 1/2 teaspoons salt or to taste
           Cayenne to taste
      1/4 cup olive oil or safflower
           oil
        2 medium onions, chopped

1. Place barley and broth in large saucepan. Bring to a boil, reduce heat to low, cover, and simmer 45 minutes. Add lentils, 2 tablespoons tarragon leaves, salt, and cayenne. Cover and simmer 20 to 25 minutes, or until tender.

2. Heat oil in skillet over medium heat. Add onions and saute, stirring often, until lightly golden. Spoon into saucepan and stir well.

3. Stir in remaining 2 tablespoons tarragon leaves. Simmer about 3 minutes. Serve hot.

SERVES 6

L iterally translated, the name of this old Armenian soup is Mustache Soup because the long feathery tarragon leaves in the soup were said to resemble a mustache.

Meatball Soup
KUFTA ABOUR

PREPARATION TIME: 15 MINUTES (plus Kibbeh)
COOKING TIME: 45 MINUTES

1/2 recipe Kibbeh (page 194)
4 tablespoons butter
1 tablespoon vegetable oil
1 medium onion, finely chopped
1/2 pound beef liver, sliced into 1/4-inch thick strips

6 cups chicken or beef broth
2 beef bouillon cubes (optional)
Freshly ground pepper to taste
1 cup cooked chick-peas
Freshly chopped parsley and scallions to garnish

1. Shape Kibbeh into 1/2-inch meatballs. Melt butter and oil in large saucepan. Saute meatballs until browned on all sides. Remove with slotted spoon and set aside.

2. Saute onion in same saucepan 10 minutes or until transparent. Add liver and saute 5 to 10 minutes. Add broth, bouillion cubes, and pepper. Bring to a boil and add meatballs and chick-peas. Bring to a boil again, reduce heat, and simmer 10 minutes, or until meatballs are done.

3. Spoon into bowls and sprinkle with chopped parsley and scallions.

SERVES 6

VARIATION: Omit beef liver and add 1 can (6 ounces) tomato paste to broth. Add 1/4 cup lemon juice just before serving.

Vegetable Barley Soup
KARI ABOUR

PREPARATION TIME: 20 MINUTES
COOKING TIME: 30 TO 40 MINUTES

3 tablespoons butter
1 large onion, finely chopped
3 peeled and diced carrots
2 celery stalks sliced
1/2 cup pearl barley

5 to 6 cups chicken broth (preferably homemade)
1 to 2 teaspoons thyme
salt and freshly ground pepper to taste
Juice of 1 large lemon
Lemon wedges to serve

1. Melt butter in a medium-size saucepan. Saute onion till transparent and golden. Add carrots, celery, and barley stirring often, saute for 3 minutes.

2. Pour liquid over vegetables, add thyme. Bring to a boil, stir, reduce to low. Cover and cook till vegetables and barley are tender.

3 Add salt, pepper, and lemon juice. Serve hot, with extra lemon wedges to squeeze into soup when serving.

SERVES 4 TO 6

Cold Yogurt Soup
AB DUG KHIAR

PREPARATION TIME: 20 MINUTES

- 3 cups plain yogurt
- 2 cups julienne, diced, or grated small cucumbers (preferably Kirby)
- 1/2 to 1 cup freshly chopped dill
- 1/4 cup chopped scallions

- 1 to 1 1/2 tablespoons dried crushed mint
  Salt and white pepper to taste
- 1/2 cup seedless raisins to garnish (optional)
- 1/2 cup chopped walnuts to garnish (optional)

1. Beat yogurt until smooth. Add 1 cup water, cucumber, dill, scallions, mint, salt and pepper. Stir well.

2. Cover and place in refrigerator until well chilled.

3. Spoon into soup bowls and sprinkle with raisins and walnuts.

SERVES 6

VARIATION: Milk may be substituted for water. Mint and scallions may be omitted. 1 cup dairy sour cream may be substituted for 1 cup yogurt.

This refreshing cold soup (soupa-sard) is prepared during the summer in Iran and is very soothing on a hot dry day. Sometimes a chopped hard-cooked egg is added and gently mixed into the soup. The soup can be thinned out by adding water or thickened by adding drained yogurt (see Labni, page 19). Sometimes ice cubes are added to keep soup cool. If possible, always use small un-waxed cucumbers because their seeds are smaller. Cucumbers are served as a fruit in Iran, and included on a fruit tray or basket. They are eaten before a meal as a "meza" or at the end of a meal as fruit.

Cold Yogurt Soup

Roasted Noodle Soup
ASHE RESHTE

PREPARATION TIME: 15 MINUTES
COOKING TIME: 1 1/2 TO 2 HOURS

According to tradition, this Iranian soup was made to celebrate a baby's first tooth. It was also served to relatives when returning home after a long journey.

6 tablespoons butter
1 medium onion, finely chopped
1/2 pound top round beef cut into 1/2-inch cubes
1/8 teaspoon turmeric (optional)
1 cup freshly chopped parsley
1 cup snipped garlic chives or spinach

1/2 cup chopped scallions
1/4 cup brown lentils
4 ounces egg noodles
1 cup plain yogurt
1/2 cup Kachick*
1 cup cooked white kidney beans
1 cup cooked chick-peas
4 large cloves garlic (crushed)
2 tablespoons dried crushed mint

1. Melt 4 tablespoons butter in 4-quart saucepan. Add onion and saute until transparent. Add meat and turmeric, cook until meat is browned on all sides. Add parsley, chives, and scallions, stirring constantly 2 to 4 minutes. Pour 8 cups water into saucepan, add lentils, and bring to a boil, reduce heat. Cover, and simmer 1 hour or until meat is tender.

2. Preahot oven to 350° F. Place noodles on baking sheet in single layer and crisp in oven 2 to 4 minutes. Stir after 1 minute and watch carefully to prevent noodles from burning.

3. Place yogurt in bowl and beat until smooth. Set aside. Mix Kachick with 1/2 cup water and stir to dissolve lumps. Pour into soup slowly, stirring constantly. Mix 1/4 cup hot soup with yogurt and add to soup. Cook over low heat about 20 minutes, stirring frequently. Add crisped noodles, chick-peas, and kidney beans. Cook 10 to 15 minutes. (Soup should be creamy but not watery.)

4. Melt remaining 2 tablespoons butter in small skillet. Add garlic and cook about 30 seconds, or just until lightly colored. Stir with wooden spoon. Add mint, mix well, and spoon over soup. Serve hot. "Noush e Djan" which means good appetite in Iranian.

SERVES 8

VARIATION: Substitute spaghetti or fettucine for egg noodles.

Kachick is a mixture of yogurt and bulgur that has been fermented and sun-dried then ground to a powder. Keeps well refrigerated. Available in Middle Eastern food stores. If you cannot find it, 1/3 cup red wine vinegar can be used instead.

The coriander and garlic, sauteed in butter, although somewhat spicy, are what makes this soup special. It is a Lebanese dish that is served on sunday in restaurants that specialize in Arabic food. Goat's milk was originally used to make the yogurt.

Dumplings in Yogurt Soup
SHISBARAK

PREPARATION TIME: 30 MINUTES (plus resting, draining, and footballs)
COOKING TIME: 45 MINUTES

6 uncooked Stuffed
Footballs (page 192)

DOUGH:

2 cups unbleached
all-purpose flour
1/4 teaspoon salt or to taste

FILLING:

1/2 pound lean ground lamb
or beef
1 medium onion, finely
chopped
2 tablespoons pine nuts
1/8 teaspoon cinnamon
1/8 teaspoon allspice
Cayenne to taste
Salt to taste
2 tablespoons butter

SOUP:

2 containers (32 ounces
each) plain yogurt
1 1/2 tablespoons cornstarch or
1 large egg white
1/2 teaspoon salt or to taste

TO SERVE:

3 tablespoons butter
2 to 4 cloves garlic, crushed
3 to 4 tablespoons chopped
fresh coriander leaves.

1. Prepare Stuffed Footballs (if using frozen, thaw completely). Set aside.

2. To make dough, place flour in large bowl, stir in salt, add 3/4 cup water, and mix well. Knead until smooth, about 8 minutes. Cover and set aside to rest 30 minutes.

3. To make filling, combine meat, onion, pine nuts, cinnamon, allspice, cayenne, and salt. Mix well and set aside.

4. Divide dough in half. Roll out half of dough on lightly floured surface to about 1/8-inch thickness. Cut into 1 1/2-inch squares or rounds. (You should have about 30 dumplings.) Place 1 teaspoon filling on one side of each square, fold over to make a triangle or half moon shape, and pinch edges together with dampened fingertips to seal. Repeat with remaining dough and filling.

5. Preheat oven to 350° F. Place dumplings on lightly greased baking sheet and dot with 2 tablespoons butter. Bake in preheated oven 10 minutes. Set aside on baking sheet.

6. To make soup, drain yogurt in several thicknesses of cheesecloth 30 minutes, if desired.

7. Place yogurt in large saucepan and stir with wooden spoon until smooth. Mix cornstarch with 4 tablespoons water or beat egg white with 2 or 3 tablespoons yogurt. Add to saucepan. Stir in salt and blend well to stabilize yogurt and prevent it from curdling. Bring to a boil slowly over medium heat, stirrring constantly in one direction only. Cook 10 minutes.

8. Add footballs and dumplings. Cook about 5 minutes, gently stirring several times to prevent burning. Reduce heat and simmer 15 to 20 minutes, stirring often.

9. Melt 3 tablespoons butter in small saucepan. Add garlic and coriander, mix well, and cook 30 seconds. Add to soup and stir gently. Spoon into serving bowls and serve hot.

SERVES 6

VARIATION: Fresh or frozen tortellini or small meat-filled ravioli may be substituted for homemade dumplings. Cook separately as directed and add to soup.

STUFFED FOOTBALLS IN YOGURT SOUP: (Kibbeh Labaneya): Substitute 1 cup cooked rice for dumplings. Increase footballs to 12. Substitute 1 tablespoon dried crushed mint for fresh coriander. Serve with radish, scallions, cheese, and bread.

HINTS: Footballs may be precooked by simmering in broth. Add to hot soup with cooked dumplings or rice and heat gently about 5 minutes. This method is somewhat easier and eliminates the risk of breaking the footballs while stirring.

Swiss Chard-lentil Soup

I n Lebanon one is frequently invited for morning coffee and then is asked to stay for lunch. On such an occasion I was served this hearty soup which is made year round. Swiss chard is abundant and can be used with a pinch of sugar instead of spinach.

Swiss Chard Lentil Soup
ADASS BI SILQK

PREPARATION TIME: 15 MINUTES
COOKING TIME: 1 HOUR

1/2 cup brown lentils, picked over and rinsed
6 cups chicken broth
3 tablespoons vegetable oil or butter
1 large onion, finely chopped
2 cloves garlic, chopped
2 carrots, diced

1 medium potato, diced
1 pound swiss chard or spinach, washed stemmed and chopped
1 tablespoon ground coriander
1/2 teaspoon allspice
1/2 teaspoon salt or to taste lemon wedges to serve

1. Place lentils in large saucepan. Add chicken broth, bring to a boil, and cook over medium heat 15 minutes.

2. Heat oil or melt butter in skillet, saute onion and garlic until onion is transparent. Add to lentils with carrots and potatoes. Stir to combine, cover and cook over medium-low heat 15 minutes or until tender. Add swiss chard, coriander, allspice, and salt. Cook 5 minutes. Adjust seasoning and serve hot with lemon wedges to squeeze over soup.

SERVES 4 TO 6

VARIATION: 1/2 pound diced lean lamb or beef or small meatballs can be added with lentils, while soup is cooking.

HINTS: To remove sand easily, wash leafy greens in warm water.

CHAPTER THREE

Salads

Most of the salads in this chapter can be used as a main course, for lunch or on a very hot day for dinner. A basic salad is tomatoes, romaine lettuce, cucumbers, and onions. The most common dressing is a good quality olive oil and freshly sqeezed lemon. Iranians substitute lime since lemons are usually not available. You will always find a plate of fresh romaine lettuce, ripe tomatoes, radishes, and scallions (green onions) resting on ice or in iced water on Lebanese and Armenian tables. The Iranians use mixed green eating herbs (Sabzi Khordan), which consists of green onions, tarragon, mint, coriander, flat leafed parsley, dill, and watercress. Bean salads are popular with the Armenian and Lebanese and are more tasty when left to marinate overnight. The yogurt salads are refreshing and filling, they are perfect for a summer buffet or barbecue. Home made breads with herb flavored butter go exceptionally well with these salads.

Yogurt Cucumber Salad
MAST VA KHIAR

PREPARATION TIME: 1 HOUR AND 10 MINUTES

4 cups yogurt
2 cups thinly sliced and
   quartered cucumbers
   (preferably Kirby)
1 tablespoon dried crushed
   mint

Salt and white pepper to
   taste
1/2 cup chopped scallions
1/4 cup seedless dark raisins
   Fresh mint leaves and
   cucumber slices for
   garnish

1. Dampen several thicknesses of cheese-cloth, place in colander. Pour yogurt into it and drain for one hour. Or use Labni (page 19) for thicker mixture.

2. Mix yogurt, cucumbers, dried mint, salt, pepper, and scallions. Stir in raisins, Decorate with mint and cucumber slices.

SERVES 6

VARIATION: YOGURT, DILL AND SCALLION SAUCE: Mix 2 cups yogurt. 1/2 cup freshly chopped dill and 1/4 cup chopped scallions, with salt to taste. Serve as an accompaniment with meats, chickens, or as a dip with crunchy crudites.

HINTS: If making salad in advance, add raisins when ready to serve, as it might give out color.

This refreshing dish lends itself to buffets and can be used as an appetizer scooped up with bread.

Cucumber Mint Yogurt Salad
JAJIK

PREPARATION TIME: 15 MINUTES

1 clove garlic
3 cups plain yogurt
1/4 cup chopped fresh mint
   leaves or 1 tablespoon
   dried crushed mint

1/4 teaspoon salt or to taste
1 1/2 cups diced cucumbers
   (preferably Kirby)

1. Mash garlic with salt in a mortar and pestle.

2. Mix together with yogurt in a bowl. Add mint, salt and cucumbers. Chill.

SERVES 4

VARIATION: Substitute 1 1/2 cups cooked swiss chard or spinach leaves drained and squeezed dry then chopped, instead of cucumbers.

An appetizing yogurt based salad from the Middle and Near East. Served in small bowls and eaten with spoons. Traditionally served in Armenian homes the night before Easter (Khoutum Kisher), with baked fish, Armenian Rice with Noodles (page 170) and spinach sauteed in butter. Also popular with Greeks and Lebanese.

Cucumber Mint Yogurt Salad
Yogurt Cucumber Salad

Brain Salad
OUGHEGHI AGHTSAN

PREPARATION TIME: 20 MINUTES (plus soaking)
COOKING TIME: 15 TO 20 MINUTES

DRESSING:

- 1 *pound lamb brain (fresh)*
- 1 *tablespoon plus 1/2 teaspoon salt*
- 3 *tablespoons white vinegar*
- 1 *large clove garlic*
- 1 *bay leaf*

- *Juice of 1 large lemon (about 1/3 cup)*
- 1/4 *cup olive oil (preferably virgin)*
- *Salt and freshly ground pepper to taste*

1. Place brain in a bowl, cover with cold water, sprinkle with 1 tablespoon salt, and 1 1/2 tablespoons vinegar. Soak for 30 minutes.

2. Drain and remove skins and veins. Rinse.

3. Transfer to a saucepan, add 1 cup water, garlic clove, 1 1/2 tablespoons vinegar, 1/2 teaspoon salt and bey leaf. Bring to a boil over high heat, reduce to low and cover. Simmer for about 15 minutes. Drain. Discard bay leaf.

4. Mix with dressing and marinate for 1 to 2 hours. Serve as a Meza.

SERVES 4

Onion Parsley Salad
SOKHI AGHTSAN

PREPARATION TIME: 15 MINUTES

2 cups freshly chopped
  parsley
1 medium onion, thinly
  sliced, (rings separated)

1 tablespoon sumac*
1/4 cup lemon juice
  Salt to taste
  Cayenne to taste

This salad is not to be served on its own, it should accompany a main course such as grilled or barbecued meats or poultry. Try it with warmed Pita Bread, Hummus, and Shish Kabob.

1. Spread chopped parsley on a serving dish. Top with onion.

2. Sprinkle with sumac, lemon juice, salt, and cayenne.

VARIATION: Add 2 medium tomatoes chopped, 1 tablespoons olive oil, 1/2 teaspoon paprika, serve with chicken or meat.

* Sumac is available in Middle Eastern stores.

SERVES 6

Chicken Pickle Salad

Chicken Pickle Salad
SALATET JAJ

PREPARATION TIME: 15 MINUTES

2 cups cooked and finely
  diced chicken
1 cup finely chopped garlic
  dill pickles
1 cup seeded and finely
  chopped tomatoes
1 cup shredded lettuce
1/2 cup freshly finely chopped
  parsley

1/2 cup finely chopped
  scallions including 2-inch
  green tops
1/3 cup lemon juice
1/4 cup olive
2 to 3 tablespons Dijon
  mustard
  Salt and freshly ground
  pepper to taste
  Cayenne to taste

1. Mix chicken, pickles, tomatoes, lettuce, parsley, and scallions in a large bowl.

2. In a measuring cup stir together lemon juice, oil, mustard, salt and peppers. Pour over salad, toss carefully and serve or sprinkle roasted pine nuts or whole almonds on top, or stuff into a small pita bread cut in half as a sandwich.

SERVES 4 TO 6

B orani in Persian means yogurt mixed with any number of vegetables. It is said that over 1000 years ago a woman ruler of Persia was very found of yogurt, so this was called Poorani after her name Poorandokt and then eventually Borani. A very versatile dish that is served as an appetizer or side dish. When it's very hot Borani is used with a rice cake (Katah) instead of a stew (Khoresht). It can be served with bread as an appetizer.

Spinach Yogurt Salad
BORANI ESFANAJ

PREPARATION TIME: 15 MINUTES (plus draining of yogurt)
COOKING TIME: 15 MINUTES

2 cups drained yogurt (page 19)
2 pounds fresh spinach or two (10 ounce) packages of frozen chopped spinach thawed
2 to 3 tablespoons vegetable oil

1 medium onion, finely chopped
1 teaspoon salt or to taste Freshly ground pepper to taste
1 cloves garlic, crushed
1 teaspoon dried crushed mint

1. Drain yogurt as for labni (page 19) but only 2 hours not the full 10 hours.

2. Rinse fresh spinach and discard stems. Chop leaves. If using frozen spinach squeeze dry then separate.

3. Heat oil in skillet, saute onions over medium heat till transparent. Add spinach, toss together, cooking till wilted.

4. Mix drained yogurt, salt, pepper, and garlic together. Add spinach-onion mix, blend thoroughly. Sprinkle with mint and serve room temperature.

SERVES 6

VARIATION: BORANI-BADEMJAN: EGGPLANT YOGURT SALAD: One large eggplant sliced or diced and salted, leave for 20 minutes, rinse and pat dry. Fry in oil about 3 tablespoons or as needed. Drain on paper towels. Mix with yogurt and garlic, salt and pepper. Chill. Sprinkle with chopped walnuts when serving.

BORANI-E-GHARCH: MUSHROOM YOGURT SALAD: Saute 2 pounds sliced fresh mushrooms in 3 to 4 tablespoons butter, over high heat to cook slightly, omit onion, mint, and garlic. Stir in yogurt and seasonings, serve warm. Or simply substitute drained canned mushrooms for spinach, continue as for Spinach Borani.

Potato and Egg Salad
KEDNAKHUNTZORI AGHTSAN

PREPARATION TIME: 10 MINUTES
COOKING TIME: 30 MINUTES

4 medium potatoes (about
1 1/2 pounds) cooked then
diced
1/4 cup freshly chopped
parsley
1/4 cup chopped chives
(optional)
1/2 cup chopped onions or
scallions

1/3 to 1/2 cup lemon juice
1/3 cup olive oil
1/4 to 1/2 teaspoon cayenne
Salt and white pepper to
taste
3 hard-boiled eggs
Paprika
10 black pitted olives whole
or sliced

From the vast range of potato salads, this one is a jewel. I remember this satisfying and inexpensive dish being made by my great grandmother. It is easily put together since all of the ingredients are staples of any kitchen.

1. Place potatoes in a saucepan cover with water, cook about 25 minutes or till fork pierces potatoes easily. Drain, cool slightly enough to handle. Dice, transfer to bowl.

2. Add parsley, chives, onion or scallions, toss, pour lemon juice and olive oil over mix and sprinkle with seasonings.

3. Toss well and let marinate 20 to 30 minutes, taste, add remaining lemon juice if needed.

4. To serve, transfer to dish, cut each hard boiled egg in quarters lenghtwise for decoration.

5. Sprinkle eggs with a little paprika. Decorate with black olives.

SERVES 4 TO 6

HINT: Can be made 1 day ahead except add some fresh parsley when serving for brighter color.

Marinated Vegetables
KARN AGHTSAN

PREPARATION TIME: 15 MINUTES (plus overnight)

1/4 pound string beans cooked, cut into 1-inch lengths
3 new potatoes, steamed
and quartered or sliced
1/2 small head cauliflower,
cooked, separated
1/2 pound mushroom caps
12 cherry tomatoes
3/4 cup pitted black olives

8 radishes
1 thin yellow squash or
zucchini, sliced
1 or 2 Kirby cucumbers
peeled and sliced
1 medium purple onion,
thinly sliced
Red cabbage leaves
garnish

DRESSING:

1/4 cup lemon juice
1/2 cup vinegar
1 large clove garlic, minced
1 tablespoon Dijon mustard
1/2 teaspoon tarragon
2 teaspoons freshly chopped dill or 1/2 teaspoon dried
Salt and freshly ground pepper to taste
1 1/3 cups olive or safflower oil

1. Combine all but oil for dressing in a large bowl. Add oil stir to blend thoroughly.

2. Stir in all of vegetables till thoroughly coated. Chill, covered in refrigerator at least 4 hours. To serve, place red cabbage leaves around platter or bowl and salad in center. Use as a salad or with toothpicks as a appetizer.
SERVES 6 TO 8

Marinated Vegetables
Potato and Egg Salad

Beet Salad
Potato and Chicken Salad

T his popular salad was brought to Iran from Russia by Armenians.

Potato and Chicken Salad
SALAD-A-OLIVIER

PREPARATION TIME: 20 MINUTES
COOKING TIME: 30 MINUTES

2 cups cooked, diced
chicken breast
4 medium potatoes, cooked,
sliced or diced
2 cups frozen, thawed baby
green peas
1 small onion, halved, very
thinly sliced
1 1/2 cups dilled pickled
cucumbers, chopped

1 teaspoon salt or to taste
1 tablespoon sugar
1/2 teaspoon white pepper or
to taste
3 tablespoons lemon juice
1 cup mayonnaise
2 cups dairy sour cream
Large black olives to
garnish

1. In a large bowl mix chicken, potatoes, peas, onion, and pickles together. Blend salt, sugar, pepper, and lemon juice, in a small bowl. Add mayonnaise 1 1/2 cups of sour cream and mix together. Add to chicken mixture and blend thoroughly.

2. Spread evenly onto serving dish. Coat surface with remaining sour cream, decorate with olives in a criss-cross pattern. This can be prepared 1 day ahead of time covered and refrigerated. Perfect for a buffet.

SERVES 8 TO 10

VARIATION: Omit chicken, increase peas to 3 cups, and add 1 cup carrots or beets cooked and diced. The beets will make salad a pink color.

Beet Salad
PANJAR AGHTSAN

PREPARATION TIME: 10 MINUTES
COOKING TIME: 1 1/2 HOURS

3 pounds beets, with 1-inch
   tops
3 tablespoons wine vinegar

3 tablespoons vegetable oil
1 teaspoon sugar
   watercress garnish

1. Wash beets. Wrap each separately in aluminum foil. Place on baking sheet and bake in preheated oven 350° F. for 1 1/2 hours or till tender.

2. Peel and cut off ends. Slice into strips.

3. Mix vinegar, oil and sugar together in a medium bowl. Add beets, toss to mix and transfer to a serving platter or bowl, garnish with watercress.

SERVES 6 TO 8

Purslane Salad
FATTOUSH

Perfect for a light dinner or a lunch in the summer when purslane grows wild.

PREPARATION TIME: 20 MINUTES

1/2 cup lemon juice
1/3 cup olive oil
   Salt and freshly ground
   pepper to taste
1 cup seeded and chopped
   tomatoes
1 cup sliced or diced
   cucumbers
1 1/2 cups purslane leaves
1/2 cup freshly chopped
   parsley

1/2 cup chopped onions or
   scallions
1 romaine lettuce (small)
   washed, dried, torn into
   bite-size pieces
1 1/2 tablespoons sumac*
2 cups toasted crisp pita
   bread cut up into 1/2-inch
   pieces

1. In a large bowl mix lemon juice, oil, salt and pepper. Add tomatoes, cucumbers, purslane, parsley, onions, and lettuce.

2. Sprinkle with sumac and toss together thoroughly.

3. Just before serving, add toasted pita bread, toss and serve.

SERVES 4 TO 6

VARIATION: If purslane is not available substitute equal parts of chopped parsley and mint. This salad is best alone but is equally good as a side dish with meats, poultry, or pastas.

* Sumac is available in Middle Eastern stores.

Red and White Bean Salad
LOOBIYAI AGHTSAN

PREPARATION TIME: 10 MINUTES

This Armenian salad has a robust lemony taste, and is a very hearty and popular dish, often found on luncheon buffet tables throughout the Middle East.

1/3 cup lemon juice
1/3 cup olive oil
     Salt and freshly ground
     black pepper to taste.
1/2 teaspoon paprika
     Dash cayenne
  2 cups cooked red kidney
     beans

2 cups cooked white kidney
   beans
1 medium purple onion,
   finely chopped
1 large tomato, seeded, and
   chopped
1/2 cup freshly chopped
     parsley

1. Place lemon juice, oil, salt and peppers in a bowl. Mix well.

2. Add beans, onion, tomatoe, parsley. Toss well to coat. Serve on a bed of lettuce with cheese and crackers.

SERVES 6

Chick-Pea Salad
SALATET HUMMUS

PREPARATION TIME: 15 MINUTES

A hearty mixture, both satisfying and delicious. Keeps well and is good to have on hand for a snack or a lunch. It is better when left to marinate overnight.

1/3 to 1/2 cup lemon juice
1/2 cup olive oil (preferably
     virgin)
  1 teaspoon Dijon mustard
  1 to 2 cloves garlic, crushed
     Salt and freshly ground
     pepper to taste
  2 cups cooked chick-peas
  1 green pepper seeded and
     diced

1/2 cup chopped scallions
     with 2-inches green tops
     or 1 small purple onion,
     chopped
1/4 cup freshly chopped
     parsley
  1 or 2 small cucumbers
     chopped (preferably
     Kirby)
1/2 cup green or black olives
     pitted
     Radish slices to garnish

1. Mix lemon juice, oil, mustard, and garlic in a bowl. Salt and pepper to taste.

2. Toss with remaining ingredients. Taste and adjust if needed. Chill covered in refrigerator.

3. When ready to serve bring salad to room temperature. Keeps for several days.

SERVES 4 TO 6

Red and White Bean Salad
Chick-Pea Salad

Cooked Peppers in Wine
BUGHBEGH AGHTSAN

PREPARATION TIME: 10 MINUTES
COOKING TIME: 40 MINUTES

1/3 cup safflower oil
1 large onion, quartered
3 carrots, cut into 1/2-inch pieces
4 green, red, or yellow, peppers, cut into 1 1/2-inch pieces
2 celery stalks, cut into 1-inch pieces
4 cornichons (small sweet pickles)
1 hot chili pepper, split and seeded
1/3 cup dry white wine
1/3 cup lemon juice
2 tablespoons freshly chopped parsley
2 teaspoon salt or to taste
  Freshly ground pepper to taste

1. Heat oil in large skillet. Add onion and carrots, saute 10 minutes, stirring often.

2. Add green, red, or yellow peppers, celery, cornichons, and chili pepper. Toss to coat in oil.

3. Reduce heat to low, add wine, lemon juice, parsley, chives, salt and pepper. Cover and simmer 30 minutes. Adjust seasoning. Spoon into bowl and set aside to cool. Serve cold or at room temperature with barbecued meat or poultry.

SERVES 6

E ggplant is very popular throughout the Middle and Near East. It is used in salads, stews, soups, and is delicious with steak, or grilled chicken. This recipe is a classic in the Armenian repertoire of eggplant dishes.

Eggplant Salad
SUMPOOGI AGHTSAN

PREPARATION TIME: 15 MINUTES
COOKING TIME: 30 MINUTES

1 *eggplant, 1 to 1 1/2 pounds*
1/2 *cup lemon juice or to taste*
1 *cup seeded, chopped, tomatoes*
1 *red pepper, seeded and chopped*
1 *green pepper, seeded and chopped*

1 *cup chopped scallions including 2-inch green tops*
1/2 *cup freshly chopped parsley*
1 *teaspoon paprika Dash of cayenne Salt and freshly ground pepper to taste*
1/4 *cup olive oil*

1. Preheat oven to 400° F. Place eggplant on foil lined baking sheet and bake in preheated oven 45 minutes.

2. Peel eggplant and slit open to drain juice. Remove seeds.

3. Place eggplant in dish and sprinkle with lemon juice. Set aside to cool. When cool, chop into bite-size pieces.

4. Place tomato, red and green peppers, scallions, and parsley in bowl. Add paprika, cayenne, salt, pepper, olive oil, and chopped eggplant with lemon juice. Stir lightly until well combined. Serve at room temperature or chilled.

SERVES 6

HINTS: To add a tart flavor, sprinkle eggplant with 1/8 teaspoon sour salt (citric acid), lemon juice is added.

Lentil Salad
VOSPOV AGHTSAN

PREPARATION TIME: 10 MINUTES (plus soaking)
OOKING TIME: 30 MINUTES

Eggplant Salad
Corn Salad
Lentil Salad

1 1/2 cups brown lentils picked
over and rinsed
1 medium purple onion,
finely chopped
1 medium tomato, seeded
and chopped (optional)
1/2 cup vinegar
1/3 cup olive oil

1/4 cup freshly chopped
parsley
Salt and freshly ground
pepper to taste
Cayenne to taste
1/4 teaspoon cumin
1/4 teaspoon coriander

1. Soak lentils several hours in enough water to cover at least 2-inches.

2. Place in saucepan, bring to a boil, simmer about 25 minutes or till tender but not mushy.

3. Drain. Cool. Mix with remaining ingredients and serve or chill.

SERVES 6

VARIATION: Substitute lemon juice for vinegar.

Corn Salad
YEKIBTAZORENOV AGHTSAN

PREPARATION TIME: 15 MINUTES

3 (12 ounce) cans corn,
drained
1 small green pepper diced
1 small onion finely
chopped
1/3 cup lemon juice

1/4 cup olive oil
Salt and freshly ground
pepper to taste
Radish or black olives
garnish

1. Mix corn, pepper, onion, lemon juice, salt and pepper together. Decorate with radish slices overlapping or olives around dish.

SERVES 6

SALADS

This piquant salad can be used with any type of barbecued meats, or chicken, or as a relish. The amount of cayenne depends on the cook.

Hot Armenian Salad
LOLIGI AGHTSAN

PREPARATION TIME: 15 MINUTES

3 large tomatoes, seeded and diced
1 large onion, finely chopped
1 cup freshly chopped parsley
1/4 cup lemon juice
2 tablespoons olive oil
1/2 teaspoon paprike
1/4 teaspoon cayenne or to taste
Salt and freshly ground pepper to taste
Tabasco sauce

1. Place all ingredients in a bowl, toss together. Taste, and adjust seasonings.

SERVES 6

VARIATION: Add 1 cup toasted pita bread cut into 1-inch pieces just before serving (or bread will turn soggy). Add 1 green pepper or cucumber chopped, increase lemon juice and oil to taste.

Cabbage Salad
Green Olive Salad

Cabbage Salad
SALATET ET MALFUF

Lebanese are fond of cabbage, they stuff, pickle, and make salad with it. A favorite Middle Eastern salad with more of this or more of that added in different countries. I dry mint springs from my garden in the summer, then crush the leaves and store them in a glass container and enjoy this salad all winter long. Mint is used in numerous dishes throughout the Middle East. A very popular herb among the Armenians, Greeks, Lebanese, and Iranians.

PREPARATION TIME: 15 MINUTES

1/4 cup olive oil
1/4 cup lemon juice
    Salt and white pepper to taste
  5 cups shredded cabbage
1/2 cup fresh mint leaves chopped, or 1 tablespoon dried crushed mint

1. Mix oil, lemon juice, salt and pepper in a bowl. Add cabbage, mint, and toss thoroughly. Serve, or marinate for more intense flavor overnight.

SERVES 4

VARIATION: One garlic clove crushed or garlic powder to taste. Shred cabbage and blanch in boiling water for 1 minute. Drain, refresh in cold water. Drain completely and toss with dressing.

Green Olive Salad
SALATET ZEITOUN

PREPARATION TIME: 10 MINUTES

1/3 cup lemon juice
1/4 cup olive oil
1/2 teaspoon paprika
    Dash cayenne
1 1/2 cups green olives pitted or stuffed pimento olives coarsely chopped
  1 cup seeded and chopped tomatoes

1 cup freshly chopped parsley
1/4 cup chopped mint leaves or 2 teaspoons dried crushed mint
4 scallions with 2-inch green tops chopped

1. Mix lemon juice, oil and pepper in a bowl.

2. Add remaining ingredients and toss to coat.

SERVES 4 TO 6

VARIATION: Add 1/2 cup diced cheese such as Swiss or Halloum.

HINTS: Test olives before making the salad for saltiness.

CHAPTER FOUR

Eggs

P opular egg dishes are used extensively in the Middle East, they are called Koo Koo's in Iran and Ijja in Lebanon similar to Fritta tas. The eggs are used to bind precooked vegetables such as string beans, potatoes or combined with freshly chopped parsley, coriander, dill, mint, spinach or romaine lettuce. Armenians love eggs with sujuk (page 39), prepared like the traditional ham and eggs. They also use Basterma, a spicy cured meat with a delicious hot strong taste, which can be found in Armenian or Greek speciality stores. The two dishes are especially good during the cold winter months.

Green Vegetable Omelet
KOO KOO-YE-SABZI

PREPARATION TIME: 15 TO 20 MINUTES
COOKING TIME: 20 TO 30 MINUTES

4 tablespoons butter
Bread crumbs
8 eggs
1/4 teaspoon saffron steeped in 2 tablespoons hot water or 1/4 teaspoon turmeric
Pinch cinnamon
Salt and freshly ground pepper to taste
2 cups shredded romaine lettuce

1 1/2 cups freshly chopped parsley
1 cup freshly chopped spinach or 1/2 cup chopped spinach and 1/2 cup chopped coriander
1 cup chopped scallions
1/4 cup freshly chopped mint or 2 tablespoons dried crushed mint
1/4 cup freshly chopped dill or 2 tablespoons dried dill

1. Preheat oven 350° F. Butter a 10-inch cake pan and dust with bread crumbs. Set aside.

2. Beat eggs in a bowl. Add saffron, cinnamon, salt, pepper, and mix. Add lettuce, parsley, spinach, and scallions. Mix well and pour into prepared pan.

3. Bake in preheated oven 25 to 30 minutes, or until omelet is set and golden on top. If necessary, run under broiler about 1 minute to brown top. Cut into wedges or squares and serve hot or at room temperature. Delicious served with dairy sour cream and chives spooned over individual portions. If desired, cook in non-stick skillet on top of stove.

SERVES 6 TO 8

VARIATION: Add 3 tablespoons coarsley chopped walnuts and 3 tablespoons currants to mixture before cooking.

Potato and Tomato Omelet
KOO KOO-YE-SIB ZAMINI

PREPARATION TIME: 15 MINUTES
COOKING TIME: 45 MINUTES

6 tablespoons butter
2 tablespoons vegetable oil
1 large onion, chopped
2 large potatoes, sliced
  1/4-inch thick
3 tablespoons lemon juice

1/4 to 1/2 teaspoon cinnamon
Salt and freshly ground
  pepper to taste
2 tomatoes seeded, sliced
6 large eggs (whisked
  together)

1. Heat 4 tablespoons butter and the oil in a 10-inch non-stick skillet. Add onion and saute till transparent and golden, stirring often (about 10 to 15 minutes). Remove with a slotted spoon to a dish. Set aside.

2. Saute potatoes on both sides till golden in same saucepan adding more butter if necessary. Leave potatoes in saucepan, spread with sauteed onion, sprinkle lemon juice over them. Dust with cinnamon, salt and pepper. Arrange tomatoes on top, salt and pepper. Cover and reduce to low. Cook 10 minutes.

3. Remove cover, and pour beaten eggs over potatoes. Lightly salt and pepper. Loosely cover and cook for about 20 to 25 minutes until eggs are set. Serve hot with salad and Lavash Bread available in Middle Eastern stores. This can also be cooked then layered in a heatproof dish and baked covered for 35 to 45 minutes in a preheated 350° F. oven.

SERVES 4

Fried Eggs with Sumac
BEIT BIL SUMAC

PREPARATION TIME: 10 MINUTES
COOKING TIME: 5 TO 7 MINUTES

1/4 cup olive oil (preferably
  virgin)
4 jumbo eggs
  Salt and freshly ground
  pepper

1 1/2 teaspoons sumac*
2 teaspoons dried crushed
  mint
2 to 4 cloves garlic, crushed,
  or 1/2 teaspoon garlic
  powder or to taste

For something really unusual try this recipe. It is served in Lebanon late at night or early morning after an all night party.

1. Heat oil in a skillet over medium-high heat.

2. Break eggs leaving whole into skillet. Sprinkle with salt and pepper, sumac, mint and garlic. Cook just till set, or cover and cook to desired doness. Serve with warm bread and fruits of the season for dessert.

SERVES 2 TO 4

* Sumac is available in Middle Eastern stores. Do not confuse with the poisonous berries.

Fish Omelet
KOO KOO-YE-MAHI

PREPARATION TIME: 15 MINUTES
COOKING TIME: 1 HOUR

Dried bread crumbs
6 *tablespoons butter*
1 *small onion, finely chopped*
1 *pound firm white fish fillets*
1/4 *cup chopped coriander leaves*

1/8 *teaspoon turmeric (optional)*
Salt and freshly ground pepper to taste
6 *large eggs*
1 *tablespoon all-purpose flour*
Sliced tomato to garnish

1. Grease an 8 x 8-inch baking dish and lightly dust with bread crumbs.

2. Heat 2 tablespoons butter in large skillet. Add onion and saute until transparent. Remove to large bowl with slotted spoon.

3. Add 2 to 3 tablespoons butter to skillet. Saute half of fish fillets on both side, transfer to bowl with onion. Repeat with remaining fish, adding more butter if necessary.

4. Preheat oven to 350° F. Flake fish with a fork. Add coriander, turmeric, salt and pepper, and mix well.

5. Whisk 1 egg. Add flour and beat until smooth. Add remaining 5 eggs and beat until well combined. Pour over fish mixture and stir to blend. Spoon into prepared baking dish.

6. Bake in preheated oven for 25 minutes or until set. Brown top lightly under broiler, if desired. Unmold onto serving plate and cut into squares. Serve hot or room temperature as an appetizer or as a main meal with sliced tomatoes and hot bread and butter.

SERVES 4 TO 6

String Bean Omelet
KOO KOO-YE-LOOBIA SABZ

PREPARATION TIME: 10 MINUTES
COOKING TIME: 20 MINUTES

Bread crumbs
1 *pound string beans, cut into 1/4-inch pieces*
3 *tablespoons butter*
1 *teaspoon tarragon (optional)*
1/4 *teaspoon nutmeg*

1 *large onion, finely chopped*
6 *large eggs, beaten together*
Pinch of saffron steeped in 2 tablespoons water
Salt and freshly ground pepper to taste

This is a lovely way to serve vegetables for lunch or as a light meal.

1. Preheat oven to 350° F. Grease an 8 x 8-inch pan and dust with bread crumbs.

2. Cook string beans in lightly salted boiling water until tender-crisp, 8 to 10 minutes. Drain and set aside.

3. Heat 2 tablespoons butter in skillet and saute onion until transparent.

4. Mix eggs, tarragon, nutmeg, saffron, salt and pepper. Add beans and onion, stir to combine.

5. Pour into prepared pan, sprinkle with bread crumbs and dot with 1 tablespoon butter. Bake in middle of preheated oven, 15 to 20 minutes or until eggs are set. cool slightly, cut into squares, and serve warm or at room temperature with meat, chicken, or fish. If desired, cook in non-stick skillet on top of stove.
SERVES 4 TO 6

VARIATION: Add half a pound lean ground beef to onion, saute, and set aside. Pour half of egg-string bean mixture into prepared pan and bake until set, about 10 minutes. Spread onion-meat mixture over cooked layer and top with remainder of egg string bean mixture. Cover and bake 15 minutes. Serve hot or room temperature.

Parsley Omelets
IJJA

PREPARATION TIME: 20 MINUTES
COOKING TIME: 3 TO 5 MINUTES

1 1/2 cups freshly chopped
    parsley
2 cloves garlic, crushed or 1
    teaspoon garlic powder
    Salt and freshly ground
    pepper to taste

1/2 cup chopped scallions
6 large eggs (whisked
    together)
    Vegetable oil or butter as
    needed (about 1/4 cup)

1. Mix parsley, scallions, garlic and seasonings together. Add eggs and blend thoroughly.

2. Heat a 10-inch, non-stick skillet with oil or butter to cover bottom.

3. Pour 2 tablespoons of mixture at a time here and there, leaving space in between each omelet, to keep roundish shape. Cook over medium-heat till edges are slightly golden, turn and cook on other side. Size of omelet should be about 2 to 3 inches. Drain on paper towels if needed. Add more oil or butter if necessary. Continue with rest of mix.

Serve warm or room temperature. Can accompany fish, Fried Eggplants (page 144), or with dairy sour cream and chopped chives.

SERVES 4 TO 6

VARIATION: Made as one large omelet. Cut into square bite-size pieces, serve with toothpicks.

Substitute 1 1/2 cups grated or finely diced zucchini for parsley.

HINTS: For slightly thicker batter add 2 tablespoons flour to mix with eggs.

Egg and Yogourt Sauce
MADZOUNOV HAVGIT

PREPARATION TIME: 20 MINUTES
COOKING TIME: 5 MINUTES

3 tablespoons butter
6 large eggs
4 small pita or sandwich
    bread lightly toasted

1 recipe Yogurt Garlic
    Sauce (page 260) room
    temperature
    Salt and freshly ground
    pepper to taste

1. Melt butter in medium-sized non-stick skillet. Scramble eggs, or make an omelet.

2. Place toast on individual plates. Spread yogurt garlic sauce equally over bread. Top with equal amounts of cooked eggs. Serve immediately while hot. Sprinkle with salt and pepper.

SERVES 4

VARIATION: Capers, crisp fried bacon bits, dried crushed mint or basil leaves may be sprinkled on top of eggs.

CHAPTER FIVE

Fish

Many restaurants in Lebanon grill their freshly caught Mediteranean fish over characoal grills. The Sultan Ibrahim (red mullet) a favorite, is fried in hot oil to a golden crispy brown. To remove the strong fishy odor, pieces of pita bread are added to the oil when fish is removed and served crackling along side the mouth watering fish.

In Iran's Caspian Sea, where the famous caviar comes from, you will find enormous sturgeon as well as Whitefish, Salmon, and Swordfish. These fish are sometimes smoked or cut into bite-sized pieces and made into kabobs. Whitefish is cooked then layered with Green Herb Rice (page 174) and steamed to perfection.

Lake Savan in Armenia has a very famous trout called Prince. I have been told it is well worth the trip just to savor it's royal flavor.

T his Armenian classic recipe was taught to me by my mother. It was usually served on a friday.

Layered Flounder
SHERDEVADZ TSOUG

PREPARATION TIME: 30 MINUTES
COOKING TIME: 25 TO 35 MINUTES

5 carrots, sliced
2 1/2 pounds flounder or sole fillets
1/2 cup olive oil
5 medium onions, sliced
4 large potatoes, peeled and sliced

1 can (6 ounces) tomato paste
1/4 teaspoon sugar
1/4 teaspoon nutmeg
Dash cayenne
Salt and freshly ground pepper to taste
1/4 cup lemon juice

1. Cook carrots in lightly salted water about 10 minutes or until almost tender. Drain and set aside. Rinse fish fillets and pat dry with paper towels.

2. Heat 1/4 cup oil in large skillet. Add onions, saute until transparent and golden. Remove with slotted spoon and set aside. Add remaining 1/4 cup oil to skillet and saute fish fillets on both sides until golden. Set aside. Saute potato slices on both sides, adding more oil if necessary. Drain on paper towels. Set aside.

3. Preheat oven to 350° F. Grease bottom of 13 x 9-inch baking dish. Place 1 layer of potatoes and onions in dish, cover with fish fillets and reserved carrots. Place remaining potatoes and onions on top.

4. Mix 3/4 cup water, tomato paste, sugar, nutmeg, cayenne, salt and pepper in saucepan. Bring to a boil and pour over fish. Cover with foil. Bake in preheated oven 25 minutes. Remove cover, add lemon juice, and bake 10 minutes. Serve with green salad, fresh bread and ice cream or sherbert and cookies for desert.
SERVES 6

HINT: Prepare ahead of time and refrigerate without liquid until ready to bake.

In Iran green eating herbs (Sabzi Khordan) are featured in their cuisine. A mixed platter of dill, mint, tarragon, watercress, garlic chives, coriander, and basil is found on every luncheon and dinner table.

Herb Stuffed Fish
MAHI A SHEKAMPOUR

PREPARATION TIME: 20 MINUTES
COOKING TIME: 40 TO 50 MINUTES

1 whole bass, snapper, or any baking fish (3 to 4 pounds)
Salt to taste
1/2 cup freshly chopped parsley
1/2 cup freshly chopped dill
1/2 cup freshly chopped watercress
1/2 cup freshly chopped coriander
1/4 cup chopped scallions
Freshly ground pepper to taste
2 limes, thinly sliced and seeded
1/3 cup olive oil
Lime wedges and parsley sprigs to garnish

1. Clean and rinse fish. Rub with salt inside and out.

2. Mix parsley, dill, watercress, coriander, scallions, and pepper. Reserve 3 lime slices. Place remaining lime slices in cavity of fish. Add herb stuffing and secure opening with toothpicks.

3. Preheat oven to 400° F. Make 3 diagonal slashes on top and bottom of fish with sharp knife. Place in baking dish and pour oil over. Rub oil into surface of fish on top and bottom. Place reserved lime on top of fish and bake in preheated oven about 30 minutes or until fish flakes when fork is inserted into thickest part. Baste with pan juices while cooking.

4. Remove fish carefully to serving platter and garnish with lime wedges and parsley sprigs. Serve with sliced tomatoes and steamed potatoes or Steamed Rice, (page 182). If served with rice, gently toss rice with stuffing before serving.

SERVES 4 TO 6

Fish with Oranges

MAHI SORKARDA BA NARENJ

PREPARATION TIME: 15 MINUTES
COOKING TIME: 5 TO 8 MINUTES

2 pounds fish fillets such as
sole, perch, halibut,
flounder, or small whole
fish or whitefish steaks 1
per person
Salt and freshly ground
pepper to taste

Flour as needed
Vegetable oil or butter as
needed
2 Seville oranges cut into
wedges
Watercress

1. Rinse and pat fish dry with paper towels. Cut into 4-inch pieces. Sprinkle with salt and pepper on both sides.

2. Coat fish thoroughly with flour, set aside.

3. Heat skillet with oil (about 1/8 of an inch), to shallow fry, over medium-high heat. Add prepared fish and fry to a golden color on both sides. Drain on paper towels. Place on serving dish and garnish with seville oranges (to be squeezed over fish) surrounded with watercress. Bread, rice or homemade potato chips are served with this dish. If Seville oranges are not available an alternative is to mix orange and lemon or lime juice in equal portions.

SERVES 4 TO 6

VARIATION: Follow step 1 above with fish. Rub over fish a mixture of 2 cloves crushed garlic, zest of one orange and 2 to 3 tablespoons olive oil. Cover, set aside 30 minutes. Dip pieces in 3 large beaten eggs, then dip in flour and fry fillets as above. Omit seville oranges. Serve with sauted spinach and onions in butter and orange wedges (to squeeze over fish if desired).

Arabs and Iranians are very fond of seville oranges (bitter orange) which is abundant in the Middle East. It is squeezed on fried fish or into soups, also eaten in sections like a grapefruit. This recipe is served often in Iran when seville oranges are in season. Whitefish from the Caspian Sea is used for its delicate flavor.

Cheese Sprinkled Sole
BANEEROV TSOUG

PREPARATION TIME: 15 MINUTES
COOKING TIME: 20 TO 25 MINUTES

2 1/2 pounds fillet of grey sole
2 tablespoons safflower or corn oil
Freshly ground white pepper to taste
1/4 cup bread crumbs, plain or seasoned (optional)

1/2 cup grated parmesan cheese
Paprika to taste
4 tablespoons butter
Parsley and lemon garnish

1. Run your finger over center of fillets, if you feel a hard rubber like cartilage strip in center, remove with a sharp knife by slitting close to it on both sides. Rinse fillets, pat dry with paper towels. Set aside.

2. Coat a large heatproof dish with 2 tablespoons oil. Place fish in pan. Sprinkle freshly ground pepper, bread crumbs, cheese, and paprika on top.

3. Preheat oven to 400° F. Dot fish with butter and bake for about 15 minutes. Garnish individual plates with parsley and lemon wedges. Serve with steamed potatoes or Armenian Rice with Noodles (page 170) and a mixed salad or sliced zucchini sauteed in butter.

SERVES 6 TO 8

This is an extremely easy dish. Any hard grated cheese on hand can be used, with any white fish fillet that is available. No matter what the combination, it still works. The recipe below is my favorite. Serve with lots of lemon to squeeze over cooked fish when serving.

Baked Whole Fish
SAMKE MATBOUKHA

PREPARATION TIME: 15 MINUTES
COOKING TIME: 35 TO 45 MINUTES

1 sea bass or striped bass about 5 pounds
Salt to taste

1 large lemon, sliced and seeded
4 sprigs of parsley or 4 bay leaves

1. Preheat oven to 450° F. Rinse fish inside and out. Pat dry with paper towels.

2. Cut piece of parchment paper large enough to wrap fish completely and place on baking sheet. Place fish on parchment paper and sprinkle with salt inside and out. Place lemon slices and parsley inside fish. Wrap fish loosely and tuck ends under, leaving space for steam to circulate inside package.

3. Bake in preheated oven about 35 to 45 minutes or until fish flakes easily.

4. Unwrap fish (remove and discard bay leaves if using) and place on serving platter. Serve with Armenian Rice With Noodles (page 170), mixed salad, and steamed vegetables.

SERVES 6

HINT: Leftover fish should be removed from bone covered and refrigerated.

This simple but excellent baked bass recipe is a Lebanese version served throughout the Middle East. The fish is thoroughly oiled, stuffed with lemon slices and parsley or coriander, wrapped in parchment paper, and baked in the oven. Originally lightly oiled brown paper or newspaper was used to wrap the fish. Arabs like to pour Tarator Sauce (page 257) over the fish and sprinkle it with roasted pine nuts. Armenians serve this dish with extra lemon juice, oil, or herb-flavored mayonnaise. Occasionally garlic is added to the stuffing.

The combination of a vinegar sauce with carrots and fish is unique. Not only does it look unusual, the pungent taste is memorable.

Fish Salad
TSOUG AGHTSAN

PREPARATION TIME: 15 MINUTES
COOKING TIME: 30 MINUTES

1 1/2 *pounds grey sole fillets or other firm white fish.*	1 1/2 *teaspoons whole black peppercorns*
2 *medium onions, thinly sliced*	2 *bay leaves*
1 *pound carrots, sliced and cooked*	1/3 *cup red wine vinegar*
	1/3 *cup olive oil*
	1/3 *cup tomato sauce*
	1/2 *teaspoon salt or to taste*

1. Preheat oven to 350° F.

2. Rinse fillets and trim if necessary. Cut into 2 1/2-inch pieces. Pat dry with paper towels and set aside.

3. Arrange onions in 2-quart baking dish. Add carrots and fish, sprinkle peppercorns over, and place bay leaves on top.

4. Place vinegar, olive oil, tomato sauce, and salt in 2-cup glass measure. Mix well and pour over fish. Bake, uncovered, in preheated oven 30 minutes. Cool to room temperature, cover, and refrigerate up to 2 days. Discard bay leaves. Serve cold or at room temperature.

SERVES 6

VARIATION: Saute onions in 3 tablespoons of olive oil until transparent, stirring frequently. Add 2 to 3 thinly sliced celery stalks, stir, and cook 1 minute. Continue as directed above.

Fish Salad

F reshly caught trout from the River Lar or Karun in south west Iran, were one of the best I have ever tasted.

Baked Trout
MAHIE GHUZALALLA

PREPARATION TIME: 15 MINUTES
COOKING TIME: 15 TO 20 MINUTES

4 *whole cleaned fresh water trout*
Salt and freshly ground pepper
Olive oil to coat

2 *tablespoons each: fresh snipped chives, fresh minced parsley, and fresh minced basil*
1/4 *cup lime juice*

1. Rinse insides and out of fish, pat dry with paper towels.

2. Salt and pepper inside and out. Rub with oil to coat. Place on oiled baking dish.

3. Preheat oven to 400° F. Mix together herbs and lime juice. Divide equally. Stuff fish, and bake in preheated oven for about 10 to 15 minutes depending on size of fish (about 8 minutes per inch thickness) or secure with toothpick and shallow fry in oil.

SERVES 4

This Armenian recipe, originated in Amasia-Turkey and was brought to Iran in 1915.

Whitefish Steaks
JERMAG TSOUG

PREPARATION TIME: 15 MINUTES
COOKING TIME: 35 MINUTES

6 *whitefish steaks, 2-inches thick*
Salt to taste
2 *cups freshly chopped parsley*
2 *cups freshly chopped scallions*
6 *cloves garlic, minced*
5 *lemons, peeled, seeded and sliced*
1/3 *cup olive oil*
Freshly ground pepper

1. Rinse fish steaks and pat dry with paper towels. Season with salt and pepper on both sides and set aside.

2. Mix parsley, scallions, and garlic in small bowl. Spread half of mixture in 4-quart non-stick saucepan. Place fish steaks on top, spread with remainder of mixture. Arrange 4 sliced lemons over surface. Combine 1/3 cup water with oil and pour into saucepan.

3. Bring to a boil over high heat, reduce to medium-low. Cover and cook 25 to 35 minutes. Remove from heat, uncover, and set aside to cool completely. Place in serving platter, cover, and refrigerate. Serve cold, garnished with remaining lemon slices.

SERVES 6

VARIATION: Omit lemon slices. Heat 1/4 cup oil in large skillet. Add fish steaks and saute on both sides. Remove to dish. Add parsley, scallions, and garlic to skillet, stir well, and cook 2 minutes. Return fish to skillet. Mix 1/ cup vinegar with 2 tablespoons tomato paste and 1/3 cup water. Pour over fish and bring to a boil. Reduce heat to medium-low, cover, and cook 10 minutes. Serve warm with bread to dip into sauce. This is served during Lent.

Curried Sea Bass
CURIOV TSOUG

PREPARATION TIME: 15 MINUTES
COOKING TIME: 15 TO 20 MINUTES

This curried fish was developed by the large Armenian community living in India.

4 small sea bass
6 tablespoons butter, room temperature
1 to 2 teaspoons curry powder

1/3 cup lemon juice
Salt to taste
Tomato wedges and fresh coriander garnish

1. Have Fishmonger select and clean fish.

2. Rinse well then pat dry with paper towels. Place on oiled baking dish.

3. Preheat oven to 500° F. Mix butter, curry powder, lemon juice, and salt together. Spread inside and out of fish.

4. Bake for 10 to 15 minutes. Basting often as fish cooks. Fish is done when fork inserted separates flesh easily. Do not turn fish or you risk them falling apart. Garnish with tomato wedges and coriander leaves. Serve hot with steamed potatoes and a mixed salad or just the filling for Spinach in Pastry (page 160) or sliced oranges and black olives surrounding platter.

SERVES 4

VARIATION: For a deeper color broil fish when almost done for 1 minute. Crushed garlic or garlic powder can be mixed into butter, and brushed over fish before cooking.

This recipe is the Lebanese version. Egyptians fry the fish and serve it with a combination of rice and onions.

Fish with Rice
SAYYADIEH

PREPARATION TIME: 20 MINUTES
COOKING TIME: 1 HOUR

1/4 cup olive oil
2 large onions, cut in half and sliced
6 cups boiling water
5 pound bass*
1/2 to 1 teaspoon salt or to taste

1/2 to 1 teaspoon cumin
2 cups long grain rice
1/4 cup lemon juice
Lemon wedges, parsley sprigs, and roasted pine nuts or slivered almonds to garnish

1. Heat oil in 4-quart skillet. Add onions and stir to coat. Brown evenly over medium heat, stirring often (do not burn). Add 6 cups boiling water and cook 10 minutes.

2. Leave fish whole or cut into pieces. Sprinkle with salt. Add to saucepan with cumin, reduce heat to low, and simmer covered. For whole fish 25 minutes, for pieces 15 minutes.

3. Remove fish carefully and keep warm. Pass liquid with onions through food mill into bowl.

4. Measure 4 cups of liquid and pour into medium-size saucepan. Reserve remainder of liquid. Add rice and bring to a boil. Reduce heat to medium low, cover and cook 15 to 20 minutes or until rice is tender and liquid is absorbed. Set aside 5 to 10 minutes before serving.

5. Pour reserved liquid into saucepan. Add lemon juice and heat. Taste and adjust seasoning. To intensify the sauce reduce by boiling 10 minutes.

6. To serve whole fish, spoon rice onto platter, place fish on top, or serve separately. Garnish with lemon and parsley. To serve fish pieces,debone, and skin. Layer rice with fish in platter, garnish with roasted pine nuts or almonds.

SERVES 6 TO 8

VARIATION: To make white Sayyadieh, cook onions until transparent but not browned. Use cooked fish fillets. Grease medium-size mold, sprinkle with roasted nuts, layer half of fish then half of cooked rice. Repeat with remainder of fish and rice. Press down to pack into mold. Heat in a preheated oven 350° F. for 45 minutes. Unmold onto platter and serve hot with sauce.

* Similar fish can be substituted.

Shrimp Kabobs
KABOB A MEYGU

PREPARATION TIME: 10 MINUTES
COOKING TIME: 8 MINUTES

2 *pounds raw jumbo shrimp*
4 *tablespoons butter, melted*

2 *tablespoons lemon juice*
Salt and freshly ground pepper to taste

1. Shell, devein shrimps and rinse.

2. Thread on skewers. Brush with melted butter, and lemon juice sprinkle with salt and pepper.

3. Cook over hot coals 2 to 4 minutes each side, brushing several times during cooking. Pour remaining sauce over shrimps when serving. Serve with bread and salad or curried rice and vegetables.

SERVES 6

VARIATION: Any firm fleshed fish cut into cubes may be substituted for shrimp. Try salmon steaks or cubes, or strugeon. Rinse shrimps, barbecue in shells. Remove shells after cooking and dip into butter lemon sauce.

Succulent shrimps caught in the Persian Gulf are not only appreciated by the neighboring countries but are shipped to Europe and Scandinavia.

Stuffed Mussels
TSGNAGANCH LETSK / MIDIA DOLMA

PREPARATION TIME: 30 MINUTES
COOKING TIME: 45 MINUTES

1/2 *cup short grain rice*
2 *pounds mussels*
1/4 *cup cornmeal*
1/2 *cup olive oil*
6 *medium onions, chopped*
1/2 *cup currants*
1/2 *cup freshly chopped parsley*

1/4 *cup pine nuts*
1/2 *teaspoon cinnamon*
1/2 *teaspoon allspice*
1/2 *teaspoon salt or to taste*
1/2 *teaspoon freshly ground pepper*
1 1/4 *cups fish stock or water*
Lemon wedges to garnish

This is an elaborate and distinguished "meza" that deserves special attention.

1. Rinse rice and set aside to soak in warm water to cover.

2. Place mussels in large bowl of cold water. Swish around and change water several times. Add cornmeal and set aside 45 minutes. Drain and scrub under cold running water. Clip off beards.

3. Use tip of a sharp knife to open mussels slowly and carefully, leaving them hinged on 1 side.

4. Heat oil in skillet. Add onions and saute until tranparent.

5. Drain rice and place in large bowl. Add onions, currants, parsley, pine nuts, cinnamon, allspice, salt and pepper. Mix well, taste, and adjust seasoning. Stuff mixture loosely into mussels close slightly and place in single layer in large saucepan. Add fish stock and bring to a boil. Reduce heat to low, cover, and simmer 30 minutes. Remove with slotted spoon. Serve at room temperature with wedges of lemon.

SERVES 4 TO 6

Stuffed Mussels

FISH

Fish with Hot Pepper I
SAMKE HARA I

PREPARATION TIME: 30 MINUTES
COOKING TIME: 1 HOUR

> 1   *buss (loukos) about 5 pounds, untrimmed*
> 1   *teaspoon salt or to taste*
> 1/2 *teaspoon cayenne or to taste*
> 1/2 *teaspoon freshly ground pepper*
> 1/4 *cup olive oil (preferably virgin)*

FLAVORED TARATOR SAUCE:
> 2   *to 4 cloves garlic, crushed*

> 1   *cup tahini*
> 1/3 *cup lemon juice*
> 1/4 *cup freshly chopped coriander leaves*
> 1   *teaspoon cayenne or to taste*
>   *Salt to taste*
> 3   *tablespoons pine nuts, pomegranate seeds, lemon wedges, coriander or parsley sprigs to garnish.*

There are two ways to prepare this dish. Both are popular in Lebanon, Egypt, and Syria. In this recipe the cooked fish is mixed with flavored Tarator Sauce (below) and reformed to resemble a fish and served cold. Snapper or other firm fish may be substituted for bass in the first recipe.

1. Preheat oven to 350° F. Rinse fish and pat dry with paper towels. Rub with salt, cayenne, pepper, and olive oil.

2. Place fish on ungreased baking sheet and bake in preheated oven 35 to 40 minutes, or until fork pierces skin easily.

3. Remove head and tail of fish very carefully, keeping them intact for decoration if desired. Discard skin and bone fish carefully. Place boned fish in dish and set aside.

4. To make sauce, place all ingredients in large bowl, add 1/2 cup water, and mix well. Taste and adjust seasonings.

5. Remove half the sauce and set aside. Add fish to sauce in bowl and mix well.

6. Spoon onto serving platter and mold or shape into fish. If desired, decorate with head and tail. Pour reserved sauce over fish to coat. Sprinkle pine nuts on top and pomegranate seed around sides of fish. Garnish platter with lemon wedges and sprigs of coriander. Serve at room temperature or chilled.

SERVES 6

VARIATION: Clean inside of fish and saute briefly on both sides. Place fish in baking dish and set aside. Prepare sauce. Preheat oven to 350° F. Spoon 1/2 of sauce into cavity of fish. Spoon remainder of sauce over fish. Bake in preheated oven 40 minutes, basting with sauce 2 or 3 times. Serve immediately.

Fish with Hot Pepper II
SAMKE HARRA II

PREPARATION TIME: 15 MINUTES
COOKING TIME: 35 MINUTES

4 *bass or salmon steaks*
1 *1/2-inch thick*
  Salt
  Vegetable oil (about 1/4 cup)
1 *medium onion, chopped or sliced*
3 *or 4 cloves garlic, minced*

1/2 *cup freshly chopped coriander leaves*
  Boiling water
1/2 *teaspoon cumin*
1/2 *cup lemon juice*
1/2 *to 1 teaspoon cayenne*
  Coriander sprigs and lemon slices or wedges to garnish

1. Rinse fish steaks and pat dry with paper towels. Sprinkle with salt on both sides and let stand 10 minutes.

2. Cover bottom of large skillet with oil and heat. Saute steaks briefly on both sides. Remove, set aside. Add more oil to skillet if necessary and saute onion, garlic, and coriander, stirring constantly 1 to 2 minutes. Drain excess oil from skillet.

3. Return steaks to skillet, placing them over onion mixture. Pour in enough boiling water to come half way up sides of steaks. Stir in cumin and simmer 10 to 15 minutes, basting steaks with liquid or carefully turning steaks over once or twice during cooking.

4. Remove steaks gently to serving platter.

5. Mix lemon juice, cayenne and salt. Pour over steaks and let cool. Garnish with coriander sprigs and lemon slices. Serve room temperature of chilled.

SERVES 4

VARIATION: 1 large tomato seeded and chopped may be added to onions, garlic, and coriander while sauteeing.

CHAPTER SIX

Chicken

The chickens used in the Middle East and Iran are delicious since they are small and free ranging. There are rotisseries full of chickens in small grocery stores in every section of town and their smell is wonderful. They are roasted, grilled and the larger ones used in stews like everywhere else, the differences being in the methods and ingredients. One particular Armenian dish is Herrisa, it looks like porridge but is chicken and whole grain skinless wheat that has been partially pureed and then topped with cumin, cayenne and melted butter. There is nothing else like it. The Lebanese have a tangy coriander dish and the Iranians mix dried fruits with their chicken.

Chicken in Tomato Sauce

Chicken in Tomato Sauce
HAVOV LOLIG

PREPARATION TIME: 20 MINUTES
COOKING TIME: 1 1/2 HOURS

2 chicken (3 1/2 pounds each) cut into 12 pieces
6 carrots
4 celery stalks
2 to 3 medium potatoes, peeled
1 1/2 teaspoons garlic powder
1/2 teaspoon allspice
1/2 teaspoon rosemary
1/2 teaspoon oregano
Salt and freshly ground pepper to taste
2 1/2 cups tomato sauce

1. Rinse chicken , pat dry with paper towels. Preheat oven to 400° F. Place chicken into roasting pan.

2. Cut carrots and celery into 1-inch pieces. Cut each potato into 6 pieces. Place vegetables around chicken.

SERVES 6 TO 8

3. Stir seasonings into tomato sauce and pour over chicken. Cover with aluminum foil, bake in preheated oven 1 hour. Uncover and cook 20 minutes. serve hot with pasta and salad.

SERVES 6

VARIATION: Leave chickens whole. Cut carrots and celery into 2-inch pieces. Cook, 1 hour longer.

Chicken with Dried Fruits and Rice
MORGH POLOW

PREPARATION TIME: 15 MINUTES
COOKING TIME: 2 HOURS

1 recipe Steamed Rice (page 182)	3/4 cup dark seedless raisins or currents
3 whole chicken breast, split, (to have 6 breasts)	3/4 cup golden seedless raisins
1/3 teaspoon cinnamon Salt and freshly ground pepper to taste	1/2 cup coarsly chopped dried apricots
8 tablespoons butter	1/2 teaspoon saffron threads steeped in 2 tablespoons hot water
1 large onion, chopped	

1. Prepare Steamed Rice in 6-quart saucepan through step 1 and 2. Rinse saucepan, set aside.

2. Rinse chicken, pat dry with paper towels. Sprinkle with cinnamon, salt and pepper on all sides.

3. Melt 2 tablespoons of butter in skillet. Add onion and saute until transparent. Place chicken over onions in skillet and saute till browned on all sides. Add 1/2 cup water, bring to a boil, cover, reduce heat to medium, cook 15 minutes. Uncover, reduce heat to low, add raisins, cover and cook 10 minutes.

4. Melt 2 tablespoons butter in 6-quart saucepan swirling to coat bottom of pan. Spoon half of reserved rice into saucepan. Drain chicken, raisins, and onion, (reserving liquid) and spoon over rice. Add apricots, cover with remaining rice. Place remaining 4 tablespoons butter over top. Pour reserved cooking liquid evenly over rice and cover with waxed paper. Wrap lid of pot in kitchen towel and place over saucepan to keep steam inside.

5. Cook over medium-heat 5 minutes, reduce heat to low and cook 55 minutes.

6. Set 1 cup rice aside. Mound rice on serving dish, place chicken, raisins, and onion around rice. Sprinkle reserved cup of rice with saffron, mix well. Sprinkle saffron rice on top of plain rice.

SERVES 6

VARIATION: Omit rice. Cook chicken with dried fruits and onion as above, till tender. Serve with bread or steamed potatoes.

Here is a decorative, exotic dish that is served by Iranian hostesses for special occasions. The raisins and apricots in this recipe may be increased or decreased. Sometimes pistachios, almonds, and hazel nuts are sauteed in butter and spooned over rice just before serving. This variation is called Jewel-Studded Rice.

Roast Chicken and Potatoes
KHOROVADZ HAV

PREPARATION TIME: 10 MINUTES
COOKING TIME: 2 HOURS

Vegetable oil
2 (3 1/2 pounds) roasting
chickens
Salt and freshly ground
pepper to taste
2 small onions

4 cloves garlic
1 teaspoon dried tarragon
or 2 fresh sprigs
8 medium potatoes, peeled
and cut in half

Roasted chicken stuffed with onions, garlic and tarragon is easy and delicious. For perfection turn the chicken while being cooked.

1. Preheat oven to 350° F. Brush roasting pan with oil. Wash chickens inside and out, pat dry with paper towels. Place in roasting pan.

2. Sprinkle chicken inside and out with salt and pepper. Place 1 onion, 2 garlic, 1/2 of tarragon inside each cavity.

3. Turn chicken in roasting pan, breast side down. Cook one-half hour. Turn both chickens onto left sides. Cook one-half hour. Add potatoes, brush lightly with oil, turn chickens to right sides. Cook one-half hour. Turn breast side up. Cook one-half hour.

SERVES 6

Skewered Chicken
SHISH TAOUK

PREPARATION TIME: 10 MINUTES (marinating 2 hours)
COOKING TIME: 8 MINUTES

3 pounds chicken cutlets or
boneless thighs
2 to 4 cloves garlic, crushed
1 tablespoon oregano
1 1/2 teaspoons dried crushed
mint
1/2 cup plus 2 tablespoons
vegetable oil

1/2 cup lemon juice
Salt and freshly ground
pepper to taste
1 green pepper
1 red pepper
1 yellow pepper
2 medium onions

Serve this tangy dish at your next barbecue with rice and a tossed green salad.

1. Cut chicken into 1 1/2 to 2-inch pieces, place in glass bowl. Add garlic, oregano, mint, 1/2 cup oil, lemon juice and pepper. stir to coat.

2. Cover and marinate in refrigerator at least 2 hours. Add salt, mix thoroughly. Thread chicken pieces on skewers and set aside.

3. Seed peppers and cut into 2-inch cubes place in bowl. Quarter onions, place in same bowl, sprinkle with salt and pepper, then the 2 tablespoons oil. Stir and thread on separate skewers.

Skewered Chicken

4. Cook over hot coals or broil about 8 minutes, turning often. Serve with fried potatoes or rice. Melted butter mixed with extra lemon juice can be poured over grilled chicken and vegetables, just before serving.

SERVES 6 TO 8

HINTS: If you like to give the chicken a pinkish tint. Mix 2 tablespoons of tomato paste to marinade. Or sprinkle with paprika and mix before cooking.

T ypically this Iranian recipe combines fruit with chicken or meat.

Tangerine Chicken
KHORESHETE MORGH VA NARENGE

PREPARATION TIME: 30 MINUTES
COOKING TIME: 2 HOURS

6 tangerines
8 tablespoons butter or vegetable oil
Flour to coat
5 pound chicken, cut into 8 pieces
2 medium onions, chopped
1/2 to 1 teaspoon saffron threads, crushed

1 1/2 cups chicken broth
1 pound carrots, julienned
1 tablespoon sugar or to taste
1/4 cup slivered almonds
2 tablespoons lemon juice
Salt and freshly ground pepper to taste

1. Peel tangerines leaving whole or separate into sections and set aside. Remove as much white from the peel as possible and cut 1 cup of very thin julienne strips. Place in small saucepan, add enough water to cover. Bring to a boil, drain, discard water and set aside.

2. Heat 6 tablespoons butter in large skillet. Sprinkle flour over chicken to coat. Saute chicken on all sides over medium-high heat until golden. Remove to large saucepan and set aside. Add remaining butter to skillet if necessary and saute onions until transparent. Transfer to saucepan. Stir in saffron, chicken broth, and reserved tangerine peel. Bring to a boil, cover reduce to medium-low and cook 40 minites.

3. Add carrots, sugar, nuts, lemon juice, salt and pepper. Mix gently together and cook 15 minutes. Taste and adjust seasonings.

4. Remove chicken, vegetables, and nuts with slotted spoon to serving platter. Keep warm. Add tangerines to saucepan, simmer 5 minutes, basting several times. Remove tangerines and place around chicken on platter. Pour sauce over entire dish. Serve with Steamed Rice, (page 182).

SERVES 4 TO 6

VARIATION: Substitute 2 cans (11 ounces each) mandarin oranges, drained, for tangerines. Substitute 1 cup candied orange peel, for tangerine peel and sugar.

Fisinjohn, a combination of duck, walnuts, and pomegranate molasses, is a Persian dish served on special occasions with fluffly Steamed Rice. Prepare this dish one day ahead to allow flavors to blend together. Chicken can be substituted for duck.

Duck in Walnut Sauce
FISINJOHN

PREPARATION TIME: 30 MINUTES
COOKING TIME: 2 HOURS

2 *duckling or one (5 pound) chicken, backbone removed and cut into 8 pieces*
1 1/2 *cups finely chopped or ground walnuts*
1 1/2 *cups coarsely chopped walnuts*
3 *tablespoons butter*

1 *large onion, finely chopped*
1/2 *cup pomegranate molasses**
4 *to 5 tablespoons sugar*
3 1/4 *cups chicken broth*
1 *to 1 1/2 teaspoons cinnamon*
Salt and freshly ground pepper to taste

1. Preheat oven to 400° F. Place ducks or chicken in baking dish and bake 30 minutes. Alternatively brown pieces in a little oil.

2. Heat heavy non-stick skillet over medium-high heat. Add walnuts and pan roast, stirring constantly with wooden spoon, about 8 to 10 minutes. Transfer to 6-quart saucepan.

3. Melt butter in same skillet. Add onion, saute until transparent. Spoon over walnuts. Add pomegranate molasses, sugar, broth, cinnamon, salt and pepper. Mix well, cook over medium-low heat 10 minutes.

4. Transfer duck or chicken to walnut-mixure in saucepan. Stir to coat, cook over low heat, covered, 1 hour, stir occasionally to prevent sticking. Serve with Steamed Rice (page 182), salad, pickles, bread, and cheese.

SERVES 8

VARIATION: Instead of duck substitute 2 1/2 pounds of ground beef or lamb shaped into small meatballs and sauteed in butter. Duck or chicken can be cooked ahead of time, deboned skinned, and cut into large pieces, then added to sauce and heated thoroughly.

* *Available in Middle Eastern speciality stores.*

Chicken Liver with Onions

Chicken Liver with Onions
SOKHOV TOK

PREPARATION TIME: 15 MINUTES
COOKING TIME: 20 MINUTES

1 pound chicken livers or calve's liver, cut into 1-inch pieces
6 tablespoons butter
2 tablespoons vegetable oil
2 large onions, halved and sliced or equal amount of scallions
2 tablespoons currents
2 tablespoons dry white wine
1 bay leaf
1/2 to 1 teaspoon allspice
Salt and freshly ground pepper to taste
Freshly chopped parsley to garnish
Lemon juice
Pita bread, to serve

1. Wash and drain liver. Pat dry with paper towels.

2. Melt butter in 12-inch skillet. Add oil and onions, saute until transparent, about 10 minutes. Add liver and stir to coat with butter. Saute 5 minutes.

3. Add currents, wine, bay leaf, allspice, salt and pepper. Cook 5 to 10 minutes. Discard bay leaf and spoon into serving dish. Sprinkle with parsley and lemon juice if desired. Serve with pita bread as part of a Meza. They can be served as a main dish with rice or noodles, over toast with watercress as an open-face sandwich with apple slices sauteed in butter.

SERVES 4

VARIATION: To make a delicious pate, cook as above, omit currents. Add dry mustard and thyme to taste. Puree cooked liver in foodmill with 6 tablespoons room temperature butter. Place in a crock or small bowl. Cover and refrigerate. (If using food processor, do not over process or pate will be grainy.)

Chicken Patties
KOTLETE MORGH

PREPARATION TIME: 30 MINUTES
COOKING TIME: 10 MINUTES

1 pound chicken cutlets
1 small onion, finely chopped
1 large egg, lightly beaten
2/3 cups fresh bread crumbs

2 tablespoons lemon juice
Salt and freshly ground white pepper to taste
Bread crumbs to coat
Butter or vegetable oil to shallow-fry

1. Grind chicken in meat grinder or food processor.

2. Transfer to a bowl. Add onion, egg, fresh bread crumbs, lemon juice, salt and pepper. Mix until thoroughly blended.

3. Divide mixture into 8 equal parts. Roll balls in bread crumbs. Reshape on waxed paper into little canoes. Sprinkle with bread crumbs to retain shapes, refrigerate on waxed paper for 10 minutes.

4. Heat enough butter or oil in skillet to come 1/8-inch up sides of pan. Add chicken patties and cook over medium-heat about 4 minutes each side, or until golden. Use additional butter or oil if necessary.

5. Drain on paper towels and serve with potatoes or rice, string beans or carrots, and salad.

SERVES 2 TO 3

VARIATION: Add 1/2 cup coarsely chopped shelled pistachios to chicken-mixture. Shape into 1-inch round balls. Deep fry or simmer in broth. Serve with cocktails. One partially cooked and grated potato can be added to patties before cooking.

HINTS: Freeze chicken patties to have on hand for unexpected guests.

Barbecued Chicken
JUJEH KABOB

Simplicity at its best. This Persian kabob is prepared with small chickens, cut into little pieces and threaded onto skewers. It was served for lunch on Thursday's the beginning of the Moslem week-end.

PREPARATION TIME: 20 MINUTES plus 1 hour)
COOKING TIME: 20 TO 25 MINUTES

12 chicken parts (breasts, thighs, drumsticks)
2 medium onions, grated Salt and freshly ground pepper to taste
1/4 cup vegetable oil

3/4 cup freshly squeezed lemon or lime juice or a mixture of both
8 tablespoons butter
1/4 teaspoon saffron steeped in 2 tablespoons hot water

1. In a large stainless steel or glass bowl mix onions, 1/2 cup of lemon or lime juice, oil and pepper. Add chicken pieces and mix to coat. Marinate, covered, for 1 hour or overnight in refrigerator.

2. Melt butter in a small saucepan. Add remainder of lemon or lime juice, saffron, and salt to taste. Brush chicken with sauce just before cooking.

3. Cook over hot charcoal, turning frequently and basting all sides with sauce as the chicken pieces cook. Chicken breasts cook in about 10 to 12 minutes, for thighs or drumsticks add an extra 10 to 15 minutes depending on individual taste. Serve with fried potatoes or rice and small or cherry tomatoes grilled several minutes along with chicken.

SERVES 4 TO 6

VARIATION: Can be broiled on middle rack in oven, turning several times during cooking, baste often. Add 1 to 2 teaspoons curry powder, and 1 teaspoon paprika to sauce.

Barbecued Chicken

Chicken with Coriander
JAJ MAAL KUZBARA

PREPARATION TIME: 20 MINUTES
COOKING TIME: 1 HOUR

3 to 4 cloves garlic, minced
1 small onion, chopped
1/2 cup chopped scallions
1 to 2 cups chopped
    coriander

1/4 cup lemon juice
3 tablespoons safflower oil
Salt and freshly ground
    pepper to taste
1 chicken (about 4 1/2
    pounds) cut into 8 pieces

This is a very simple way to cook chicken, veal cubes may be substituted with excellent results. Use crusty Italian or French bread for dipping into this delicious sauce.

1. Preheat oven to 350° F. Place garlic, onion, scallions, coriander, lemon juice, oil, salt and pepper in baking dish, mix well. Add chicken and stir.

2. Bake uncovered in preheated oven 1 hour, basting several times. Serve with noodles or rice.

SERVES 4

VARIATION: Add 1/2 pound carrots sliced, and 4 medium potatoes halved and lightly brushed with oil. Sprinkle extra chopped coriander for color over chicken before serving.

Saffron Chicken with Carrots
KHORESHTE MORGH

PREPARATION TIME: 15 MINUTES
COOKING TIME: 1 1/2 HOURS

8 chicken thighs
    Salt and freshly ground
    pepper to taste
6 tablespoons butter
1 1/2 cups hot chicken broth
1 medium onion, finely
    chopped

1 1/2 pounds carrots, sliced, or
    matchsticks
3 tablespoons sugar or
    honey
1/2 teaspoon saffron threads
    crushed, steeped in 2
    tablespoons hot water
1/4 cup orange juice
12 pitted prunes

1. Rinse chicken, pat dry with paper towels. Sprinkle with salt and pepper on both sides. Melt 4 tablespoons butter in large skillet. Brown chicken over medium-heat on both sides (about 25 minutes). Transfer to a medium-size saucepan and pour hot broth over chicken. Cover and cook over medium-low heat 10 minutes.

2. Add remaining 2 tablespoons butter to skillet and saute onion till transparent. Add carrots and sugar stir to coat, cook stirring frequently 5 minutes. Transfer to saucepan with chicken.

Saffron Chicken with Carrots

3. Strain saffron if desired and pour liquid into saucapan over chicken. Cook covered over medium-low for 20 minutes.

4. Add orange juice and prunes, reduce heat to low, cook 15 to 20 minutes. Taste adjust seasoning. Serve with rice, noodles, or potatoes.

SERVES 4

CHICKEN

Upside Down Chicken
MA LUBE

PREPARATION TIME: 20 MINUTES
COOKING TIME: 2 HOURS

1 *chicken (3 1/2 pounds) or*	1 *recipe Spiced Rice*
2 whole chicken breast	*(page 181)*
2 *-inch cinnamon stick*	2 *tablespoons vegetable oil*
4 *peppercorns*	2/3 *cup pine nuts*

1. Place whole chicken in a large saucepan. Add enough water to come half-way up sides of pan. Add cinnamon and peppercorns. Bring to a boil, reduce heat to medium-low, cover and simmer about 1 hour or until chicken is tender (Chicken breasts cook in 20 to 30 minutes).

2. Prepare Spiced Rice and set aside.

3. Heat oil in small skillet. Saute nuts in oil stirring often till golden. Set aside.

4. Remove chicken from liquid and set aside until cool enough to handle. Strain and reserve liquid for use another time. Remove and discard skins and bones from chicken. Cut chicken meat into 2-inch strips. set aside.

5. Preheat oven to 400° F. Lightly grease a 10-inch cake pan. Place roasted nuts in center of pan and arrange chicken strips in ring around nuts. Spread rice over nuts and chicken. Place waxed paper over rice and press down firmly, remove and discard. Cover with foil and heat in preheated oven 20 to 30 minutes, remove foil. Place serving dish over pan and invert. Remove pan carefully and serve hot with tossed green salad.

SERVES 6

A Lebanese dish made with cooked chicken, rice, and roasted pine nuts. The ingredients are layered in a mold, pressed down, baked, and unmolded on a platter. The first time I saw this very attractive dish it was served on a shinny silver platter and I could almost taste it with my eyes. It was as delicious to eat as it was to look at.

VARIATION: Cooked, diced meat can be substituted for chicken. Fried slices of eggplant (page 144) can be layered before rice is added. Substitute roasted whole blanched almonds for pine nuts or use a mixture of both.

HINTS: Can be prepared 2 days ahead of time, covered, refrigerated, and reheated in preheated 400° F. oven about 55 minutes. It can also be frozen, then placed directly in preheated 450° F. oven for 1 1/2 hours.

Chicken and Wheat
HERRISA (KESHKEG)

PREPARATION TIME: 15 MINUTES (plus overnight)
COOKING TIME: 3 HOURS

1 chicken (about 4 pounds)	*8 tablespoons butter*
1 1/2 cups whole grain skinless wheat or pearl barely*	*2 teaspoons cumin or to taste*
Salt and freshly ground pepper to taste	*Cayenne to taste*

1. If skinless whole grain wheat is available, rinse with cold water, place in bowl. Add enough water to cover and soak overnight. Alternatively, rinse barley and set aside.

2. Place 4 cups water in saucepan, add whole chicken, bring to a boil, reduce and simmer covered 45 minutes. Remove chicken and set aside to cool, strain liquid into a large non-stick saucepan. Remove and discard skin and bones, shred chicken or cut into small pieces. Add to reserved liquid. Add wheat or barley and 4 more cups water to chicken. Bring to a boil, stir. Reduce heat to medium-low, cover and cook 1 hour, stirring occasionally with wooden spoon.

3. Reduce heat to low and cook 2 hours, stirring often. If liquid is absorbed before grains are tender, add 1/2 cup of water as needed.

4. When wheat or barley is tender, remove from heat. Place 1/3 of mixture in electric mixer bowl and beat till half of mixture is pureed (not completely smooth). Repeat with remainder of mixture. Add salt and pepper to taste and mix well.

5. Melt butter in small saucepan. Spread Herrisa on platter and smooth surface. Make indentations on surface with back of spoon. Pour melted butter on top and sprinkle with cumin and cayenne. Serve hot with tossed salad.

SERVES 8

VARIATION: Mix cumin into Herrisa with half the butter, pour remainder on top. Substitute 2 pounds lamb or beef cut into small pieces instead of chicken. Large bulgur may also be used instead of whole grain wheat.

* Whole grain skinless wheat is available in Armenian and Middle Eastern speciality stores.

This mixture of whole grain skinless wheat (dzedzvadz) and chicken or meat is cooked and pureed to a coarse, porridge-like consistency. Bubbling hot butter is poured over the finished dish, and it is sprinkled with cumin and cayenne. Leftover turkey can be used instead of chicken.

Roast Leg of Lamb (see variation page 119)

CHAPTER SEVEN

Meats

Although beef is readily available lamb is the favored meat of the Middle East. Armenians, Greeks, Cypriots, and Christian Lebanese occasionally use pork. Muslem and Jews are forbidden to eat it by dietary laws.

Meats are used in many ingenious ways, stuffed with pine nuts and seasonings into tiny eggplants and squashes, or in cleverly spiced stews and casseroles with dried beans or peas and fresh herbs. Delicious meat balls in herb or onion sauces make an irresistable tasting meal.

When preparing meat for kabobs it is very important to remove excess fat and membranes to insure tenderness.

Ground Meat Kabobs
LULEH KABOB

PREPARATION TIME: 20 MINUTES
COOKING TIME: 5 TO 8 MINUTES

1 1/2 pounds lean ground lamb
    or beef
1 medium onion, grated or
    pureed

1 teaspoon salt or to taste
    Freshly ground pepper to
    taste
1/4 teaspoon cinnamon or
    turmeric

1. Place all ingredients in food processor. Blend together to a paste-like consistency. Scrape mixture into a bowl.

2. Shape meat mixture onto skewers in 4-inch thin sausage shapes. Dip hands frequently in water to prevent sticking if needed.

3. Cook over hot coals, turning as needed, or broil 3-inches away from heat turning twice about 5 to 8 minutes. Cooking time varies according to taste. Serve with rice, broiled tomatoes and fresh basil, or with Onion Parsley Salad (page 58) in warmed buttered pita bread.

SERVES 6

VARIATION: (Armenian) add 1/4 cup chopped parsley. Substitute 3/4 teaspoon allspice for cinnamon. Cayenne to taste.
(Syrian) Kabobs with Cherry Sauce:
Shape kabobs into 2-inch long pieces and cook. Make cherry sauce in step 2 of Sour Cherry Rice (page 166), and cook about 10 minutes till thickened. Add Kabobs, heat thoroughly. Serve over warm pita bread wedges on a heated platter.

Persian Hamburgers
KOTLETE GUSHT

PREPARATION TIME: 30 MINUTES
COOKING TIME: 20 MINUTES

1 pound lean sirloin
1 medium onion, finely
    chopped or grated
1 egg
1/2 teaspoon cinnamon
1/2 teaspoon turmeric
    Salt and freshly ground
    pepper to taste

1 small potato, cooked,
    peeled and grated
1 garlic clove crushed
    Dry bread crumbs or
    all-purpose flour to coat
    Vegetable oil (about 4 to
    6 tablespoons)

A very interesting sandwich can be made by placing cut up patties on a flat bread, topped with fresh green eating herbs such as basil, tarragon, mint and scallions and dipped into a bowl of yogurt.

1. Place meat in a large bowl. Add onion, potato, garlic, egg, cinnamon, turmeric, salt and pepper. Mix thoroughly.

2. Divide mixture into 8 equal-size portions. Shape into balls and roll in bread crumbs. Place on clean work surface, pat down, and shape into large teardrops. Flatten to about 1-inch thickness. Sprinkle with extra bread crumbs to hold shape.

3. Heat oil in large skillet. Add patties and saute over medium heat until browned on both sides, 15 to 20 minutes. Serve with peppers, onions and garlic sauteed in oil or with Taboule (page 200).

SERVES 6 TO 8

VARIATION: Omit potato and use small onion. Soak 2 slices white bread in milk until absorbed. Squeeze dry and add to meat. Add 1/2 cup chopped parsley to meat before shaping. This can also be made into small round or oval shape patties. Cook as above and serve with chutney sauce as accompaniment for cocktails.

Persian Hamburgers

MEAT

Skewered Meat Kabobs
SHISH KABOBS

PREPARATION TIME: 15 MINUTES (plus overnight)
COOKING TIME: 8 TO 12 MINUTES

Perhaps the most famous and popular of Middle Eastern dishes known throughout the western world. Skewered pieces of marinated meat grilled to perfection are the high light of any dinner. Served with grilled vegetables or lots of salad and rice. Also delicious in pita bread with some Hummus or Tarator Sauce.

2 pounds beef sirloin or boneless leg of lamb cut into 1-inch cubes
4 medium onions, sliced
1 teaspoon allspice
1/2 teaspoon freshly ground pepper or to taste

1/4 teaspoon cayenne or to taste
1/3 cup lemon juice or wine vinegar
1/3 cup corn or safflower oil
1 teaspoon salt or to taste

1. Place meat in glass bowl. Add onions, allspice, pepper, cayenne, lemon juice or vinegar and oil. Slip on plastic gloves and mix together thoroughly.

2. Cover with foil and marinate 1 to 2 days in refrigerator.

3. Bring to room temperature. Sprinkle with salt, mix and thread meat on skewers. Cook over hot coals turning often for 8 to 10 minutes. Roast a few small onions, green and red peppers, chunks of eggplant or zucchini on skewers, alternating with meat or separately. Lightly oil, salt and pepper vegetables before cooking. Serve hot with rice.

SERVES 4 TO 6

VARIATION: Omit allspice. Add one bay leaf (to be discarded before cooking) and 2 teaspoons oregano, thyme or crushed coriander seeds, continue as above.

HINT: Always remember to add salt just before cooking so the juices stay inside the meat making it more tender. This also applies to chicken.

Meatballs and Onion Sauce
DAOUD BACHA

PREPARATION TIME: 30 MINUTES
COOKING TIME: 1 HOUR

Pasha means prince in Arabic and prince Daoud loved this dish so much it was named after him.

3 to 4 large onions, finely chopped
2 teaspoons salt
1 pound lean ground sirloin
2 tablespoons pine nuts
All-purpose flour to coat
8 tablespoons butter

2 tablespoons vegetable oil
3 tablespoons lemon juice
1 beef bouillon cube
1/2 to 1 teaspoon paprika
1/4 teaspoon cinnamon
Salt and freshly ground pepper to taste

1. Mix onions and salt in a bowl. Cover with plastic wrap and let stand 30 minutes (this is to extract the bitter juices from the onions). Place in colander and rinse under cold running water. Squeeze out excess liquid. Set aside.

2. Combine meat and nuts, shape into 3/4-inch balls. Coat with flour. Heat 2 tablespoons butter and 1 tablespoon oil in large skillet. Add meatballs, cook over medium-heat until browned on all sides (about 10 minutes). Remove to dish, set aside.

3. Add remaining 6 tablespoons butter and 1 tablespoon oil to skillet. Saute onions, stirring occasionally, until transparent and golden (about 20 minutes). Add 1 cup water, lemon juice, bouillon cube, paprika, cinnamon, salt and pepper. Add meatballs, cover and cook over low-heat 20 minutes. Taste and adjust seasoning. Serve with egg noodles or rice, mixed salad and crusty bread. Oranges for dessert.
SERVES 4 TO 6

VARIATION: Add 1/2 cup chopped parsley to meat and make larger meatballs. Pour sauce over meatballs and sprinkle with 1/4 cup roasted nuts. Tomato paste may be added to the sauce. Delicious over spaghetti.

A lthough veal shanks take a long time to cook, it is very easy to prepare, and can be done a day in advance.

Dilled Veal Shanks
SAMITOV MEES

PREPARATION TIME: 20 MINUTES
COOKING TIME: 4 TO 5 HOURS

> *Vegetable oil about 1/4 cup)*
> 5 *pounds veal shanks, cut into 2-inch thick slices or 3 to 4 lamb shanks trimmed*
> 1 *large onion, chopped*
> 2 *beef bouillon cubes (optional)*
>
> 2 *or 3 large bunches of fresh dill*
> 2 *to 3 bunches of scallions trimmed and peeled Salt and freshly ground pepper to taste*

1. Heat oil in large skillet. Add veal shanks and saute until browned on all sides. Remove to heavy bottom saucepan.

2. Saute onion in same skillet. Add to saucepan. Dissolve bouillon cubes in small amount of water, add to saucepan with 1 1/2 cups water.

3. Place dill sprigs and scallions over shanks. Add salt and pepper and cook 4 1/2 hours over low heat. (Meat should almost fall apart when pierced with fork). Serve with plain rice or buttered egg noodles.
SERVES 6

Persian Meat Patties

This is a variation of Falafel made with meat. It is considered to be an Iranian family dish, and was not to be served to company.

Persian Meat Patties
SHAMI

PREPARATION TIME: 25 MINUTES
COOKING TIME: 50 MINUTES

1 *pound lamb or beef stew,* *cut into 1-inch cubes*
1 *medium onion, quartered*
1 *cup yellow split peas*
2 *eggs*
1/2 *teaspoon cinnamon*

1/4 *teaspoon nutmeg*
1/4 *teaspoon turmeric*
1 1/2 *teaspoons salt or to taste*
1/2 *teaspoon freshly ground* *pepper*
Flour for coating
Vegetable oil for frying

1. Place meat and onion in saucepan. Add 1 cup water, bring to a boil, reduce heat to low, and simmer 45 minutes or until meat is tender. Skim surface as necessary. Drain.

2. Place split peas in separate saucepan. Add 3 cups water, bring to a boil, reduce heat to low, and simmer 45 minutes. Drain.

3. Place meat and split peas in container of food processor. Add eggs, cinnamon, nutmeg, turmeric, salt and pepper. Process until pureed. Taste and adjust seasoning. Transfer to bowl and set aside until cool.

4. Divide mixture into 12 equal-size balls. Roll balls in flour and flatten into patties about 3/4-inch thick. Make hole in center of patties to resemble doughnuts. Sprinkle surface of holes with flour to hold shape.

5. Heat oil in large skillet, fry 2 minutes on each side. Serve warm, room temperature, or cold.

MAKES 12

SERVING SUGGESTION: This is quite dry when served alone. It should be served with pickles, salad, or an herb platter (Sabzi Khordan) of watercress, chives, scallions flat leaf parsley, and dill. It can also be served with Cucumber and Yogurt (page 56).

VARIATION: Make 36 patties and cook as above. Serve as an hors-d'oeuvre on a bed of watercress with pickles or a spicy sauce for dipping.

Chelo Kabob is the national dish of Iran and certainly one of the most popular. Quite simply, it is steamed rice (Chelo) served with marinated kabobs. A restaurant that specializes in Chelo Kabobs will serve mixed green eating herbs on a platter (Sabzi Khordan), sumac, herb mixed pickles, or garlic pickles, and raw egg yolks in half shells that are mixed into the steaming hot rice. Each portion is brought out on large covered platter with a slice of butter embedded in the rice and kabobs on the side. The butter and egg yolk have to be mixed evenly and quickly so the rice is still hot when eaten. When a slightly sour or tart flavor is desired, sumac is sprinkled over rice. I personally prefer to use lots of butter and sumac rather than raw egg yolk.

Although strips of lamb loin are used in Iran, I have substituted beef tenderlion because it is more easily available.

Kabobs with Steamed Rice
CHELO KABOB

PREPARATION TIME: 20 MINUTES (plus overnight)
COOKING TIME: 5 TO 8 MINUTES

3 *pounds beef tenderlion, cut into 2 x 1-inch strips*
2 *large onions, sliced mixed with 1/2 teaspoon salt*
6 *tablespoons lemon or lime juice*
4 *tablespoons mild vegetable oil (peanut or safflower)*
Freshly ground pepper to taste
Chelo (page 182)
Melted butter

8 *small regular tomatoes (optional)*
8 *slices butter, room temperature, to serve*
8 *egg yolks (optional)*
Sumac, if available
Salt and freshly ground pepper to taste
Mixed green eating herbs (Sabzi Khordan)

1. Place meat in glass bowl. Add onion, lemon or lime juice, oil, and pepper. Cover with plastic wrap and refrigerate at least 4 hours or overnight.

2. Prepare Chelo. Keep warm over low heat until ready to serve.

3. Discard onion. Salt meat if desired. Thread meat on skewers and tap lightly with back of heavy bladed knife to flatten. Brush with melted butter and cook over hot coals 2 to 4 minutes on each side, or desired doneness. Thread tomatoes on separate skewers and grill until skins blisters. Serve with Chelo, sliced butter, egg yolk, sumac, and green eating herbs. Sprinkle salt and freshly ground pepper over kabobs.

SERVES 6 TO 8

VARIATION: Omit lemon juice and oil, add 2 cups plain yogurt with onion slices, mix thoroughly with meat and continue as above.

HINTS: If using raw egg yolks, balance them in their shells on a dish of flour.

Roast Leg of Lamb
ROAST EL FAKHET

PREPARATION TIME: 15 MINUTES
COOKING TIME: 2 1/2 HOURS

1 leg of lamb, (about 8 pounds)
2 to 4 cloves garlic, slivered
1 teaspoon cinnamon

1/2 teaspoon allspice
Salt and freshly ground pepper to taste
8 small onions
2 cups boiling water

1. Preheat oven to 400° F. Place leg of lamb in roasting pan. Make small slits in meat with tip of a sharp pointed knife. Insert garlic slivers into slits. Season all over with cinnamon, allspice, salt and pepper.

2. Bake in preheated oven 1 hour. Add onions and 2 cups boiling water. Cover lightly with foil. Reduce heat to 350° F. and bake 1 hour, basting several times.

3. Let stand 10 to 15 minutes before carving. Serve with steamed vegetables and salad or Okra in Oil (page 152).

SERVES 8

VARIATION: Cover lamb with foil and cook an additional 1 1/2 hours or until meat pulls away from bone easily. Cool until easy to handle. Remove meat in chunks and place in baking dish. Set aside and keep warm. Make Spiced Rice (page 181). Heat about 2 tablespoons vegetable oil in non-stick skillet. Saute 1/3 cup pine nuts, 1/3 cup blanched whole almonds, and 1/3 cup pistachios stirring often until golden. Spoon rice onto large platter. Top with chunks of lamb and sprinkle with nuts Serve sauce from lamb with onions on the side.

Armenian Style Lamb Roast:

Make 8 slits in lamb and insert 1 clove garlic in each slit. Spread 1 1/2 cups Labni, (page 19), over surface of lamb. Place in glass dish, cover and refrigerate overnight. Season with salt and pepper and cook as Roast Leg of Lamb recipe. Or roast on a rack without water to desired doness.

MEAT

Marinated Lamb Chops
KHOROVADZ MEES

PREPARATION TIME: 10 MINUTES (plus 1 hour)
COOKING TIME: 8 TO 10 MINUTES

4 *tablespoons tomato paste*
2 *tablespoons allspice*
  Salt and freshly ground
  pepper to taste

1/8 *teaspoon freshly ground*
  nutmeg
1/4 *cup corn or safflower oil*
8 *large lamb chops, rib*
  chops, or shoulder chops

1. In a glass bowl, mix tomato paste, with allspice, salt, pepper, nutmeg, and oil. Rub over lamb chops coating thoroughly. Cover with foil and marinate for 2 hours or more in refrigerator.

2. Grill over hot charcoals for 2 minutes on each side or more depending on size and thickness of chops. Serve with thick french fries or rice and crisp tossed green salad or sauteed zucchini in butter. Fresh oranges or fruit of the season go well after this meal.

SERVES 4

Marinated Lamb Chops

Kabobs with Tomato Sauce
KABOBOV YEPVATZ LOLIG

PREPARATION TIME: 20 MINUTES (marinating overnight)
COOKING TIME: 35 MINUTES

2 pounds leg of lamb or
beef tenderlion cut in
1-inch cubes
2 tablespoons tomato paste
1 teaspoon allspice
1/2 teaspoon paprika
3 tablespoons vegetable oil
2 tablespoons vinegar or
lemon juice
1 onion, sliced
Parsley to garnish

SAUCE:

4 tablespoons butter
2 large onions, diced
2 large tomatoes seeded
and diced
1/2 teaspoon paprika
Dash cayenne
1/2 teaspoon allspice
Salt and freshly ground
pepper to taste

1. Place cubes of meat in glass bowl. Mix with tomato paste, allspice, paprika, oil, vinegar, and onion. Cover with foil and refrigerate overnight.

2. Heat skillet, add butter. Saute onions till lightly golden. Add tomatoes. Cook for 15 minutes. Add seasonings. Taste and adjust. Keep sauce warm.

3. Thread meat onto skewers. Grill over hot coals for about 3 to 5 minutes, each side depending on your taste. Transfer sauce to warmed serving dish. Place kabobs over sauce and garnish with parsley. Serve with rice or potatoes. This sauce goes very well with Luleh Kabobs (page 112) as well.

SERVES 4 TO 6

Grilled Liver
ASBEH MESHWI

PREPARATION TIME: 20 MINUTES
COOKING TIME: 5 MINUTES

1 pound lamb or calf liver
1 tablespoon dried crushed
mint
Salt and freshly ground
pepper to taste

1 clove garlic, crushed
(optional)
3 tablespoons vegetable oil
1 lemon cut into 6 wedges

1. Rinse liver thoroughly with cold water, drain in colander, pat dry on paper towels. Cut into small bite-size pieces.

2. Place liver in glass bowl. Sprinkle with mint, salt, pepper, garlic, and oil. Mix thoroughly.

3. Thread on skewers and cook over hot coals for 2-minutes each side. Remove from skewers and garnish with lemon. Serve as a meal with vegetables, rice, or potatoes, or as a Meza with warm pita bread and drinks.

SERVES 4

VARIATION: Omit mint. Sprinkle with cumin and cayenne, grill or saute in butter.

Tongue Stew
LESOUI PACHA

PREPARATION TIME: 15 MINUTES
COOKING TIME: 2 HOURS

1 *tongue, (about 3 pounds)*	8 *tablespoons butter,*
1 1/4 *teaspoon salt or to taste*	*melted*
2- *inch cinnamon stick*	*Plain croutons (about 3*
1/2 *to 3/4 cup lemon juice*	*cups)*
3 *to 4 cloves garlic, crushed*	*Freshly ground pepper or*
2 *tablespoons dried crushed*	*cayenne to taste*
mint	*(optional)*

1. Rinse tongue and place in large saucepan. Cover with water and bring to a boil over high-heat. Add 1 teaspoon salt and cinnamon stick. Reduce heat to medium-low, cover, and simmer 2 hours.

2. Remove tongue and let cool slightly. Peel off skin and cut into 1-inch chunks. Strain cooking liquids into a saucepan. Add chunks of tongue to liquid and keep warm.

3. Place lemon juice in small bowl, add crushed garlic. Stir mint into melted butter.

4. Place 1/2 cup croutons in each serving bowl and drizzle some mint butter over croutons. Add tongue, garlic-flavored lemon juice, and some liquid. Season with salt and pepper.

SERVES 6

Lamb Shanks with Chick-Peas
LOLIGOV MEES

PREPARATION TIME: 10 MINUTES
COOKING TIME: 2 HOURS

A rmenians find this a common dish, but my non-Armenian friends rave over it.

Vegetable oil	1/2 *teaspoon paprika*
4 *small lamb shanks,*	*Dash cayenne*
trimmed	*Salt and freshly ground*
4 *large tomatoes, peeled,*	*pepper*
seeded and chopped	2 1/2 *cups hot water*
2 *medium onions, sliced or*	1 *can (20 ounces)*
chopped	*chick-peas, rinsed and*
4 *cloves garlic, minced*	*drained 2 cups cooked*
1/2 *teaspoon dried rosemary*	
or oregano	

1. Preheat oven to 450° F. Rub oil on bottom of large roasting pan. Place lamb shanks in pan and turn to coat lightly with oil. Bake in preheated oven 30 minutes, turning from time to time to brown evenly.

2. Remove roasting pan from oven. Spread tomatoes and onions over lamb. Sprinkle with garlic, rosemary, paprika, cayenne, salt and pepper. Pour hot water around meat.

3. Cover and bake 1 hour. Uncover, stir sauce, and bake 15 minutes. Add chickpeas, stir into sauce, bake 15 minutes or until meat is tender. Serve meat and sauce spooned over it with bread or Cracked Wheat with Noodles (page 199), and a tossed green salad. Fresh fruit for dessert.

SERVES 4 TO 6

VARIATION: Add 4 medium potatoes, peeled and quartered, with onions. Increase water to 3 cups, an extra 1/2 cup may be added during baking if liquid is absorbed.

Potato and Meat Bake
KEDNAKUNTZOROV MEES

PREPARATION TIME: 30 MINUTES
COOKING TIME: 1 HOURS

An easy dish which is quite inexpensive and children love it.

1 pound potatoes
1 pound ground beef or lamb
1/4 cup freshly chopped parsley
Dash paprika
Dash cayenne
Salt to taste

1/4 cup bread crumbs
1 small onion, finely chopped
1 green pepper seeded and sliced
1 medium tomato, sliced
3 tablespoons tomato paste
2 tablespoons oil (corn or olive)

1. Preheat oven to 400° F. Wash , peel and cut potatoes into 2-inch pieces.

2. In a bowl mix together meat, parsley, spices, bread crumbs, and onion. Shape into 2-inch size pieces, (same as potatoes). Place in heatproof dish, alternately with potatoes.

3. Arrange pepper slices and tomatoes over meat.

4. Mix together tomato paste, 1 cup water, oil, salt and pepper. Pour over potatoes and meat. Bake in preheated oven for 45 minutes to 1 hour. Serve with a crisp green salad or pickles.

SERVES 4

VARIATION: Omit tomato paste and substitute cooked artichoke bottoms for potatoes. Place tomatoes and peppers on sides of dish, the last 10 minutes of cooking.

HINT: Can be assembled covered and refrigerated several hours before cooking.

Herb Meatballs in Sauce
KUFTA SABZI

PREPARATION TIME: 25 MINUTES
COOKING TIME: 1 HOUR

1/4 cup yellow split peas
3 tablespoons short grain rice
2 cups finely chopped flat leaf parsley
1 cup finely chopped scallions
1 pound lean ground beef or lamb
2 eggs, lightly beaten
3/4 to 1 teaspoon cinnamon
Salt and freshly ground pepper to taste
All-purpose flour

SAUCE:

2 tablespoons butter
2 tablespoons vegetable oil
1 large onion, finely chopped
1 can (8 ounces) tomato sauce
1/4 teaspoon cinnamon
Salt and freshly ground pepper to taste
1/4 cup lemon juice
Bread, pickles, and olives to serve.

1. Place 2 1/2 cups water in large saucepan. Add split peas, bring to a boil, reduce heat to medium, and cook uncovered 10 minutes. Add rice and cook 20 minutes. Drain. Place in large bowl and set aside to cool.

2. Add parsley, scallions, meat, eggs, cinnamon, salt and pepper to peas and rice. Mix thoroughly. Dip hands in flour. Roll mixture in floured hands, forming 1 1/2 to 2-inch balls. Reflour hands as needed. Place on waxed paper.

3. To make sauce, melt butter in 12-inch skillet. Add oil and onion, stir to coat, cook over medium-heat 10 minutes. Add tomato sauce, 2 1/4 cups water, cinnamon, salt and pepper. Stir well.

4. Add meatballs to sauce. Bring to a boil, reduce heat to medium-low. Cover and cook 25 minutes. Uncover, add lemon juice, and tilt skillet slightly to mix. Cook 5 minutes. Spoon into soup bowls and serve with bread, pickles, and olives.

SERVES 4

VARIATION: To make soup, increase water in sauce to 4 cups and add a second onion.

HINT: Freeze meatballs and sauce separately. Reheat together slowly over low heat.

This popular Iranian stew is very unsophisticated. It can be easily turned into a hearty soup by increasing the sauce.

Meat and Coriander Bake
KUFTA BIL SINIYE

PREPARATION TIME: 15 MINUTES
COOKING TIME: 1 HOUR, AND 10 MINUTES

Fresh coriander gives this dish an interesting flavor.

1 pound lean ground beef or lamb
1 teaspoon allspice
1/4 teaspoon cinnamon or nutmeg
1 cup freshly chopped coriander or parsley
Salt and freshly ground pepper to taste

2 medium potatoes, sliced 1/4-inch thick
1 large green pepper, seeded and thinly sliced
2 large tomatoes, sliced or 1 (16 ounce) can whole tomatoes, drained
2 tablespoons vegetable oil

1. Preheat oven to 350° F. Place meat, allspice, cinnamon, coriander, salt and pepper in a 8 x 8-inch baking dish, mix well.

2. Pat meat mixture evenly over bottom. Layer with potatoes, peppers, and tomatoes. Drizzle with oil, generously salt and pepper.

3. Cover with foil and bake in preheated oven 50 minutes. Remove foil and bake 20 minutes or until potatoes are fork tender. Serve with crusty French bread, cheese, and pickles or a plate of radishes and scallions.

SERVES 4 TO 6

Spiced Meat
SHAWERMA

This dish is as popular with Lebanese and Arabs, as hamburgers are with Americans. There are special rotisseries used to cook Shawerma. The meat is layered with fat and roasted vertically on a large skewer with heat surrounding the meat on three sides. While the meat is cooking, individual portions are sliced off. It is usually sold as a take out food or served in a restaurant that specializes in Arabic foods. If desired, you can cut the recipe in half.

PREPARATION TIME: 20 MINUTES (plus overnight)
COOKING TIME: 40 MINUTES

4 pounds boneless leg of lamb, trimmed and cut into about 3 x 5-inch pieces, or beef flank steak cut into 1/8-inch thick strips
2 to 2 1/2 tablespoons ground sumac
2 to 2 1/2 tablespoons cinnamon
1 to 1 1/2 teaspoons freshly ground pepper
1 to 1 1/2 teaspoons ground cardamom

1/2 to 1 teaspoon allspice
1/2 to 1 teaspoon miskee (gum mastic)
1/2 cup vegetable oil
3/4 cup whisky
Salt to taste
Tomatoes, peppers, scallions, or eating onions, fresh mint, or basil leaves, Tarator Sauce (page 257), pita bread to serve.

1. Place meat in large glass bowl. Mix sumac, cinnamon, pepper, cardamom, allspice, and miskee. Blend with oil and whisky. Add to meat and toss to coat. Cover and marinate in refrigerator at least 3 hours or overnight.

2. Remove meat from refrigerator and bring to room temperature. If meat seems dry, add 1/4 cup oil and 1/4 cup whisky. Mix well. Sprinkle salt over meat and mix again.

3. Preheat oven to 375° F. Place meat in baking dish in single layer. Bake in preheated oven about 25 minutes or to desired doneness.

4. If using lamb slice paper thin and keep warm until ready to serve. Spiced Rice (page 181) and Turnip Pickles (page 24) often accompany this dish.
SERVES 12

HINTS: Try this dish at your next informal party. Place bowls of chopped or sliced tomatoes, green, red, or yellow peppers, fresh mint or basil leaves, Tarator Sauce, pita bread and Shawarma on a table and let your guests make their own sandwiches.

Eggplant with Meat
SUMPOOGOV MEES

PREPARATION TIME: 15 MINUTES (plus 30 for eggplant)
COOKING TIME: 1 HOUR, 20 MINUTES

Small eggplants are sliced crosswise, stuffed with meat, and baked in tomato sauce. If small eggplant are not available, substitute large eggplant, quartered and cut into 5-inch lenghts.

2 1/2 *pounds baby or Japanese eggplants*
2 *tablespoons oil*
1 *pound lean ground lamb or beef*
1/2 *cup freshly chopped parsley*
1 *medium tomato, finely chopped*
1 *teaspoon allspice*
1/4 *teaspoon cayenne or to taste*
Salt and freshly ground pepper to taste
1 *green pepper, thinly sliced*
1 *large tomato, sliced and cut in half*
3 *tablespoons tomato paste*

1. Wash and dry eggplants and cut off stems. Make crosswise slits 3/4-inch apart almost all the way down, separate slightly to hold meat. Sprinkle with salt in between slits, set aside to sweat 30 minutes. Pat dry with paper towels.

2. Preheat oven to 350° F. Mix meat, parsley, chopped tomato, allspice, cayenne, salt and pepper. Pinch off pieces of meat and stuff slits in eggplant, place in a 13 x 9-inch baking dish. Arrange pepper and tomato slices over eggplant. Mix tomato paste with 1 cup water, pour over stuffed eggplant. Salt and pepper generously.

3. Cover and bake in preheated oven 1 hour or till tender. Uncover and bake 20 minutes. Serve with Cracked Wheat with Noodles (page 199).
SERVES 6

HINT: Can be made in advance and reheated.

This dish originated in Izmir, a town in Turkey on the Aegean Sea. It is prepared in many ways by the Armenians and Greeks.

Cumin Meatballs
CUMINOV KUFTA

PREPARATION TIME: 20 MINUTES
COOKING TIME: 30 MINUTES

1 *pound lean ground lamb or beef*
1 *large egg*
1/4 *cup dry bread crumbs*
3 *to 5 cloves garlic, crushed*
1/2 *teaspoon cumin*
Salt and freshly ground pepper to taste
2 *tablespoons vegetable oil*

TOMATO SAUCE:

1 *tablespoon tomato paste*
2 *tablespoons lemon juice*
1/4 *teaspoon garlic powder*
Salt and freshly ground pepper to taste

1. Mix meat, egg, bread crumbs, garlic, cumin, salt and pepper. Divide into 20 equal-size balls. Roll each ball into egg shape. Set aside.

2. Heat oil in a large skillet over medium-heat. Add meatballs, brown on all side. Remove from skillet, and set aside. Drain skillet.

3. Pour 3/4 cup water into skillet. Add tomato paste, lemon juice, garlic powder, salt and pepper. Bring to a boil, reduce heat to medium, cook 5 minutes. Return meat to skillet and cook just until heated through. Serve with Cracked Wheat with noodles (page 199).

SERVES 4

VARIATION: Make 40 meatballs, and serve with half of tomato sauce for dipping as hors-d'ouvres. Garnish with fresh basil leaves.

CHAPTER EIGHT

Vegetables
and
Stews

Vegetables are delicious when cooked in a tomato sauce flavored with sauteed onions, garlic and olive oil (preferably virgin). Lemon juice is added for a slightly tart flavor. They may be served at room temperature or chilled. Another way is using cabbage or tender grape leaves stuffed and rolled or hallowed out zucchinis, baby eggplants, peppers or tomatoes and filled with a mixture of rice and meat, topped with Yogurt Garlic Sauce (page 260) The meat in the vegetable stews can be omitted.

VEGETABLES & STEWS

String Bean Stew
KHORESHTA LOOBIA-SABZ

PREPARATION TIME: 20 MINUTES
COOKING TIME: 1 HOUR

> 2 *pound fresh string beans*
> 4 *tablespoons butter*
> 1 *tablespoon vegetable oil*
> 2 *large onions, chopped*
> 1 1/2 *pounds lamb shoulder or*
> *4 to 5 trimmed lamb*
> *shanks*
> 1 *teaspoon turmeric*
> 1 *teaspoon allspice*
> *(optional)*

> 1 *(28 ounces) can plum*
> *tomatoes slightly crushed*
> 2 *tablespoons tomato paste*
> 1 *teaspoon cinnamon*
> *Salt and freshly ground*
> *pepper to taste*
> 4 *to 5 tablespoons fresh*
> *lemon juice*

1. String the beans. Wash. Cut into 1/2 or 1-inch lengths. Set aside.

2. Heat large skillet. Add butter, oil, and onions, saute till transparent. Add meat brown on all sides. Drain excess fat. Stir in turmeric, allspice, and tomatoes with liquids, tomato paste and 1 1/2 to 2 hours or till meat pulls away from bone.

3. Add beans and cook for 20 minutes. Add cinnamon, lemon juice, salt and pepper. Mix cook another 20 minutes or till beans are tender. Serve with rice or Cracked Wheat with Noodles (page 199).

SERVES 6 TO 8

VARIATION: Substitute one medium head of cauliflower cut into flowerets for beans, omit turmeric.

ARMENIAN STRING BEAN STEW: Substitute 1 pound ground lamb or beef for chunks. Omit turmeric, and lemon juice. Add an extra 1/2 teaspoon allspice, 1/2 teaspoon paprika, dash cayenne and 4 cloves garlic minced. Saute onions, add meat, brown, drain excess fat. Then add remainder of ingredients.

Eggplant with Lamb Chops
SHERDEVADZ SUMPOOGOV MEES

PREPARATION TIME: 20 MINUTES
COOKING TIME: 1 1/2 HOURS

Vegetable oil
6 lamb chops
3 medium onions, chopped
6 baby eggplants or 2 thin
    medium-size

6 green peppers seeded and
    cut into 1 1/2-inch pieces
Salt and freshly ground
    pepper to taste
4 medium tomatoes seeded
    and sliced

1. Heat enough oil to cover bottom of a heavy skillet (preferabley non-stick). Brown lamb chops on both sides. Remove to a dish.

2. Add more oil as needed. Saute onions till lightly golden. Remove to dish.

3. Slice eggplants lenghtwise into thin slices. Saute on both sides. Drain on paper towels. Set aside.

4. Saute green peppers briefly. Set aside.

5. Preheat oven to 350° F. Place a single layer of chops in a baking dish. Spread with half of peppers. Salt and pepper each layer. Place onions over peppers, then eggplants, tomatoes and top with remainder of pepper. Cover with foil and cook for 25 to 30 minutes in preheated oven. Uncover. Cook for 10 minutes longer. Serve with hot buttered noodles or rice.

SERVES 6

VARIATION: 1 1/2 pounds ground beef or lamb substituted for chops. Pat ground beef or lamb into baking dish salt and pepper. continue with recipe.

Carrots & Dill Stuffed Peppers

A longtime favorite of Russian-Armenians living in Iran, this stuffed vegetable (dolma) is both attractive and delicious, served room temperature or chilled. The filling can be used in hollowed out small tomatoes as well as a side dish for grilled fish.

Carrots and Dill Stuffed Peppers
BUGHBEGHI LETSK

PREPARATION TIME: 20 MINUTES
COOKING TIME: 1 HOUR

5 tablespoons olive oil (preferably virgin)
4 medium green peppers
Salt and freshly ground pepper to taste
1 dill sprig

2 cups peeled and diced carrots
2 cups chopped onions
1/3 cup freshly chopped dill
1 tablespoon sugar
3 tablespoons lemon juice

1. Lightly oil bottom of heat-proof baking dish, large enough to hold peppers in one layer, with 1 tablespoon of the olive oil. Cut stems off of peppers. Cut in half crosswise, remove seeds and white membrane. Place in baking dish, salt and pepper insides of peppers. Place a piece of the dill sprig in bottom of each half. Set aside.

2. Bring 2 1/2 cups water to a boil. Add carrots. Reduce to medium-low cover and cook till tender about 10 minutes. Strain, reserve liquids.

3. Heat remainder of oil in a skillet. Add onions. Saute till transparent and slightly golden. Transfer to a medium-size bowl. Cool slightly.

4. Preheat oven to 400° F. Add carrots, dill, sugar, lemon juice, salt and pepper to onions. Mix completely. Taste, adjust seasonings. Pour 1/2 cup of reserved liquids into mixture, stir together.

5. Spoon filling into prepared peppers. Pour remaining liquids, into dish. Cover with foil. Bake in preheated oven for 20 minutes. Reduce to 325° F. and continue for 20 minutes longer or till peppers are easily pierced with a fork. Remove foil. Cool, serve as a starter with some bread and butter or next to roast chicken or meat.
SERVES 8

Corn on the Cob
BALALL

PREPARATION TIME: 5 MINUTES
COOKING TIME: 10 TO 20 MINUTES

12 ears fresh corn, husked
8 cups boiling water

3 to 4 tablespoons sea salt
Butter to serve

1. Mix salt with boiling water, keep hot.

2. Roast corn on grill of barbecue over hot coals turning often until well browned.

3. Dip corn into salted water for 30 seconds. Remove and roll over butter. Serve immediately.

SERVES 6

Layered Potato, Lamb and Rice
SHERDEVADZ KEDNAKHUNTZOR

PREPARATION TIME: 20 MINUTES
COOKING TIME: 1 1/2 HOURS

This Armenian recipe originated in Amasia Turkey. Served straight from the pot. A hearty winter meal.

Vegetable oil (about 1/4 cup)
6 large potatoes, peeled, sliced 1/2-inch thick
1 pound ground lamb or beef

Salt and freshly ground pepper to taste
1 cup rice long grain
1 (6 ounces) can tomato paste
4 cups chicken or beef broth

1. Heat enough oil to cover bottom of a 4-quart saucepan (preferably non-stick) over medium-high heat. Shallow fry potato slices on both sides till light golden, remove to a dish. Set aside. Continue with remainder of potatoes, adding oil as needed. Set aside.

2. Drain excess oil from saucepan. Add meat. Saute till brown, stirring frequently about 8 minutes. Drain excess fat. Add salt and pepper, mix, taste and adjust. Stir in rice with the meat. Remove to a bowl, set aside.

3. Layer bottom of same saucepan with half of browned potatoes. Spread with meat-rice mixture. Top with remainder of potatoes.

4. Mix thoroughly tomato paste with a little of broth. Stir into remainder of broth and pour over potatoes in saucepan. Bring to a boil. Reduce to medium-low heat, cover and cook for about 35 to 45 minutes, or till rice is cooked and liquids absorbed. Serve from the pot or invert onto a serving platter with slices of cucumbers, olives, and watercress or a tossed green salad.

SERVES 4 TO 6

Okra Stew
MEESOV BAMEEYA

PREPARATION TIME: 20 MINUTES
COOKING TIME: 1 HOUR AND 30 MINUTES

1 *pound fresh okra (preferably small ones)*	1/2 *teaspoon sugar*
1/4 *cup vegetable oil*	1/2 *teaspoon allspice*
2 *medium onions, chopped*	1/4 *teaspoon nutmeg*
3/4 *pound lamb or beef stew, cut into 1-inch cubes*	1 *teaspoon dried basil*
2 *cloves garlic, minced*	*Salt and freshly ground pepper to taste*
1 1/2 *cups peeled and chopped tomatoes*	1 *potato, peeled and diced (optional)*
	1/4 *cup lemon juice*

1. Wash and carefully trim okra, cutting around stems, do not cut off tops.

2. Heat half of oil in medium-size saucepan. Add trimmed okra. Saute, turning okra to brown slightly on all sides. Remove with a slotted spoon to dish and set aside. Add remaining oil and onions, cook till transparent. Add meat and garlic. Saute, stirring often for 5 to 8 minutes. Pour 1/2 cup of water, and tomatoes into saucepan. Bring to a boil. Cover, reduce to medium-low, cook for 45 minutes or till meat is tender.

3. Add sugar, allspice, nutmeg, basil, salt and pepper, mix together, then add potatoes, okras and lemon juice. Cover and cook for about 20 minutes or till potatoes and okras are cooked. Taste and adjust seasonings. Serve with Cracked Wheat with Noodles (page 199), rice or crusty bread. Extra lemon wedges may be served for squeezing over individual portions.

SERVES 4

VARIATION: For a brighter colored dish, add 1 or 2 tablespoons tomato paste mixed with the water to cook with meat. Cut off stems of okras completely. Soak for 10 minutes in 2 to 3 tablespoons lemon juice, add water to cover. Drain, saute and continue as above.

HINT: Substitute frozen okras and canned plum tomatoes for fresh. Do not saute frozen okras, simply place them into meat sauce and continue as directed.

Mixed Vegetable Bake
KHARN PANCHAREGHEN

This is a popular Armenian vegetable and meat casserole. The vegetables change according to what is in season. Frozen okra or peas may be added. If you prefer a vegeterian dish, omit the meat and add half-way through, cooked beans such as black eyed peas, lentils, or chickpeas.

PREPARATION TIME: 20 MINUTES
COOKING TIME: 2 1/2 HOURS

1 pound lamb or beef cut into 1-inch cubes
3 tablespoons tomato paste
3 medium potatoes, cut into 1-inch cubes
1/2 pound string beans, cut into 1-inch lengths
2 zucchinis, cut into 1-inch slices
4 carrots, cut into 1-inch slices
6 scallions with green tops, cut into 1-inch lengths

2 medium onions, coarsely chopped
1/2 to 1 head cloves garlic, peeled
2 tomatoes, seeded and cut into wedges
1 green pepper, seeded and sliced
Salt and freshly ground pepper to taste
Juice of 1 or 2 lemons
Lemon wedges, bread, cheese, and olives to serve

1. Heat 2 to 3 tablespoons oil in a large non-stick skillet. Saute meat over medium-high heat until browned on all sides. Remove to large saucepan. Combine tomato paste with 1 cup water and stir well. Pour over meat, cover, and cook over medium-low heat 30 minutes.

2. Saute potatoes in 2 tablespoons oil until lightly browned on all sides. Remove with slotted spoon and place in 3-quart casserole or 13 x 9-inch baking dish. Repeat with string beans, zucchinis, carrots, scallions, onions, and cloves garlic, adding additional oil as necessary. Add tomatoes and green peppers to casserole.

3. Preheat oven to 400° F. Add cooking liquid to vegetables. Season with salt and pepper, stir gently. Cover and cook in preheated oven about 1 1/2 hours. If necessary, add 1/2 cup water half-way through cooking time.

4. Add lemon juice, stir gently, and bake 5 more minutes. Serve with lemon wedges, bread, cheese, and olives.

SERVES 6

VARIATION: Omit meat and do not saute vegetables. Add 1 package (10 ounces) frozen okra. 1 or 2 bouillon cubes can be mixed into 1 cup water with tomato paste before cooking.

Swiss Chard and Chick-Peas
NIVIK

PREPARATION TIME: 10 MINUTES
COOKING TIME: 20 TO 30 MINUTES

The ribs of the swiss chard that have been removed can be chopped and added to a soup, or boiled, drained and served warm with a lemon, garlic and olive oil dressing.

2 1/2 pounds swiss chard or spinach, washed, stemmed, chopped
4 tablespoons olive oil (preferably virgin) or butter
1 medium onion, chopped
2 tablespoons tomato paste

2 tablespoons freshly chopped coriander
2 to 3 cloves garlic, crushed (optional)
Salt and freshly ground pepper to taste
Cayenne to taste
2 cups cooked chick-peas
Lemon wedges to serve

1. Bring a large saucepan with about 2 cups water to a boil. Add swiss chard and cook for several minutes. Push leaves down with back of spoon to cook evenly. reduce to low, cook till tender about 5 minutes.

2. Heat oil in a skillet. Saute onion till transparent. Stir in tomato paste with onions. Add coriander, garlic, swiss chard, salt, pepper, and cayenne. Mix well and gently stir in chick-peas. Heat thoroughly. Serve hot or room temperature with lemon wedges to squeeze over dish.

SERVES 6

VARIATION: Omit cayenne and garlic. Add instead, 1/2 cup each: chopped walnuts and dark raisins or currants.

Eggplant Stew
KHORESHTA BADEMJAN

PREPARATION TIME: 15 MINUTES
COOKING TIME: 2 HOURS

A Persian stew made with something a little different dried whole limes (Limon Amoni). An alternative is to use fresh sliced and seeded limes and discard after cooking. Traditionally served with rice.

2 1/2 pounds thin long Japanese or baby eggplants
Vegetable oil as needed
4 tablespoons butter
1 large onion, halved and sliced
1 pound lamb or beef stew cut into 1-inch cubes
1 can (28 ounces) plum tomatoes slightly crushed

2 to 3 dried limes (Limon Amoni) pierced several times or 1 1/2 to 2 fresh limes cut into 4 parts and seeded
1 tablespoon yellow split peas (optional)
1/4 teaspoon turmeric (optional)
1/4 teaspoon nutmeg
Salt and freshly ground pepper to taste

Eggplant Stew

1. Peel eggplants in 1-inch intervals lenghtwise. Cut around, not through stem, leave stem area pointed. For large eggplants, cut each into 4 to 6 lenghtwise pieces.

2. Preheat oven to 400° F. Cover baking sheet with foil. Place eggplants (if large ones, skinside down) on sheet and brush with vegetable oil. Cook for 20 to 30 minutes.

3. In a medium-size saucepan melt butter. Saute onion till transparent. Add meat, brown on all sides. Add 1/2 cup water, tomatoes, limes, yellow split peas, and turmeric into saucepan. Cook over medium-low heat, covered for 45 minutes or till tender. Add nutmeg, salt and pepper.

4. Place eggplants in baking dish (large enough to hold them in one layer) top with meat-sauce. Cover, cook for 45 minutes in preheated oven. Discard limes.

SERVES 6 TO 8

VARIATION: EGGPLANT WITH CHICK-PEAS Slice 1 large onion, saute in 1/2 cup olive oil till transparent. Add 1 large eggplant peeled and cut into 2-inch pieces. Salt and pepper, mix gently, reduce to low, cover, and cook 15 to 20 minutes. Add 2 to 3 tomatoes seeded and chopped, 2 cups cooked chick-peas, simmer until eggplant is tender. Serve room temperature.

String Beans in Olive Oil

String Beans in Olive Oil
LOUBIA SYAMEE

PREPARATION TIME: 15 MINUTES
COOKING TIME: 45 MINUTES

S ince this dish is a perfect meatless meal with bread and cheese, vegetarians love it.

1/3 to 1/2 cup olive oil
1 large onion, chopped
1 1/2 pounds string beans, trimmed and cut into 1-inch lenghts or halved lenghtwise

1 (28 ounce) can whole plum tomatoes, slightly crushed
3 to 4 cloves garlic, minced
Salt and freshly ground pepper to taste

1. Heat oil in a medium-size saucepan. Saute onion till transparent. Add string beans, stir to coat, cook for 5 to 10 minutes.

2. Add tomatoes and garlic. Cover. Cook 15 minutes. Salt and pepper. Reduce to low, cook until beans are tender. Taste and adjust.

3. Serve at room temperature or chilled.
SERVES 6

Sour Eggplant
TOTOYOV SUMPOOG

PREPARATION TIME: 40 MINUTES
COOKING TIME: 1 1/2 HOURS

2 medium eggplants (about 2 pounds) cut into 2-inch pieces
2 tablespoons sumac or 1/4 cup lemon juice
2 1/2 cups hot water
3 tablespoons vegetable oil
1 large onion, halved and sliced
1 pound lamb or beef stew, cut into 1-inch cubes
2 cloves garlic, minced
3 tablespoons tomato paste
1/8 teaspoon nutmeg
1/4 teaspoon cayenne or to taste
Salt and freshly ground pepper to taste

1. Sprinkle eggplant pieces with salt. Set aside. Steep sumac in 2 1/2 cups hot water for 20 minutes. If using lemon juice, add last 25 minutes of cooking

2. Meanwhile, heat oil in medium-size saucepan. Saute onion, until lightly golden. add meat and garlic. Saute for 5 minutes.

3. Strain liquid into saucepan and discard sumac. Bring to a boil. Cover. Reduce to medium-low cook for 45 minutes or until meat is tender.

4. Add tomato paste, nutmeg, cayenne, salt and pepper. Pat moisture off eggplant pieces with paper towels. Add to pan and cook 25 minutes, or till tender. Taste and adjust seasonings. Serve with crusty bread in bowls or with Mechugov Kufta (page 202).

SERVES 6

VARIATION: ZUCCHINI STEW: Substitute 6 medium zucchinis, cut lengthwise in half and then cut into 1 1/2-inch lengths, for eggplant. Do not sprinkle with salt. Add 1 green pepper, seeded with white membrane removed, cut into 1-inch pieces, and one tablespoon dried crushed mint. Use lemon juice instead of sumac. 1 cup drained cooked chick-peas and 1/2 cup extra hot water may be added. Serve with rice or Cracked Wheat with Noodles (page 199).

PUMPKIN STEW: Substitute 1 1/2 to 2 pounds peeled pumpkin for eggplant. Reduce tomato paste to 1 tablespoon. Mix pumpkin, tomato paste, and 1 tablespoon dried crushed mint with 1 small onion, chopped. Cover, set aside. Saute onion, garlic, and meat. Add 4 cups hot water, cook 45 minutes. Add pumpkin and lemon juice, cover, cook over low-heat for about 35 to 45 minutes or till tender. More mint and lemon juice may be added if desired.

Fried Eggplant
DABGEVADZ SUMPOOG

PREPARATION TIME: 10 MINUTES (plus 30 minutes for eggplant)
COOKING TIME: 5 TO 8 MINUTES

2 *pounds eggplant*
Salt and freshly ground
pepper to taste
Vegetable oil as needed
(about 1/2 cup)

Parsley, onion rings,
paprika, cherry tomato,
and lemon to garnish

1. Rinse eggplants and pat dry with paper towels. Slice into 1/2-inch thick slices, crosswise or lenghtwise. Sprinkle both sides with salt. Set aside to sweat 30 minutes (this is to bring out bitter juices). Pat dry with paper towel.

2. Heat half of oil in skillet. Saute eggplants till golden (do not crowd). About 5 minutes, turning once. Drain on several thicknesses of paper towels. Arrange on serving platter overlapping each other and garnish.

3. Serve hot or cold sprinkled with salt and pepper, or make a sandwich with toast, mayonnaise, fried eggplant.and sliced tomatoes with lettuce, salt and pepper to taste.

SERVES 4 TO 6

VARIATION: Dip eggplant into flour to coat, then in slightly beaten eggs and saute. Substitute zucchinis for eggplants eliminate 20 minutes sweating time. Use olive oil and saute cauliflowerets, sprinkle with salt, pepper, lemon juice, garlic powder and toss. Serve room temperature or cold.

Braised Leeks
BRAHS

PREPARATION TIME: 15 MINUTES
COOKING TIME: 30 MINUTES

9 *leeks (small if available)*
1/4 *cup olive oil (preferably virgin)*
1 *medium onion, halved and sliced*
1 *cup chicken broth*
2 *tomatoes, seeded and chopped*

3 *tablespoons lemon juice*
3 *tablespoons freshly chopped dill*
Salt and freshly ground white pepper to taste
Chopped dill or dill sprigs to garnish

1. Cut root ends and all but 1 1/2-inches of green parts off leeks. Make a slit down one side to about 1-inch of base, (do not slit through keep whole). Run under warm water to remove sand particles. Soak in warm water 5 minutes, and rinse again. Drain on paper towels.

2. Heat oil in a large skillet. Add onion and saute, until transparent.

3. Add leeks and turn to coat in oil. Add chicken broth, tomatoes, lemon juice, dill, salt and pepper. Cover and simmer until leeks are fork tender, about 15 to 20 minutes. Arrange in serving dish and pour liquid over.

Garnish with additional chopped dill or dill sprigs. Serve cold or room temperature.

SERVES 4

Stuffed Zucchini
TOUTOUMI LETSK

PREPARATION TIME: 30 MINUTES
COOKING TIME: 1 HOUR

3 1/2 **pounds long thin zucchinis**
1 **pound ground lamb or beef**
1 **cup long-grain rice**
1 **large onion, finely chopped**
1 **tomato, finely chopped**
1 **green pepper, finely chopped**
2 **tablespoons tomato paste**
1/2 **teaspoon sugar (optional)**
1/4 **teaspoon each: allspice, ginger, nutmeg**
   Salt and freshly ground pepper to taste
   Dash cayenne
3 **tablespoons lemon juice**

COOKING LIQUIDS:

2 **cups hot water**
1 **tablespoon tomato paste**
3 **tablespoons lemon juice**
   Salt and freshly ground pepper to taste
1/8 **teaspoon sour salt (citric acid optional)**

TOPPING SAUCE:

4 **tablespoons butter**
3 to 4 **cloves garlic, crushed**
1 **tablespoon dried crushed mint**
   Juice of one lemon

Letsk in Armenian means stuffed. Better known to the Western world as Dolma. Do not throw away the insides of the zucchini since they make a good vegetable dish served warm or cold. See Zucchini in Oil (page 154).

1. Rinse zucchinis under warm water. With the pronges of a fork scrape skins lenthwise, leaving a striped effect. Rinse under warm water. Cut off stem end. Cut zucchinis into 3-inch pieces. Using an apple corer, or vegetable peeler, hollow insides of each piece, leave 1/4-inch thickness on bottom end, (only one side should have a hole). Salt and pepper inside walls of zucchinis.

2. In a large bowl mix together meat, rice, onion, tomato, chopped pepper, tomato paste, sugar, allspice, ginger, salt, pepper, cayenne, and lemon juice. Stuff zucchinis to about 1/4-inch on top, (rice will expand). Place in a saucepan, in rows.

3. Mix cooking liquids together. Pour over stuffed vegetables. Invert a dish over zucchinis to keep in place during cooking.

4. Bring to a boil. Reduce heat to medium-low. Cover. Cook for 35 minutes. Tilt pan slightly to distribute liquids, continue cooking 20 minutes longer or till easily pierced with a fork and rice is cooked. Remove dish. Melt 4 tablespoons butter till bubbling in small saucepan. Add crushed cloves garlic, stir, cook 30 seconds. Add 1 tablespoon dried mint and lemon juice, stir to blend, pour over vegetables in pot. Tilt to distribute. Serve, with yogurt or Yogurt Garlic Sauce (page 260) and omit topping sauce.

SERVES 6 TO 8

VARIATION: Substitute 1 (16 ounce) jar grape leaves rinsed and drained for zucchinis. Follow direction for wrapping as in Stuffed Grape Leaves (page 20). Place thin lamb chops or thin beef steaks on bottom of pot and rolls on top.

Stuffed Zucchini

Substitute 10 small 4-inch eggplants, 4 tomatoes, 3 green peppers. Cut off 1/2-inch of stems and reserve, hollow out insides, salt and pepper stuff and cook.

HINT: If you have any extra stuffing. Simply take one extra green pepper hollow out, stuff and cook.

Mushrooms are relatively new to Persian Cuisine. This dish is similar to Beef Stroganoff but with the use of egg yolks whisked with lemon juice instead of dairy sour cream. Chopped parsley may be sprinkled on top for color.

Mushroom Stew
KHORESHTA GHARCH

PREPARATION TIME: 15 MINUTES
COOKING TIME: 1 1/2 HOURS

4 tablespoons butter
1 large onion, chopped or sliced
1 pound veal or lamb stew, cut into 1-inch cubes
1 to 1 1/2 cups beef broth

1 1/2 pounds mushrooms sliced or quartered
Salt and freshly ground pepper
2 egg yolks
3 tablespoons freshly squeezed lemon juice

1. Melt butter in a medium-size non-stick saucepan. Add onion, saute till transparent. Add meat, mix thoroughly and brown. Pour in 1 cup beef broth, bring to a boil, cover, simmer, 35 to 45 minutes, or till meat is tender.

2. Add mushrooms, salt and pepper. Bring to a boil, reduce and simmer loosley covered 20 minutes. Stew can be made up to this point several hours ahead of time.

3. Combine egg yolks in small bowl. Pour in lemon juice and whisk together till smooth. Slowly pour into saucepan stirring constantly. Simmer 5 minutes longer. Serve hot with rice or noodles, a tossed green salad and fruit of the season.

SERVES 4 TO 6

VARIATION: Several lamb shanks, 4 cloves garlic, and 1/2 cup extra broth used instead of meat cubes. Cook about 1 1/2 hours or until tender. Debone, return to saucepan and continue as above.

Stuffed Cabbage Leaves
MIHSHI MALFUF

PREPARATION TIME: 1 HOUR
COOKING TIME: 1 HOUR

The magic ingredients in this Lebanese version of stuffed cabbage are mint and garlic. The Armenians add chopped tomatoes to stuffing and tomato paste to cooking liquid.

1 large head of cabbage (about 3 pounds)
3 tablespoons butter
1 teaspoon vegetable oil
1 large onion, finely chopped
1 clove garlic, minced
1 pound ground lamb or beef
1 cup rice (preferably short grain)

1 to 1 1/2 teaspoons allspice
1 teaspoon dried crushed mint
1 teaspoon salt or to taste
1/2 cup lemon juice
8 whole cloves garlic

TOPPING SAUCE:

6 tablespoons butter
3 to 5 cloves garlic, crushed
2 tablespoons dried crushed mint

1. Carve out center core of cabbage 3/4 way down. Place in a large pot of boiling water, carved side up. Gently pull leaves away with wooden fork as cabbage cooks, this should take about 15 minutes. Leaves must be soft or limp. Drain in colander. When cool, cut the large ribs from leaves, and place as a liner in bottom of a medium-size saucepan. If leaves are too large, cut in half.

2. Melt butter in a skillet. Add oil and onion saute till lightly golden, add minced garlic, stir and transfer to medium bowl. Mix together with meat, rice, allspice, mint, salt and half of lemon juice.

3. Spread a few leaves at a time on work surface. Place one tablespoon filling at edge of each leaf. Tuck sides in and roll. Arrange rolls in saucepan lined with cabbage ribs seam side down. Place whole cloves garlic here and there between rolls. Pour about 2 1/2 to 3 cups water over rolls, (just enough to cover) and invert a dish over rolls to keep in place, during cooking. Bring to a boil. Cover. Reduce to medium-low and cook for 45 minutes or till tender when pierced with a fork and rice is cooked (try one to see if its done).

4. Remove dish. Pour remainder of lemon juice over rolls. Tilt pan to distribute evenly. Cook over low 5 minutes.

5. Meanwhile in a small saucepan, melt butter. Add crushed garlic, mix and cook 30 seconds. Add dried mint, mix and pour into saucepan over rolls. Tilt pan to distribute evenly. Serve from pot or pour out liquid and invert as a cake, remove pot carefully.

SERVES 6

VARIATION: Substitute 1 (16 ounces) jar grape leaves rinsed and drained, instead of cabbage. Omit mint in stuffing step 1 and topping sauce. Place 5 to 6 slightly flattened thin lamb chops on bottom of saucepan. Stuff and roll leaves, cook as above. Serve with Yogurt Garlic Sauce (page 260) or spoon plain yogurt over portions.

HINT: This can be assembled and cooked the day before. Cool before removing from saucepan, so they don't fall apart. Drain liquid, reserve. To heat, pour over rolls.

King of Stuffed Eggplants
SHEIKH EL MAHSHI

PREPARATION TIME: 20 MINUTES
COOKING TIME: 1 HOUR

In the past, when meat was not readily available, the Arabs called this dish sheikh, meaning best or great.

2 1/2 *pounds thin baby eggplants about 3 to 4-inches long*
Vegetable oil as needed (about 1/4 cup)
1 *large onion, chopped*
1 *pound ground lamb or beef*
3 *tablespoons pine nuts*
1/4 *cup freshly chopped parsley*
1/4 *teaspoon allspice*

1/4 *teaspoon cinnamon*
Salt and freshly ground pepper to taste

SAUCE:

1 *(28 ounces) can whole tomatoes, chopped or slightly crushed*
Salt and freshly ground pepper to taste
2 *tablespoons lemon juice*

1. Peel eggplants in 1/2-inch intervals lenghtwise, to give striped effect. Leaving whole. Cut around (not through) stem. Leave stem area pointed.

2. Heat enough oil to cover bottom of a skillet. Add eggplants. Saute on all sides till golden. Remove to heatproof baking dish. Sprinkle with salt and pepper.

3. To same skillet, add oil as necessary with onion, saute till transparent. Mix in meat and nuts. Cook about 8 minutes over medium-heat, stirring often. Drain off excess fat. Stir in parsley, allspice, cinnamon, salt and pepper.

4. Preheat oven to 350° F. Make one slit lengthwise 3/4-inch deep, along center of eggplant (to hold filling). Spoon filling into slit and remainder over eggplants.

5. Mix tomatoes, salt, pepper, and lemon juice together. Pour over meat-mixture. Cover. Cook in preheated oven for 45 minutes or till tender. Uncover, cook another 10 minutes to evaporate extra juices if needed. Serve hot with rice or tossed salad and thickly sliced crusty bread.

SERVES 6 TO 8

VARIATION: Substitute large eggplants for baby ones. Slice lenghtwise, saute in oil, layer eggplants then meat-mixture, 1 sliced green pepper and sauce, cook as above.

Okras in Oil
BAYMEE SYAMEE

PREPARATION TIME: 10 MINUTES
COOKING TIME: 30 MINUTES

1 large onion, chopped
1/4 cup olive oil
3 cloves garlic, chopped (optional)
1 (16 ounce) can plum tomatoes

2 teaspoons sugar
Salt and freshly ground pepper to taste
1 pound frozen baby okra, thawed
1/3 cup lemon juice
1/4 cup freshly chopped coriander of parsley

1. Heat oil in a medium-size saucepan. Saute onion till lightly golden. Add garlic, tomatoes, sugar, salt and pepper, cook 10 minutes.

2. Add okra, lemon juice, and coriander. Mix gently (not to crush okra) and cook till tender. Taste and adjust seasonings. Remember this is served chilled or room temperature so it must be slightly stronger as chilling reduces flavor.

SERVES 4

Celery Stew
KHORESHTA KARAFS

PREPARATION TIME: 20 MINUTES
COOKING TIME: 1 HOUR

1 large bunch celery (about 3 pounds)
4 tablespoons butter
1 large onion, chopped
3 cups freshly chopped parsley
1/4 teaspoon saffron (optional)

2 cups chicken or beef broth
2 to 3 tablespoons dried crushed mint
Salt and freshly ground pepper to taste
1/4 cup lemon juice (optional)

1. Wash and cut celery into 1-inch pieces.

2. Melt butter in a 4-quart (preferably non-stick) saucepan. Saute onion till transparent. Add celery, saute 5 minutes. Add half of parsley, saffron, and broth, stir to mix. Bring to a boil. Cover. Reduce to medium-low and cook 30 minutes.

3. Add remainder of parsley, mint, salt, pepper, and lemon juice. Stir and cook for 10 minutes or until celery is tender. Serve with rice.

SERVES 6

VARIATION: A few chicken or beef bouillon cubes can be thrown into saucepan for some extra flavor. 1 1/2 to 2 pounds lamb shoulder cut into 1-inch cubes, can be sauteed with onion, and increase broth to 3 cups. Cook covered, over medium-low heat 45 minutes. Add celery and continue as recipe directs.

Whenever I see celery stalks, I remember one of our cooks, a former apprentice to the chef of Reza Shah's palace in Iran making this marvelous stew. He could not read or write so he prepared his accounts by drawing the items and the amounts next to it. Traditionally meat is added to most stews (khoreshts).

Celery Stew

For a slightly sweet and sour stew, add 2 tablespoons tomato paste, 3 tablespoons sugar and 1/3 cup lime juice instead of lemon.

RHUBARB STEW: Decrease parsley or coriander to 1 1/2 cups. The last 30 minutes of cooking, subsititute for celery 5 to 8 trimmed rhubarb stalks cut into 1-inch lengths.

ARMENIAN CELERY STEW: 3 lamb shanks cooked with 1 large onion, chopped and just enough water to cover till meat is tender and pulls away from bone easily. 1 large bunch celery washed, and cut into 1-inch pieces, salt and pepper to taste. Cook till celery is tender. Serve in soup bowls with Yogurt Garlic Sauce (page 260) spooned over it.

Zucchini in Oil
KOUSA MOUTABAL

PREPARATION TIME: 10 MINUTES
COOKING TIME: 15 MINUTES

1/2 cup olive oil
1 large onion, chopped
3 to 5 cloves garlic
Insides of 2 1/2 pounds zucchinis

1 tablespoon dried crushed mint or more to taste
Salt and freshly ground pepper to taste
Dash sour salt (citric acid) optional
1/2 cup lemon juice

A resourceful way of using the insides of the zucchini when making a stuffed zucchini recipe.

1. Heat oil in a large skillet. Saute onion till transparent and golden

2. Add garlic and zucchini meats, saute over high-heat till tender crisp, (about 10 to 15 minutes).

3. Add mint, salt, pepper, sour salt, and lemon juice. Chill and serve with crusty bread, and cheese.

SERVES 6

VARIATION: Substitute a mixture of zucchinis and eggplants sliced paper thin.

Zucchini in Oil

Split Yellow Pea Stew
KHORESHTA GHEIMEH

PREPARATION TIME: 20 MINUTES
COOKING TIME: 1 HOUR AND 15 MINUTES

3 tablespoons vegetable oil, plus oil to fry potatoes
1 large onion, finely chopped
1 1/2 pounds ground lamb or beef or lamb shoulder 1 inch cubes
1/2 teaspoon turmeric
4 dried limes (Limon Amoni)* pierced several times or 1 1/2 fresh limes cut in thirds and seeded

1 1/2 cups split yellow peas
3 tablespoons tomato paste
1/2 teaspoon cinnamon
1/4 teaspoon nutmeg
Salt and freshly ground pepper to taste
3 large potatoes, peeled, cut into thin matchsticks

1. Heat oil in a medium-size saucepan. Saute onion till transparent. add meat, brown on all sides. Drain extra fat from pan. Add turmeric, stir, add 4 cups water and limes (if using meat cubes cook 30 minutes).

2. Add peas, tomato paste, stir. Bring to a boil. Reduce to medium-heat, cover, cook 15 minutes. Extract juices by pressing down on limes with wooden spoon. Add cinnamon, nutmeg, salt and pepper. Reduce to medium-low. Cover. Cook 20 minutes, or until peas are tender but not mushy.

3. Heat about two-inches oil in deep skillet. Fry potato-sticks in three batches till golden. Drain on paper towels.

4. Remove limes from saucepan and discard. Serve, topped with crisp potato-sticks. Or with rice, boiled or baked potatoes.

SERVES 6

VARIATION: Subtitute 2 tablespoons curry powder for turmeric. Add 1 1/2 to 2 cups peeled, seeded and chopped fresh tomatoes.

* Dried limes are available in Middle or Near Eastern specialty shops.

Chick-Peas with Yogurt
FATTE

PREPARATION TIME: 15 MINUTES

2 pita breads, peeled apart
   and toasted
2 tablespoons butter
1 teaspoon dried crushed
   mint

2 cups cooked chick-peas
   Yogurt Garlic Sauce
   (page 260), warmed or
   room temperature

1. Break up toasted pita bread into bite-size pieces or larger wedges. Place on serving platter.

2. Heat butter in small saucepan. Add half of mint, stir and cook 30 seconds. Drizzle evenly over toast.

3. Top toast with chick-peas. Pour yogurt sauce over peas. Sprinkle remainder of mint over top. (For extra color sprinkle lightly with paprika). Serve warm or room temperature.

SERVES 4

VARIATION: Place 1 pound diced lamb or beef stew, 1 small onion chopped, and just enough water to cover in saucepan, cook till tender about 30 minutes. Spoon meat and several spoons of liquid over peas, continue as above. Or layer with Ground Meat with Rice (page 167), 2 cups cooked shredded chicken, double recipe for Yogurt garlic Sauce. Layer toast, meat-rice mixture and chicken, then sauce and sprinkle with some roasted pine nuts and paprika. Serve hot. This will serve 6 to 8.

Meat Stuffed Zucchini
ABLAMA

PREPARATION TIME: 30 MINUTES
COOKING TIME: 1 1/2 HOURS

2 1/2 pounds thin zucchinis
   Salt and freshly ground
   pepper to taste
3 tablespoons vegetable oil
1 medium onion, chopped
1 pound ground lamb or
   beef
3 tablespoons pine nuts

1 tablespoon tomato paste
1/4 teaspoon allspice or to
   taste

SAUCE:

1 (28 ounces) can whole
   tomatoes, slightly crushed
1/8 teaspoon cinnamon
2 tablespoons lemon juice

1. Wash zucchinis under warm running water, soak in a bowl of warm water for 10 minutes. Rinse again. Cut stem end off. Carefully scoop out pulp with apple corer or peeler (do not throw away pulp, make Zucchinis in Oil (page 154). Leaving outer skin intact, do not puncture skins.

2. Salt and pepper insides of hollowed out zucchinis. Place in colander opened end down.

3. Heat oil in a skillet. Add onion and saute till transparent. Add meat and nuts, brown over medium-heat about 8 minutes. Drain excess fat. Add tomato paste, allspice, salt and pepper, stir together, cook 2 minutes. Cool slightly.

4. Preheat oven to 350° F. Stuff prepared zucchinis with meat-mixture. Place in an ovenproof baking dish, in one layer.

5. Mix tomatoes, cinnamon, and lemon juice. Pour over zucchinis, cover with foil. Cook in preheated oven for 1 1/2 hours. Serve hot with extra lemon wedges to be squeezed over individual portions if desired. Rice or Cracked Wheat with Noodles, and a bowl of yogurt or Yogurt Drink (page 258).

SERVES 6 TO 8

The most important ingredient of this lamb, bean and herb stew is fenugreek (Shambalileh) that makes the recipe authentic. Sometimes it is eliminated because of its strong aroma. The greens can be varied and should be chopped by hand. Take care not to puree if using a food processor.

Lamb Herb Stew
KHORESHTA GHORMEH SABZI

PREPARATION TIME: 25 MINUTES
COOKING TIME: 2 HOURS

8 tablespoons butter
2 tablespoons vegetable oil
2 pounds shoulder of lamb or beef stew, cut into 1-inch cubes
1 large onion, chopped
4 cups broth
3 or 4 dried limes (Limon Amoni)* pierced several times or 1/3 cup fresh lime juice
1/2 cup dried black eyed beans

3 1/2 cups chopped scallions with 2-inch green tops
3 1/2 cups snipped garlic chives or a good alternative is equal portions of spinach and regular chives
3 1/2 cups freshly chopped flat leaf parsley
3 tablespoons dried crushed fenugreek leaves or to taste
1/2 to 1 teaspoon turmeric Salt and freshly ground pepper to taste

1. Melt 4 tablespoons butter with oil in saucepan large enough to hold all ingredients. Saute meat with onion, stirring frequently over medium-high heat. Add broth, dried limes (if fresh lime juice is used reserve for last 15 minutes of cooking time) and cook for 1 hour, covered over medium-low heat. Add beans, cook for 35 minutes or till meat and beans are tender.

2. Meanwhile heat a large non-stick skillet over medium-high heat, add chopped greens, stir constantly but gently to remove excess moisture (about 5 minutes). Reduce to medium-low, add remainder of butter, stir frequently for about 10 minutes (do not burn). Mix with fenugreek, turmeric, salt and pepper. Pour into saucepan with meat, cook 10 to 20 minutes. Serve with rice. Can be made in advance up to 2 days.

SERVES 6

* Dried limes are available in Middle or Near Eastern specialty shops.

Curried Potato Stew

Curried Potato Stew
KHORESHTA SIB ZAMINI

PREPARATION TIME: 20 MINUTES
COOKING TIME: 2 HOURS

4 *tablespoons butter*
1 *tablespoon vegetable oil*
1 *large onion, finely chopped*
1 1/2 *to 2 pound lamb or beef shoulder cut into 1-inch or 4 to 5 lamb shanks*
3 *to 4 dried limes (Limon Amoni)* pieced several times or 1 1/2 fresh lime sliced and seeded*

1 *(6 ounces) can tomato paste*
1 1/2 *to 3 tablespoons curry powder*
Salt and freshly ground pepper to taste
4 *large potatoes, peeled and cut into 1-inch cubes.*

1. In 4 quart-saucepan melt butter. Add oil, and onion. Saute until transparent. Add meat, brown on all sides. Pour 3 cups water and limes into saucepan, bring to a boil. Cover, reduce to medium-low and cook for 1 hour, (for shanks 2 hours). If using shanks, pull meat apart into chunks. Discard bone.

2. Stir in tomato paste, add curry, salt and pepper. Taste and adjust. Add potatoes, cook over medium-low heat for about 20 to 25 minutes. Serve with rice or crusty bread, or in small bowls with a plate of raw vegetables.

SERVES 6

VARIATION: Decrease potatoes to 2. Add 1 1/2 cups frozen green peas, cook as above. Or add 1/2 cup split yellow peas last 30 minutes of cooking time for meat.

* Dried limes are available in Middle or Near Eastern speciality stores.

Spinach in Pastry
SHOMINOV KHUMOREGHEN

PREPARATION TIME: 30 MINUTES (plus dough)
COOKING TIME: 45 MINUTES

PASTRY:

1 3/4 cups all-purpose flour

8 tablespoons butter, sliced and chilled

1 egg

1/4 cup dry white wine

1 1/2 tablespoons vegetable oil

1/8 teaspoon salt or to taste

1 egg yolk, lightly beaten for glaze

FILLING:

1/2 cup olive oil

2 medium onions, chopped

3 packages (10 ounces each) frozen chopped spinach, thawed and squeezed dry

1/2 cup pine nuts or coarsely chopped walnuts

1/2 cup lemon juice

1/2 teaspoon paprika

1/8 teaspoon cayenne or to taste

Pinch of sour salt (citric acid optional)

Salt to taste

1. To make pastry, put flour in container of food processor. Place butter evenly over flour. Turn motor on-off a few times, until mixture resembles coarse crumbs.

2. mix egg, wine, oil, and salt in 1-cup glass measure.

3. With motor running, pour egg-mixture through feed tube and process until dough forms ball around blade. Scrape down sides and place dough on waxed paper. Wrap, place in refrigerator several hours.

4. To make filling, heat oil in skillet. Add onions, saute until transparent. Place spinach in large bowl. Add onions, nuts, lemon juice, paprika, cayenne, sour salt and salt. Mix well.

5. Lightly grease 17 x 14-inch baking sheet. Roll out pastry on lightly floured surface to 16 x 8-inch rectangle. Cut edges even (reserve trimmings). Place on prepared baking sheet and spoon filling down center of pastry. Spread filling out toward one long side, leaving 1-inch edge on side and at top and bottom. Fold unfilled pastry over and press edges together to seal. Tuck ends under.

6. Cut reserved trimmings into attractive shapes and attach to top. Brush with egg glaze. Refrigerate 15 minutes. Preheat oven to 375° F.

7. Bake in preheated oven 40 minutes or until golden. Cool tray on rack (about 1 hour).

SERVES 6 TO 8

VARIATION: For smaller pastries divide pastry and filling in 2 or 3 parts, combine as indicated and bake about 25 minutes or until golden.

HINT: To freeze, cook, cool completely, wrap in foil. Remove from freezer let thaw, wrapped, about 3 hours. Unwrap, place on baking sheet, bake in preheated 400° F. oven 15 minutes to crisp pastry.

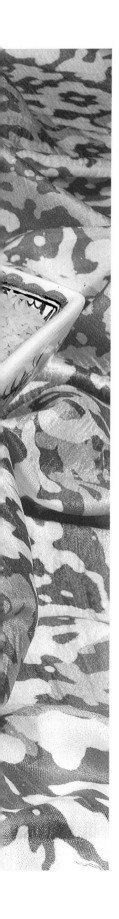

CHAPTER NINE

Rice

Rice is called Rez in Arabic, Berenj in Persian and Printz in Armenian. It is the basic ingredients of most Middle Eastern and especially Near Eastern Cuisines. There are many types of rice such as Berenj Domsiah, preferred by the Persians, which is similar to the Indian Basmati availble in Near Eastern stores.

To make pilaf or polow all the ingredients are cooked together. Another method used by Persians is to parboil the rice and then adding butter and steaming. Layer with vegetables, herbs, fruits or meats. Real connoiseurs prefer Persian style rices because in the preparation the excess starches are removed making it much fluffier and lighter.

Potatoes are used in the Middle East and Iran but they take second place to a steaming rice dish. In Iran if one isn't served rice once a day they feel they have not had a complete meal. Our butler Ahmad would eat a heaping platter everyday. The amounts I have seen consumed in one sitting still amazes me.

It is important to know that every type of rice is different so the amount of water or broth used will vary. In Iran they say the older the rice the better. I always give it a good rinse until the water runs clear, this removes the dust particles and starch. The more exotic rices need picking over, often I find small stones or unidentifiable objects that are definitely not for eating. An iron nail or bay leaf should be used in rice for storing.

This exotic Iranian dish can be served with plain yogurt spooned over the rice, or with roast chicken, barbecued lamb chops, or steak. A straight-sided, non-stick, saucepan is the best kind of pot to use for this recipe.

Lima Bean with Dill Rice
BAGALI SHEVID POLOW

PREPARATION TIME: 20 MINUTES (plus soaking for rice)
COOKING TIME: 45 MINUTES

1 recipe Steamed Rice
(page 182)
14 tablespoons butter
3 medium potatoes, cut
into 1/4-inch slices
(optional)
Salt and freshly ground
pepper to taste

1 package (10 ounce) frozen
baby lima beans, thawed
3 cups freshly chopped dill
1/4 teaspoon saffron threads
crushed and steeped in 2
tablespoons hot water

1. Prepare Steamed Rice through steps 1 and 2. Melt 4 tablespoons butter in a non-stick 6-quart saucepan. Arrange potato slices in single layer in saucepan.

2. Spread one-third of prepared rice over potatoes. Salt and pepper. Cover with half of lima beans, and half of dill. Cover with half of remaining rice and remainder of lima beans and dill. Top with remaining rice. Keep ingredients mounded high in center so steam can circulate. Sprinkle 1/4 cup water over rice. Slice remaining butter, place over rice. Cover rice with waxed paper. Wrap cover of pot in kitchen towel and place over saucepan to keep steam inside.

3. Cook over medium-high heat 8 minutes, reduce heat to low, and cook 35 minutes or until rice is soft and fluffy.

4. Set 1 cup rice aside. Mound remaining rice on serving dish. Remove potatoes from saucepan with spatula and place around rice or in separate dish. Sprinkle reserved cup of rice with saffron and mix well. Spread saffron rice on top of plain rice. Season with salt and pepper.

SERVES 6 TO 8

VARIATION: When layering rice, add 1 large onion, chopped and sauted in butter, 6 broiled lamb chops or 1 1/2 pounds cooked boneless lamb shoulder cubes, or 6 cooked chicken cutlets. Increase cooking time by 15 minutes.

Sour Cherry Rice
ALBALOW POLOW

PREPARATION TIME: 20 MINUTES (plus soaking for rice)
COOKING TIME: 1 1/2 HOURS

5 tablespoons vegetable oil	1/3 cup sugar
Salt and freshly ground pepper to taste	1/2 teaspoon cinnamon
8 large chicken pieces	10 tablespoons butter
1 1/2 to 2 pounds (about 4 cups) ripe, tart, pitted sour cherries	1 Recipe Steamed Rice (page 182)
	1/2 teaspoon crushed saffron threads, steeped in 2 tablespoons hot water

Although sour cherries of Iran are not available here, a fresh, tart, sour cherry will do. It has a beautiful bright appearance and is very decorative for a buffet. With a bit more sugar added and some orange rind, fresh cranberries can be substituted. Omit chicken and have a very different dish to go with a Thanksgiving turkey.

1. Heat oil in skillet. Salt and pepper chicken pieces. Brown on all sides. Drain pan. Pour 1 1/2 cups water over chicken. Bring to a boil. Cover, reduce to low, cook for 45 minutes. or till tender.

2. In a medium-size saucepan combine cherries and sugar. Mix gently together. Bring to a boil. Reduce, cook over low-heat for 5 minutes. Cherries must retain their shape and should not be mushy. Stir in cinnamon, and 2 tablespoons butter. Set aside.

3. Prepare steamed rice through step 1 and 2. Melt 2 tablespoons butter in a 6-quart (preferably non-stick) saucepan.

4. Spread half of rice into buttered saucepan. Reserve liquids from skillet. Place chicken pieces over rice and top with cherrie-sauce mixture. Spread with remaining rice. Keep ingredients mounded high in center so steam can circulate. Sprinkle with 1/3 cup of reserved liquids from skillet. Slice remaining 4 tablespoons butter, place over rice. Cover with waxed paper. Wrap cover of pot in a kitchen towel, place over saucepan to keep steam inside.

5. Cook over medium-high heat 5 minutes. Reduce to medium-low and cook for 25 to 35 minutes or till soft grains of rice are obtained.

6. Melt remaining 2 tablespoons butter. Remove about 1 cup rice to a bowl. Sprinkle saffron, melted butter over rice. Mix thoroughly to coat and turn bright shinny yellow. Serve rice pilled onto platter, chicken around edge, and saffron-rice topping.

SERVES 8

VARIATION: 8 large pieces of roasted duck may be used instead of chicken. Or 2 pounds lean ground beef shaped into small meatballs and sauteed in butter briefly. Although not authentic and bright in color an alternative is to substitute 2 cups dried sour cherried for fresh (check for pits). Add 1/2 cup water with sugar cook 10 minutes, and continue as directed. Dried sour cherries are available in Near or Middle Eastern stores.

Fruit Market in Beirut, Lebanon

Ground Meat and Rice
REZ MAGH LAHIM MAFRUMA

PREPARATION TIME: 10 MINUTES
COOKING TIME: 30 MINUTES

4 *tablespoons butter*	1 *cup long grain converted*
1 *tablespoon vegetable oil*	*rice (Uncle Ben's)*
3 *tablespoons mixed*	2 *cups beef or chicken broth*
almonds and pine nuts	*Salt and freshly ground*
1/2 *pound ground sirloin*	*pepper to taste*

1. Heat a small skillet over medium. Add 1 tablespoon butter, oil, then almond and pine nuts, stir to coat. Saute nuts stirring often for about 5 minutes or till golden. Remove with a slotted spoon. Drain on paper towels. Set aside.

2. Heat a medium saucepan (preferably non-stick), add meat, brown stirring often. Drain fat. Add remaining butter, and rice, stir constantly 1 minute. Add broth and seasonings to taste. Bring to a boil. Cover, reduce heat to medium-low and cook for 15 to 20 minutes or until rice is done and liquids are absorbed.

3. Remove from heat and let stand 10 minutes. Stir gently with fork to loosen, spoon onto serving platter. Sprinkle roasted nuts on top. Goes well with roast lamb or chicken. Some carrots boiled and sauteed in butter for color.

SERVES 4

VARIATION: Ground Meat and Bulgur: Substitute 1 cup large bulgur (cracked wheat) for rice. Add 1 small green pepper finely chopped, 3 tablespoons tomato paste, and 1/2 teaspoon allspice, stir to mix with liquids. Continue as above.

Sweet Orange Peel Rice
SHIRIN POLOW

PREPARATION TIME: 30 MINUTES, (plus soaking for rice)
COOKING TIME: ABOUT 2 HOURS

SAUCE:

1 **cup dried orange peel* or 4 medium oranges**	1/2 **cup slivered almonds**
1/2 **cup shelled and skinned pistachios**	1 1/2 **teaspoon saffron threads**
1 1/4 **cups sugar**	1/2 **teaspoon cinnamon**
16 **tablespoons (1/2 pound) butter**	1/8 **teaspoon nutmeg**
	1 1/4 **cups orange juice**
	1 **recipe Steamed Rice (page 182)**

1. Place dried orange peels in a medium-size saucepan. Or, if using fresh oranges, peel, scrape off the white insides, as much as possible and cut into thin julienne strips. Cover with water, bring to a boil. Cover, reduce to medium-low and cook 20 minutes or till tender.

2. Drain peels in a colander, discard liquid. Rinse and return to pan. Add pistachios, almonds, sugar, 8 tablespoons of butter, saffron, cinnamon, nutmeg, and orange juice. Stir, cook over medium-low heat for 30 to 40 minutes, stirring occasionally.

3. Prepare Steamed Rice through steps 1 and 2. Melt 2 tablespoons butter in a 6-quart (preferably non-stick) saucepan. Reserve 1/4 of sauce, set aside.

4. Spoon one-third of Steamed Rice into buttered saucepan. Cover with half of sauce. Spoon over half of remaining rice and the sauce. Top with remainder of rice. Keep ingredients mounded high in center so steam can circulate. Sprinkle with 3 tablespoons water. Slice remaining 6 tablespoons butter, place over rice. Cover rice with waxed paper. Wrap cover of pot in kitchen towel and place over saucepan to keep steam inside.

5. Cook over medium-high heat 5 minutes, reduce to low, cook for 30 to 40 minutes or until rice is soft amd fluffy. Pile rice onto a platter and top with reserved 1/4 of sauce.

SERVES 6 TO 8

VARIATION: Two medium-size cooked, skinned and deboned chickens or ducks cut into large pieces may be layered with sauce over rice, then continued as above. Reduce orange peels by, 1/4 cup for dried peels, or 2 oranges for fresh ones. Add 3 carrots, peeled and cut into 1-inch by 1/4-inch strips to the sauce after step 1.

DRIED ORANGE PEELS: Wash and dry 6 squeezing oranges. Cover a baking sheet with a paper towel or waxed paper, set aside. With a sharp knife quarter each orange and peel of skins. Scrape off most of white part underneath the peel. Cut into thin julienne strips. Place on sheet, dry several days in a cool place. Store in an airtight container or freeze.

* Dried orange peel is available in some Middle or Near Eastern stores.

HINT: Sauce may be cooked 2 days in advance, covered and refrigerated, or frozen up to 1 month.

The unusual combination of orange peel, nuts, and saffron is favored by Iranians, they use them in stews (Khoreshts) or layer them between rice as below. Prepared for weddings and feasts because it is outstanding in taste and colorful for the eyes. In Iran one could buy these ingredients in a store specializing in freshly roasted nuts, seeds, dried fruits, and peels of all kinds. These stores are called Ajeel Fourosh decorated with mirrors and bows. The aroma from the ovens usually downstairs in the cellar was incredible. One would always buy more then one needs. I always looked forward to going shopping with my mother to one of these stores. There was something almost magical about them.

Armenian Rice with Noodles
ARISHDAOV PRINTZ

PREPARATION TIME: 5 MINUTES
COOKING TIME: 30 MINUTES

1 cup long grain rice
2-3 tablespoons butter
1 teaspoon oil

1/2 cup very thin egg noodles
or vermicelli cut into
1-inch pieces
2 cups chicken stock
1/2 teaspoon salt or to taste

1. Wash rice by raking fingers through rice in a bowl until water runs clear. Drain, set aside.

2. Heat butter and oil in saucepan over medium-heat. Add noodles, stir to coat. Cook about 5 to 10 minutes, stirring often. At this point butter will start to foam. Stir and toss with wooden spoons or forks constantly, until golden.

3. Add rice and saute 1 minute. Pour liquid and salt into pan, bring to a boil. Cover, reduce to medium-low. Cook for 15 to 20 minutes or till liquid is absorbed. Turn heat off let rest for 10 minutes and serve, or sprinkle with some roasted nuts, freshly ground black pepper over rice, or some chopped parsley or paprika for color.

SERVES 4 TO 6

VARIATION: Omit noodles, add to butter, 1 medium onion, chopped and sauteed till transparent. Add rice, broth, 1/4 teaspoon allspice, salt, and 1 cup cooked chickpeas, cook as above.

Armenian Rice with Noodles (see variation)

Molded Shiraz Rice
SHIRAZY POLOW GHALEBI

PREPARATION TIME: 15 MINUTES (plus soaking for rice)
COOKING TIME: 2 HOURS

1 medium eggplant (about 3/4 pound)
14 tablespoons butter
1 1/2 cups dried barberry or currants*
1/8 teaspoon nutmeg
1/3 cup sugar
1 Recipe Steamed Rice (page 182)
2 egg yolks
1 cup unflavored yogurt
1/2 teaspoon saffron threads steeped with 2 tablespoons hot water
Salt and white pepper to taste
1 1/2 cups cooked and diced chicken

An unusual layered rice, with chicken, eggplant, saffron, yogurt and dried barberry berries (Zarashk), that originated in the city of Shiraz, where they are known for growing the best quality saffron.

1. Peel and slice eggplants (about 1/2-inch thick). Sprinkle with salt on both sides, set aside for about 15 minutes to bring out bitter juices. Pat dry with paper towels. Heat skillet with 3 tablespoons butter. Saute eggplants over medium-heat on both sides. Add more butter as needed to brown. Set aside.

2. Pick over berries. Rinse well, place in a saucepan. Add enough water to cover 1-inch above berries. Bring to a boil, reduce to medium-low heat, cook for 10 minutes, if using currants this step is not necessary. Drain and rinse. Return to saucepan. Add 3 tablespoons butter, nutmeg and sugar, stir well. Place over low-heat stirring often, till butter melts and sugar dissolves. Set aside.

3. Prepare Steamed Rice through steps 1 and 2. With 2 tablespoons butter, grease a 13 x 9-inch pyrex baking dish or a 11-inch round cake pan preferably non-stick. Set aside.

4. Preheat oven to 350° F. or 400° F. for non-pyrex pan. In a large bowl, beat egg yolks. Add yogurt saffron, salt and pepper. Mix completely. Add two-thirds of the rice, mix to blend thoroughly. spread mixture on bottom of prepared baking dish and go up slightly on the sides. Press down on mixture with back of spoon.

5. Arrange eggplant slices over rice-mixture, sprinkle with salt and pepper. Layer with the chicken, salt and pepper, then spread with berries. Top with remaining rice. Slice remaining 6 tablespoons butter place over rice. Cover with foil. Bake for 2 hours or until a crisp golden crust has formed around bottom and sides. Remove from the oven, let stand for 5 minutes. Run a sharp knife around edge and invert onto a serving platter. Serve with pickles or tossed green salad.

SERVES 8 TO 10

HINT: Place baking dish in cold water about half-way up pan for one minute to insure easy removal.

* Available at Middle or Near Eastern specialty shops.

Molded Rice Cake

🌹

Molded Rice Cake
KATEH GHALEBI

PREPARATION TIME: 5 MINUTES
COOKING TIME: 1 HOUR 30 MINUTES

A popular way of making rice in the Caspian Sea region of Iran. Omit butter and it can be served cold in hot weather with yogurt.

2 cups basmati rice or other long-grain white rice

1 1/2 teaspoon salt or to taste
3 tablespoons butter

1. Wash rice in a bowl, until water runs clear, (rake fingers through rice to wash) drain.

2. In a medium-size non-stick saucepan, add 3 1/2 cups water, rice, salt and butter. Bring to a boil. Cover, reduce to medium-low, cook 35 minutes. Reduce to low and continue cooking for 1 hour longer.

3. Loosen if necessary, a good shake should be enough or with a knife around sides. Place a large serving dish over saucepan, then hold firmly, and invert (as for a cake). Cut through crust into wedges or pieces and spoon rice into dish, serve with stew (khoresht).

SERVES 6

VARIATION: Add 1 cup tomato sauce, decrease water to 2 1/2 cups, or 3 tablespoons tomato paste, mixed with water and 1/2 teaspoon oregano. Cook as above.

T a Dig, is the bottom crust that forms when butter and rice, potato, or bread turns to a golden crust. Rice lovers think of it as the best part. When you have mastered the art of Ta Dig, you are considered a good cook by Iranian standards. Please read both recipes before starting.

Crusty Bottom of Rice
TA DIG

1 *Recipe Steamed Rice*
(page 182) up to step 2
9 *tablespoons butter*

RICE CRUST:

Add 1/2 cup extra rice to steamed rice recipe

POTATO CRUST:

4 *medium potatoes, scrubbed and sliced 1/4-inch thick*

BREAD CRUST:

Cut enough pita into squares or wedges, pull apart place inside out in a single layer over buttered pot

1. Prepare rice as indicated, set aside. Melt 4 tablespoons butter in a 4-quart heavy bottomed saucepan, swirling to coat bottom of pan. Choose one of above for the crust. Top with rice. Slice remaining 5 tablespoons butter and place over rice. Sprinkle with 1/4 cup water. Cover rice with waxed paper.
Wrap cover of pan with kitchen towel and place over saucepan to keep steam inside while cooking.

2. TO COOK OVER DIRECT HEAT: For regular saucepan, cook over medium-heat 5 minutes. Reduce to low for 45 minutes. To serve spoon fluffy rice onto a platter, invert crust with a spatula by breaking into serving size pieces, place around rice or in separate dish. Crust may also be removed whole. For non-stick coated saucepan, cook 10 minutes over medium-heat. Reduce to medium-low, 10 minutes longer and then to low for 50 minutes. To serve place large serving dish over pot and hold carefully invert (as for a cake). or spoon onto platter as above.

3. TO COOK IN OVEN: Preheat oven to 400° F. generously butter casserole large enough to hold rice. Add rice, sprinkle with water as directed and cover with foil. Bake in a preheated oven for 1 1/2 hours. To serve, run knife around sides of casserole to loosen and invert onto serving platter. Serve by cutting through crust and spoon rice along with a piece of crust onto individual plates.

HINT: If bottom crust sticks to saucepan or casserole, place into a pan of cold water for 1 minute to loosen. If using a pyrex baking dish lower heat to 350° F. and bake for 2 hours or till golden crust forms on bottom and sides.

Green Herb Rice
SABZI POLOW

PREPARATION TIME: 15 MINUTES (plus soaking for rice)
COOKING TIME: 40 MINUTES

1 *Recipe Steamed Rice (page 182)*
1 *cup freshly chopped flat leaf parsley*
1 *cup chopped dill*
1 *cup snipped garlic chives or spinach*
1 *cup freshly chopped coriander*

1 *teaspoon dried crushed fenugreek (optional)*
1 *clove garlic, minced (optional)*
14 *tablespoons butter*
Salt to taste
1/2 *teaspoon saffron steeped in 2 tablespoons hot water*

1. Prepare steamed rice through steps 1 and 2.

2. Mix parsley, dill, garlic chives, coriander, fenugreek, and garlic together. Set aside.

3. Melt 2 tablespoons butter in a 4-quart saucepan, swirling to coat bottom of pan. Spoon one-third of rice into saucepan, lightly, salt top of rice. Cover with half of herb mixture. Spoon half of remaining rice over herbs and salt lightly. Add remainder of herb mixture. Top with remaining rice. Keep ingredients mounded high in center so steam can circulate. Sprinkle 1/4 cup water over rice. Slice remaining 12 tablespoons butter, place over rice. Cover rice with waxed paper. Wrap cover of pot in kitchen towel and place over saucepan to keep steam inside.

4. Cook over medium-heat 5 minutes, reduce to low, cook for 30 minutes or till rice is soft and fluffy.

5. Set 1 cup of rice aside. Mound rice on serving dish. Sprinkle reserved cup of rice with saffron and mix well. Spread saffron rice on top of plain rice. Season with salt and freshly ground pepper if desired.
Serve with fish, roast turkey or duck, yogurt and pickles.

SERVES 6
VARIATION: Melt 4 tablespoons butter in saucepan instead of 2. Add 1 1/2 pounds cooked lamb, cut into 1-inch pieces on bottom of buttered pot, continue as above. The meat will become crusty on the bottom of the pot. Or make a Ta Dig (page 173).

A fresh herb studded rice, steamed to perfection is one of the most popular and delicious rices of Iran. This is accompanied by fried, baked or smoked whitefish from the Caspian Sea. Served for New Year (No Rooz) the most important holiday in Iran. It lasts 13 days. During this time each family sets up a table with seven items (Haft-Sin) that must start with the letter S. Sometimes fresh fenugreek leaves are used, I have not listed it since it is hard to find.

Red Rice
Lentil Raisin Rice
Green Herb Rice

RICE & PASTAS

Red Rice
ESTAMBOLI POLOW

PREPARATION TIME: 15 MINUTES (plus soaking time for rice)
COOKING TIME: 1 1/2 HOURS

12 *tablespoons butter*
2 *large onions, chopped*
2 *pounds shoulder of lamb diced*
1 *(28 ounces) can whole tomatoes slightly crushed*
2 *to 3 tablespoons tomato paste*

1/2 *teaspoon cinnamon*
1/4 *to 1 teaspoon turmeric (optional)*
Salt and freshly ground pepper to taste
2 *to 3 tablespoons freshly squeezed lemon juice*
1 *Recipe Steamed Rice (page 182)*

1. Melt 4 tablespoons butter in a medium-size (preferably non-stick) saucepan. Saute onion till transparent. Add meat, brown on all sides. Pour in tomatoes. Stir in tomato paste, cinnamon, turmeric, salt, pepper, and lemon juice. Bring to a boil. Reduce to medium-low, cover, cook for 20 to 30 minutes. Or till meat is tender.

2. Prepare steamed rice through step 1 and 2. Melt 3 tablespoons butter in a 6-quart (preferably non-stick) saucepan.

3. Spoon one-third of steamed rice into buttered pot. Cover with half of meat-tomato mixture. Spoon in half of remaining rice, and remainder of meat-tomato mixture. Top with remaining rice. Keep ingredients mounded high in center so steam can circulate. Slice remaining 5 tablespoons butter and place over rice. Cover rice with waxed paper. Wrap cover of pot in kitchen towel, place over saucepan to keep steam inside.

4. Cook over medium-high heat 5 minutes. Reduce to medium-low for 15 minutes, then low for 15 minutes. Pile onto a serving dish. Serve with green vegetables, tossed salad or a bowl of yogurt to be spooned over rice. This dish may be baked in a buttered casserol covered in an oven preheated to 350° F. for 40 to 50 minutes. For a Crusty Bottom Rice see (page 173).

SERVES 8

VARIATION: Ground lamb or beef may be substituted for chunks, saute with onions, drain excess fat, cook 10 minutes continue as above. Omit meat. Add peas and carrots instead, cook 10 minutes with tomatoes and continue with recipe.

Lentil, Raisin Rice
ADAS POLOW

PREPARATION TIME: 10 MINUTES (plus soaking for rice
COOKING TIME: 45 MINUTES

14 tablespoons butter
1 medium onion, finely chopped
1 pound lamb stew, diced
1/4 teaspoon cinnamon
1/4 teaspoon nutmeg

Salt and freshly ground pepper to taste
1 cup raisins
1 Recipe Steamed Rice (page 182)
1 1/4 cup brown lentils

1. Melt 3 tablespoons butter in a skillet. Add onion, saute till transparent. Add meat, stir, cook 5 minutes. Add 1/2 cup water, bring to a boil. Cover, reduce to low, and cook about 20 minutes or till tender. Sprinkle with cinnamon, nutmeg, salt and pepper. Stir in raisins, set aside.

2. Prepare steamed rice through step 1. Bring 4-quarts water to a boil in a 6-quart saucepan. Add lentils, cook for 5 to 8 minutes. Then add drained rice to lentils, bring back to a boil, stirring occasionally, and cook 4 minutes longer or until rice is just firm. Drain and rinse with warm water.

3. Rinse saucepan thoroughly. Melt 2 tablespoons butter in saucepan, swirling to coat bottom of pan. Transfer half rice-lentil mixture into saucepan. Spoon meat-onion mixture over rice with a slotted spoon, reserve liquids. Top with remaining rice. Keep ingredients mounded high in center so steam can circulate. Pour reserved liquids evenly over rice. Slice remaining 9 tablespoons butter, place over rice. Cover rice with waxed paper. Wrap cover of pot in kitchen towel, place over saucepan to keep steam inside.

4. Cook 5 minutes over medium-heat, reduce to low, cook 35 to 45 minutes or until rice and lentils are soft and fluffy.

5. Spoon rice into serving dish. Serve with yogurt, salad or pickles, and (Sabzi Khordan) mixed platter of eatng herbs.

SERVES 6

VARIATION: Omit meat and raisins. Add 2 cups dried pitted and halved dates to sauteed onions in skillet. Stir in spices and 1/4 cup water cook 2 minutes. Continue as above. Sprinkle 1/4 cup water over rice in pot before covering and cooking 25 to 35 minutes.

String Beans with Rice
LOOBYA POLOW

PREPARATION TIME: 10 MINUTES (plus rice and stew)
COOKING TIME: 45 MINUTES

The stew can be made ahead of time and frozen. If desired omit the meat.

1/2 **Recipe String Bean Stew**
   (page 132)
  1 **Recipe Steamed Rice**
   (page 182)

12 **tablespoons butter**
   Yogurt and pickles to
   serve

1. Prepare String Bean Stew. Set aside.

2. Prepare Steamed Rice through Step 1 and 2. Melt 2 tablespoons butter in a 6 quart (preferably non-stick) saucepan.

3. Spoon one-third of steamed rice into buttered pot. Cover with half of string bean stew. Spoon half of remaining rice, and then remainder of stew. Top with rice. Keep ingredients mounded high in center so steam can circulate. Sprinkle with 1/4 cup water. Slice remaining 10 tablespoons butter, place over rice. Cover rice with waxed paper. Wrap cover of pot in kitchen towel. Place over saucepan to keep steam inside.

4. Cook over medium-high heat 5 minutes, reduce to low, cook 35 to 45 minutes or until rice is soft and fluffy. Serve with a bowl of yogurt and pickles.
For a Crusty Bottom Rice see (page 173).
SERVES 8

String Beans with Rice

Molded Carrot Rice
HAVIDJ POLOW GHALIBI

PREPARATION TIME: 25 MINUTES (plus soaking for rice)
COOKING TIME: 1 TO 2 HOURS

8 tablespoons butter	1 teaspoon turmeric or to taste
1 tablespoon vegetable oil	
1 large onion, finely chopped	Salt and freshly ground pepper to taste
2 pounds carrots, peeled and cut 1/4-inch by 1-inch long	3 tablespoons lemon juice
	3 tablespoons sugar
	1 Recipe Steamed Rice (page 182)

1. Heat large skillet Add 6 tablespoons butter and oil. Saute onion over medium-heat until transparent. Add carrots, turmeric, salt and pepper, mix thoroughly. Cook 5 minutes. Pour in lemon juice and sugar, mix, cook about 5 minutes. Reduce to low, cover, cook until carrots are tender about 15 to 20 minutes. Set aside.

2. Prepare steamed rice through steps 1 and 2. Butter a 13 x 9-inch pyrex or 11-inch round baking dish with remaining 2 tablespoons of butter.

3. Preheat oven to 350° F. Add two-thirds of the rice to prepared baking dish, spread evenly and press down with back of a spoon. Spoon carrot mixture evenly over rice. Top with remainder of rice. Press down on surface to pack down the rice. Sprinkle 3 tablespoons water on top. Cover with foil. Bake for 1 1/2 to 2 hours or till a golden crust forms around bottom of baking dish. (Crust may form sooner then baking time indicated but it will not be crisp enough).

4. Remove, let stand 5 minutes, run a sharp knife around edges if needed. Invert onto a serving platter. Cut into squares or just break through crust with a spoon, serve a piece of the crust then rice-mix onto each plate.

SERVES 8

VARIATION: 2 pounds cooked chicken cutlets or meatballs, that have been rolled in flour to coat and sauteed in butter can be layerd with carrots and rice. Or omit rice and use as a carrot stew.

HINT: If turmeric is not desired use cinnamon to taste.

This carrot sauce, layered with rice and baked to form a crust is one of my favorites. The yellow color of the rice is very festive. Goes well with breaded veal cutlets. Try throwing a handful of currants into the carrot sauce. For a sweet-sour taste add more sugar and lemon juice to carrots while cooking.

Pureed Lentil and Rice
MUJADARAH

PREPARATION TIME: 10 MINUTES
COOKING TIME: 1 HOUR

1/4 cup olive oil (preferably virgin)
1 large onion, finely chopped
1 1/2 cups brown lentils picked over

1/2 cup rice (preferably short grain)
1/2 teaspoon allspice
Salt and freshly ground pepper to taste

1. Heat oil in skillet, saute onion until transparent and lightly golden. Set aside.

2. In medium-size saucepan add 4 cups water and lentils, bring to a boil. Cover, reduce to medium-low and cook till tender, about 20 minutes.

3. Pass lentils with liquid through food mill into a bowl. Return mixture to saucepan. Add fried onion, rice, allspice, salt and pepper. Cook for about 25 minutes over low-heat stirring often, or until rice is tender. Pour into a shallow dish and cool. Serve as part of meza (hors d'oeuvre).

SERVES 4 TO 6

VARIATION: LENTILS AND RICE: MOUDARDARA: Place 1 cup picked over brown lentils in a medium-size saucepan. Add 4 cups broth, bring to a boil, reduce to medium. Cook uncovered about 10 to 15 minutes or till almost tender. Drain liquids into a 2 cup measure (add some water if needed to make 2 cups). Return liquids to saucepan with 1 cup rice, salt and freshly ground pepper to taste. Throw in a chicken bouillon if desired. Add 4 tablespoons (2 ounces) butter, bring to a boil, cover, reduce heat to medium-low, cook for 15 to 20 minutes or till liquids are absorbed and grains are tender but not mushy. Set aside 10 minutes. Serve with salad.

LENTILS WITH BULGUR: ARMENIAN MUJADARAH: Cook lentils as for lentils and rice above. Drain liquids into a 2 cup measure. Measure 1 3/4 cups liquids. Return to saucepan with lentils. Add bouillon cube (chicken or beef) if desired, 1 cup large bulgur (cracked wheat) 6 tablespoons butter, salt and freshly ground pepper, to taste. Bring to a boil, cover reduce heat to medium-low and cook for 20 to 25 minutes or till liquids are absorbed and grains are tender.

To serve garnish with tomato wedges around serving platter. 1 large onion, halved, and sliced, then sauteed in 1/4 cup olive oil to a dark golden brown may be placed over any of the above dishes when serving. Watch onion carefully so it does not burn.

In this dish. The lentils are cooked, passed through a food mill, recooked with rice and mixed with a fried onion. The result is a pudding like dish, served room temperature. Goes well with salads and fried vegetables such as eggplant, zucchini, cauliflower, tomatoes and fresh mint or basil. In the variations below the lentils are not pureed but left whole and then cooked with rice or bulgur.

Pureed Lentil and Rice

Spiced Rice
REZ MAGH BAHARAT

PREPARATION TIME: 10
COOKING TIME: 25 MINUTES

> 6 *tablespoons butter*
> 2 *cups long-grain converted*
>   *rice (Uncle Ben's)*
> 4 *cups chicken broth*
> 1/2 *teaspoon allspice*
> 1/4 *teaspoon freshly ground*
>   *pepper*
> 1/8 *teaspoon cloves*
> 1 *teaspoon cinnamon*
>   *Salt to taste*

1. Melt butter in medium-size saucepan, over medium-heat. Add rice, stir constantly 1 minute. Add broth, allspice, pepper, cloves, cinnamon and salt, stir. Bring to a boil cover. Reduce to medium-low and cook 15 to 20 minutes or until rice is soft and liquids are absorbed. Serve with roast lamb, turkey or chicken.

SERVES 6

VARIATION: Brown 1 pound ground beef or lamb. Drain fat. Add butter, rice, stir and cook 1 minute, continue as above. Sprinkle with chopped parsley for color.

Steamed Rice
CHELO

This is the basic recipe for steamed rice which is a specialty of Iran. If you have not tasted rice prepared by this method, by all means try it. You will be delighted. It is served plain with stew or kabobs. A variety of chopped green herbs, vegetables, cooked meat, chicken, or dried fruit, may be added to the parboiled rice before it is steamed.

PREPARATION TIME: 10 MINUTES (plus soaking for rice)
COOKING TIME: 40 MINUTES

> 3 cups Basmati or white long-grain rice
>
> 3 tablespoons coarse sea salt
> 6 tablespoons butter

1. Wash Basmati rice in a bowl under cold running water, raking fingers through rice until water runs clear. Drain and cover rice with enough warm water to come 3-inches above rice. Sprinkle with 1 1/2 tablespoons sea salt, set aside to soak at least 3 hours. Rice may be soaked 24 hours. Drain before cooking.

2. Bring 3 1/2-quarts water to a rolling boil in 6-quart saucepan. Add remaining 1 1/2 tablespoons sea salt and drained rice. Stir to loosen lumps of rice, return to a rolling boil, cook 4 minutes or until rice is just firm. Drain and rinse under warm water.

3. Rinse saucepan thoroughly. Melt 2 tablespoons butter in saucepan, swirling to coat bottom of pan.

4. Mound rice into pan so steam can circulate. Slice remaining 4 tablespoons butter and place over rice. Sprinkle with 1/4 cup water and cover rice with waxed paper. Wrap cover of pan in kitchen towel and place over saucepan to keep steam inside.

5. Cook 3 to 4 minutes over medium heat, reduce heat to low, and cook 20 minutes or until rice is soft and fluffy.

6. Loosen rice and spoon into serving dish.

SERVES 6 TO 8

NOTE: for Crusty Bottom Rice, see (page 173). It is not absolutely necessary to soak rice, but soaking will make rice more fluffy.

Rice with Lamb
TAH CHIN

PREPARATION TIME: 20 MINUTES (plus soaking for rice)
COOKING TIME: 3 1/2 HOURS

3 1/2 to 4 pounds leg of lamb
1 recipe Steamed Rice (page 182)
Salt and freshly ground pepper to taste
2 1/2 cups plain yogurt

1/2 teaspoon saffron threads crushed and steeped in 2 tablespoons hot water
3 egg yolks
10 tablespoons butter
Parsley garnish

1. Preheat oven to 450° F. Place lamb in a roasting pan. Cook in preheated oven for 15 minutes. Reduce to 325° F , continue cooking for 1 hour and 45 minutes longer. Cool till easily handled. (This can be made a day ahead).

2. Prepare steamed rice through step 1 and 2. Butter a 13 x 9-inch pyrex baking dish, or a 11-inch round cake pan with 2 tablespoons of butter. Set aside.

3. Pull lamb meat away from bone into bite-size chunks, (do not slice or cut to be authentic). Place in a large mixing bowl. Salt and pepper meat. Add 2 cups of the yogurt and half of the saffron, mix thoroughly to coat. yogurt must coat lamb generously, if needed add 1/4 cup extra yogurt. Set aside.

4. Preheat oven to 350° F. In a medium mixing bowl, beat egg yolks together slightly. Add remainder of yogurt and saffron, stir to combined. Add half of rice and mix thoroughly.

5. Spread egg-rice mixture in buttered baking dish going up sides (about 1 inch). Add yogurt-lamb over rice-mix and press down with back of spoon in an even layer. Top with remaining plain rice. Slice remaining 8 tablespons butter, place over top of rice. Cover with foil.

6. Cook for 1 1/2 to 2 hours in preheated oven. Remove foil. Run a sharp knife around edge and invert onto a serving platter. See Hints (page 173).

SERVES 8

VARIATION: With Chicken and Spinach: Substitute 2 pounds chicken cutlets for lamb, sauteed in 4 tablespoons butter 8 minutes. 2 (10 ounce) packages frozen spinach leaves, cooked and squeezed dry. A handful of pitted prunes or dried apricots. Mix chicken with yogurt, saffron. Layer spinach over egg-rice mixture in baking dish. Place chiken over spinach, then prunes over chiken and continue with recipe.

Macaroni, Dill, Cheese Mold
BANEEROV ARISHDA

A molded pasta dish both deliciously easy and attractive. Try it with fresh tomato sauce.

PREPARATION TIME: 15 MINUTES
COOKING TIME: 15 MINUTES

>   1 teaspoon salt
>   1 pound macaroni
>   3/4 cup feta cheese, rinsed,
>   patted dry
>   3/4 cup freshly chopped dill
>   1 tablespoon oil
>   4 tablespoons breadcrumbs
>   4 tablespoons butter

1. In a saucepan of boiling water, add salt, macaroni, cook till just firm to the bite, drain in colander, and rinse. Set aside. Coat 10-inch non-stick skillet with oil. Dust bottom and sides with 2 tablespoons breadcrumbs.

2. Add half of macaroni, press down to flatten. Sprinkle with crumbled cheese and dill. Then add remainder of macaroni and press down. Dot with butter. Sprinkle with remainder of breadcrumbs.

3. Cook covered over medium-heat, for 10 minutes. Uncover cook for 5 minutes, so that the bottom forms a crust. Place serving dish over skillet and invert carefully but quickly. Serve hot with fresh seeded chopped tomatos or stewed tomatoes with some fresh basil and salt and pepper.

SERVES 4 TO 6

VARIATION: Mix 4 tablespoons melted butter with cooked macaroni, add 2 cups freshly chopped dill, 3/4 pound feta cheese crumbled, toss and mix together. Place in a 4-quart greased and bread crumb dusted non-stick saucepan. Cook over direct medium-heat, 25 minutes, or bake in 400° F. oven for 45 minutes covered. Cool 5 minutes then invert onto serving dish and serve.

S paghetti birds nests; take about 30 strands at a time of cooked, drained, and rinsed thin spaghetti, twist around two fingers making a round shaped birds nest. Fill with meat filling (page 195) or your favorite recipe and pour a spicy tomato sauce over it, sprinkle with oregano. Heat thoroughly in preheated 350° F.

Spaghetti Rounds

Lebanese Cous-Cous
MOUGHRABIA

PREPARATION TIME: 20 MINUTES
COOKING TIME: 1 HOUR

3 cups Moughrabia	2 tablespoons allspice
10 tablespoons butter	1 tablespoon cumin
1 (16 ounce) bag, frozen pearl onions, thawed	(optional) Salt and freshly ground pepper to taste
1 cup cooked chick-peas	4 cups chicken broth
3 to 4 tablespoons powdered caraway seeds	

T his pasta type dish is spiced with caraway and allspice. Although it is traditionally made with both lamb and chicken, I have omitted them and prefer to just roast a chicken and serve it on the side. Moughrabia is found in Middle Eastern speciality stores.

1. Bring water to a boil in a medium-size saucepan. Add moughrabia, cook till just firm to the bite. Drain. Set aside.

2. Melt half of butter in a non-stick 12-inch skillet. Add pearl onions, brown on all sides. Remove to a dish with a slotted spoon, set aside. Add remainder of butter, melt, add moughrabia stir to coat, over medium-heat. Pour in half of broth and half of spices. Stir frequently for 5 minutes. Reduce to medium-low, cook till liquid is absorbed. Add remaining broth, spices, salt, pepper, chick-peas, and onions. Cook stirring often until liquid is absorbed and moughrabia is tender. Taste and adjust. Serve with roasted chiken pieces around platter of moughrabia. Fruit of the season for dessert. Extra sauce can be made with broth, spices and a little cornstarch to thicken with.

SERVES 6 to 8

VARIATION: 1 pound of lamb cut into chunks cooked in 1 cup water till tender may be added to sauteed onions, and 1/2 teaspoon turmeric added with spices.

Pastries in Yogurt Sauce
MANTI

PREPARATION TIME: 1 HOUR
COOKING TIME: 1 HOUR·

DOUGH:
- 3 1/2 cups unbleached all-purpose flour
- 3/4 cup water
- 4 tablespoons olive oil
- Pinch salt

FILLING:
- 1 pound ground lamb or beef (not too lean)
- 1 small onion, finely chopped
- 1/8 teaspoon cayenne or to taste
- Salt and freshly ground pepper to taste
- 4 tablespoons butter
- 1 cup broth

SAUCE:
- 2 cups chicken broth
- 1 cup Drained Yogurt (page 19)
- 2 or 3 cloves garlic
- 1/2 teaspoon salt or to taste
- 1 egg, slightly beaten
- Dried basil, mint, and sumac* to serve

1. Combine ingredients for dough in a large bowl. Knead, smooth, flouring your hands as needed to prevent sticking. Or mix in a food processor. Place flour and salt in workbowl fitted with plastic blade, turn motor on, pour liquids through feed tube. Mix until dough forms a ball around blade. Remove dough, cover, set aside to rest 30 minutes.

2. Mix meat, onion, cayenne, salt and pepper together, set aside.

3. Butter a large baking dish. Set aside, divide dough into two equal parts. Roll each separately, on a lightly floured work surface or use a pasta machine to about 1/16-inch thick. Cut into 1 1/2-inch squares. Place 1 teaspoon filling in center of each square. Fold opposite edges, pinch together to seal on both sides, (making miniature canoe like shapes, opened in the center).

4. Preheat oven 375° F. Place pastries close to each other on prepared baking sheet. Top with a small piece of butter on each pastry or melt butter, and brush surface to coat.

5. Bake in preheated oven 30 minutes. Remove, pour 1 cup broth over pastries, return to oven for 10 minutes longer. Meanwhile prepare sauce.

6. Crush garlic with salt in a mortar and pestle. In a medium-size saucepan combine the drained yogurt, broth, and garlic. Warm sauce stirring constantly over medium-heat with a wooden spoon. Blend in the slightly beaten egg, stir till thickened.

7. Transfer Manti to a serving dish or individual dishes and spoon sauce over it. Sprinkle with dried crushed basil, mint, and sumac, serve immediately. Pastries freeze well uncooked or cooked without sauce.

SERVES 6

VARIATION: Boil pastries in enough boiling broth to cover. Drain. Serve in soup plates with hot sauce spooned over it, then sprinkle with basil, mint, and sumac.

* Sumac is available in Middle Eastern stores.

When Manti is mentioned to someone who has tasted the authentic dish you can see their mouths watering. In order for you to succeed you must start from scratch. I have seen recipes substituting won-ton wrappers for home made dough, definitely not the same. I suggest making large batches and freezing the meat pastries adding the sauce when ready to assemble.

Water Dipped Pastry with Cheese Filling
BANEEROV KHUMOREGHEN (SOU BOUREK)

PREPARATION TIME: 1 1/2 HOURS
COOKING TIME: 1 HOUR

DOUGH:
- 4 cups all-pupose flour
- 5 large eggs
- 2 tablespoons olive oil
- 3/4 teaspoon salt or to taste
- 10 tablespoons melted butter

FILLING:
- 2 pounds mixed light colored mild grated cheeses such as:
- brick cheese
- farmed cheese
- monterey Jack
- munster cheese
- Halloum, if available
- Salt to taste
- 1/4 cup parsley (optional)

This very old Armenian recipe is similar to meatless lasagna. The traditional way of preparing is layering it into a round cake pan and cooked over direct heat, turning the pan constantly to brown evenly. It is then inverted into an identical pan and browned on the other side, very tricky.

1. Sift flour in a bowl or on work surface. Make a well in center of flour. Break eggs in center of well. Add oil and salt. With a fork (as for making fresh pasta) mix eggs, oil, salt, together gently. Then start to incorporate flour from inner ring around middle. When about half of flour is absorbed, knead with palms of your hands to finish. Cover and let rest for 30 minutes.

2. Mix cheeses, salt and if using parsley together. Set aside.

3. Divide dough into 12 equal-size parts. Roll each to make a round ball set aside. Lightly flour work surface, roll one ball at a time into a thin round to fit a 10-inch cake pan. Stack pastry rounds with paper towels in between, until all are rolled out and ready to be cooked.

4. Bring a large saucepan full of water to a boil. Have a large bowl, half filled with water, a colander, and paper towels handy.

5. Preheat oven to 400° F. Take one round of pastry at a time, and dip into boiling water. Cook for 1 minute, pushing it down to keep pastry submerged. Remove and immediately place in cold water (careful not to tear) until cool. Drain in colandar. Pat dry on paper towels.

6. Brush a 10-inch cake pan with the melted butter. Place one cooked pastry round into pan brush with butter. Do the same with the next five rounds brushing them with butter. Spread with cheese mixture evenly. Top with one-layer of pastry, brush with butter, continue until all is used up. Pour remainder of butter evenly over surface.

7. Bake in preheated oven for about 30 to 40 minutes or until golden. Cut into squares with a very sharp knife. Serve immediately with a tossed salad or as a side dish to chicken or meats. Also good with okras or string beans in oil (see vegetables). Freezes well cooked or uncooked.

SERVES 6 TO 8

HINT: The dough can be made in a food processor and rolled out with a pasta machine into wide strips and placed in a rectangular baking dish. Freeze very soft cheeses before grating.

CHAPTER TEN

Bulgur
(Cracked Wheat)

Bulgur is used primarily by Armenians, Lebanese, Syrians and in the Caucasus of Russia. It is whole grains of wheat that have been par boiled in a small amout of water, sun dried and then cracked between stone rollers. It is found in three sizes fine, used with meat for Kibbehs, medium for taboule salads, and coarse for pilafs. It has a delightful nutty taste, a firm texture and is a favorite of health food enthusiasts. Less water is used to cook bulgur than rice and very little vitamin content is lost since the expanding grains absorb them.

Raw Meat with Bulgur

This dish has a similarity to steak tartar since it is eaten uncooked with the addition of bulgur. It is favored by Middle Easterners, especially the men.

Raw Meat with Bulgur
KIBBEH NAYE

PREPARATION TIME: 30 MINUTES

1 Recipe Ground Meat with Bulgur (page 194). Meat must be fresh and has to be ground same day as used.

GARNISH:

1 cup chopped scallions including 2-inch green tops, fresh mint sprigs, olive oil, pita bread, pickles, radishes

1. Smooth prepared kibbeh onto platter with fingertips that have been dipped into water. Make a criss-cross indentation over surface with side of your hand.

2. Pour some olive oil over entire surface, surround platter with scallions and mint sprigs. Serve with pita bread, pickles and radishes. Or serve oil and whole scallions, mint sprigs in a separate bowl.

SERVES 4 TO 6

VARIATION: ARMENIAN CHI-KUFTA: Add cayenne to taste and mix well. Pinch off about 2-inch portions of mixure and shape into cylinders. Roll in finely chopped parsley and chopped scallions. Serve with drinks as a Meza.
Make Kibbeh Naye as above. Make half recipe of FILLING for Kibbeh bil Siniyeh (page 195). Cook filling as directed. Serve warm filling with Kibbeh Naye and warm bread, pickles, fresh mint leaves, and radishes. Goes well with Arak, a favorite Middle Eastern drink.

Stuffed Footballs
KIBBEH MEKLEE

PREPARATION TIME: 30 MINUTES (plus Kibbeh and Hashwe)
COOKING TIME: 25 MINUTES

*1/2 recipe of filling for
Layered Meat with
Bulgur (page 195)*

*1/2 recipe of Ground Meat
with Bulgur (page 194)
vegetable oil as needed*

1. Follow instructions for filling, cook, set aside to cool. This may be prepared one day in advance.

2. Prepare Ground Meat with Bulgur. Cover, set aside.

3. Divide Kibbeh into 30 equal parts. With hands slightly dipped in water, take one part at a time, roll into a ball. Make a hole in center, about 3/4 of the way in (not all the way) with your finger. Enlarge hole to make it as thin as possible. This will act as the shell for the cooked filling.

4. Place about 1 tablespoon of cooked filling inside shell. Close opening. If any cracks occur in shell, seal with wet finger tips. Mold and smooth out into a football or torpedo shape. Place on a flat baking sheet and continue with remainder.

5. Heat about 4-inches of oil in a deep fryer or heavy saucepan to a temperature of 370° F. Fry few at a time till it turns golden brown about 3 to 5 minutes. Drain on paper towels. Serve hot or room temperature as a Meza.
If prepared in advance, to heat, place in a non-stick pan. Sprinkle with water, cover, and warm over direct heat tossing several times to heat evenly. Freezes well. Heat directly from freezer in heatproof dish, covered in a preheated 450° F. oven, about 20 to 30 minutes.

MAKES 30

VARIATION: Shape kibbeh mix into small bite-size balls. Uncooked Kibbeh may be mixed with 3 tablespons fresh chopped mint before cooking. Fry in oil or saute in a little butter. Serve with yogurt garlic sauce (page 260), or yogurt with 1 tablespoon dried mint and salt to taste.

*Stuffed Footbals
Flying Saucer*

Flying Saucer
KIBBEH SAJE

PREPARATION TIME: 30 MINUTES
COOKING TIME: 30 MINUTES

1/2 recipe Kibbeh (page 194)	cayenne to taste
6 tablespoons butter	1/8 teaspoon nutmeg
1 1/2 cups finely chopped onions	1/2 teaspoon salt or to taste
2 tablespoons pine nuts	1/8 teaspoon freshly ground pepper
3/4 teaspoon cumin	1 tablespoon lemon juice
1/4 teaspoon paprika and	Butter or vegetable oil

1. Prepare Kibbeh Mix and set aside.

2. Melt butter in skillet (preferably non-stick). Saute onions to cook almost to a mush, stirring often. Add nuts, cumin, cayenne, nutmeg, salt and pepper, and cook 5 minutes. Stir in lemon juice and set aside to cool. Can be prepared a day in advance.

3. Divide Kibbeh Mix into 16 equal-size portions. Roll out each portion on waxed paper to 3 1/2-inch round. Set aside.

4. Place about 1 tablespoon filling in center of 8 Kibbeh rounds. Top each round with second round. Moisten edges and press firmly together to seal. Preheat oven to 425° F.

5. Brush both sides of rounds with melted butter or oil. Place on greased baking sheet and bake in preheated oven 15 minutes, turning over once or twice with spatula. Alternatively, shallow-fry in clarified butter until golden on both sides. Serve immediately with Baba Ghanoush, (page 26), Roasted Peppers, (page 35), Labni, (page 19), or tossed green salad.

MAKES 8 SAUCERS

HINT: Assemble and open freeze uncooked in single layer 30 minutes to harden. Stack between sheets of waxed paper and place in rigid container. Thaw before using.

Kibbeh is a mixture of pounded meat mixed with bulgur (cracked wheat). Many Lebanese and Syrians consider this dish to be a national treasure. The old-fashioned way to make Kibbeh was to pound the lamb, bulgur, and onions to a paste in a large-stone mortar and pestle. Some village women were said to be blessed with a special "hand" for making kibbeh and were envied. However, today, with a food processor, Kibbeh is easy to make and can be used as a shell for stuffings, or can be rounded into small cocktail-size balls, fried, and served with a sauce. It can be served as an appetizer with drinks or in soup, it feeezes well, and is easy to reheat in the oven.

Ground Meat with Bulgur
KIBBEH

PREPARATION TIME: 20 MINUTES

1 1/2 to 2 cups small bulgur
    1 medium onion, quartered
    2 pounds lean lamb or beef,
       cut into 1-inch cubes
    2 teaspoons salt or to taste
    1 teaspoon freshly ground
       pepper or to taste
  1/2 teaspoon allspice
  1/4 cup small ice chips
       (optional)

1. Wash bulgur in bowl, drain, and cover with water. Set aside.

2. Place onion in container of food processor and process until pureed. Remove half set aside. Add half of meat and half of seasonings. Cover and process to a paste. Remove cover and scrape mixture into large bowl. Repeat with remaining pureed onion, meat and seasonings. Mix well.

3. Drain bulgur and press out excess liquid with back of spoon.

4. Divide meat mixture in half. Place half of mixture in container of food processor. Sprinkle a few ice chips (if using) over and add half of bulgur. Process until well mixed, scrape into large bowl. Repeat with remaining meat, ice chips, and bulgur. Blend thoroughly. Use this basic recipe to make Layered Meat with Bulgur (page 195), Stuffed Footballs (page 192), Raw Meat with Bulgur (page 191), or little meatballs in a soup, and in many other recipes.

SERVES 6 TO 8

Layered Meat with Bulgur

Layered Meat with Bulgur
KIBBEH BIL SINEYA

PREPARATION TIME: 30 MINUTES
COOKING TIME: 60 MINUTES

1 Recipe Kibbeh *(page 194)*

FILLING   (Hashwe):

  2 *tablespoons safflower oil*
  1 *large onion, chopped*
  1 *pound lean ground lamb
     or beef*
  1/4 *cup pine nuts*
  2 *teaspoons allspice*
  1/4 *teaspoon cinnamon or
     nutmeg*

  1 *teaspoon cumin
     (optional)*
  1/4 *teaspoon paprika
     (optional)*
  2 *tablespoons corn or
     safflower oil*
  2 *tablespoons butter or
     vegetable shortening*

I n this recipe half the kibbeh is spread in a baking dish and topped with cooked meat filling. The remainder is patted over the cooked meat and the pie is cut into diamond shapes or squares before baking.

1. Prepare Kibbeh and set aside.

2. Heat oil in skillet. Add onion and saute until transparent. Stir in meat, and nuts, cook until meat is browned, stirring occasionally. Blend in spices and set aside to cool.

3. Preheat oven to 450° F. Lightly grease 13 x 9-inch or 11-inch round pan. Pat half of Kibbeh in prepared pan. Spread filling over. Pat remainder of Kibbeh over filling and smooth top with damp fingertips. Cut three-fourth of the way down, making diamond shapes or squares. Combine oil and butter. Pour evenly over top.

4. Bake in preheated oven 10 minutes. Tilt pan to distribute oil. Reduce oven temperature to 350° F. and bake 25 to 35 minutes. Tip pan once or twice during cooking to coat surface of Kibbeh with oil. Serve hot with Baba Ghanoush, or yogurt, tossed green salad, radishes, or pickles Kibbeh can be wrapped and frozen cooked or uncooked.

SERVES 6 TO 8

A hearty wholesome food, a favorite with my vegetarian friends, that can be prepared quickly and from staples found on hand in any Armenian home. A mixture of bulgur (cracked wheat) orange lentils, onions, and olive oil. Serve with lots of mixed pickles and fresh tomato wedges. Also known as Majmackly Kufta.

Orange Lentil and Bulgur
VOSBOV KUFTA

PREPARATION TIME: 15 MINUTES
COOKING TIME: 25 MINUTES

1 cup orange lentils picked over and washed
1 cup small bulgur rinsed
1 large onion, finely chopped
Salt and freshly ground pepper to taste
1/8 teaspoon cayenne or to taste

1/2 to 3/4 cup olive oil (preferably virgin)
1 cup freshly chopped flat leaf parsley
1 cup chopped scallions with 2-inch green tips included

1. Pour lentils into a medium-size saucepan. Cover with 2 cups water, bring to a boil over high heat, stirring occasionally. Reduce to low, cook until tender about 15 to 20 minutes.

2. Heat olive oil in skillet. Saute onions until transparent and golden.

3. Remove lentils from heat. Mix in bulgur, cover pan and set aside for 10 minutes. Transfer mixture to a large bowl, add onions and oil, blend together very well. Season with salt, pepper and cayenne, taste, adjust, then mix 2 tablespoon parsley into mixture. Arrange on serving dish. Sprinkle remaining parsley and scallions on top. Or as it is served more traditionally formed into 2-inch long sausage shapes then rolled into chopped parsley and scallion mixture to coat entire surface and placed on a round platter in a circle.

SERVES 4 TO 6

Meat and Bulgur Kabobs
KHOROVADZ MEES ANANOUKOV

Delicous grilled on charcoal and served in pita bread with Parsley Onion Salad (page 58) and tomato slices. Also known as Orouk.

PREPARATION TIME: 15 MINUTES
COOKING TIME: 8 MINUTES

3/4 cup small bulgur	1/4 teaspoon paprika
1 1/2 pounds ground lamb or beef	Dash cayenne
2 tablespoons dried crushed mint	1/8 teaspoon freshly grated nutmeg
Salt and freshly ground pepper to taste	Pita bread
	Parsley Onion Salad

1. Rinse and soak bulgur in warm water to cover for 15 minutes. Drain, and squeeze out excess moisture.

2. In a large bowl, mix meat, bulgur, mint, salt, peppers, and nutmeg together.

3. Pinch off pieces the size of an egg and shape onto skewers to make about 4-inch thin kabobs (dip hand in cold water frequently to keep from sticking).

4. Cook over hot coals, or broil turning often for about 6 to 8 minutes. Serve with steamed vegetables and potatoes, lightly buttered.

SERVES 6

Cracked Wheat with Lamb Shanks
MEESOV TZAVARI YEGHINTZ

Spoon yogurt on top and serve with tomato wedges. This filling dish can be made in advance.

PREPARATION TIME: 10 MINUTES
COOKING TIME: 2 HOURS

6 tablespoons butter	2 cups cooked chick-peas
1 tablespoon vegetable oil	1 1/2 teaspoons allspice
3 medium onions chopped	1/2 teaspoon cumin
2 lamb shanks (about 2 pounds) trimmed	Salt and freshly ground pepper to taste
1 1/2 cups large bulgur, rinsed	

1. Melt butter in medium non-stick saucepan. Saute onions in butter with oil till transparent. Add lamb shanks, brown. Pour in 2 cups water, bring to a boil, cover, reduce to medium-low, cook for 1 1/2 hours. Transfer shanks to a dish, debone, trim excess fat cut into bite-size chunks. Pour liquids from pan into a measuring cup and add water till it measures 2 3/4 cups. Pour into same saucepan. Add bulgur, chick-peas, allspice, cumin, salt and pepper. Return meat to saucepan.

2. Bring to a boil, reduce to medium-low, cover and cook about 25 minutes. Remove from heat, rest for 10 minutes. Serve with extra cumin sprinkled on top if desired.

SERVES 4

This is an Armenian version for the stuffing, for Lebanese use rice, and parsley instead of bulgur and mint.

Meat Bulgur Sausage
MUMBAR

PREPARATION TIME: 1 HOUR
COOKING TIME: 1 HOUR

1 *whole intestine (lamb) about 15 feet thin casings*
1 3/4 *pounds beef and 1/4 pound suet ground together*
1 *small onion, finely chopped*
2 *tablespoons dried crushed mint*
1/4 *to 1 teaspoon cayenne or to taste*

1 *teaspoon freshly ground pepper or to taste*
1 1/2 *teaspoon salt or to taste*
1/2 *to 1 teaspoon cinnamon*
1 *teaspoon allspice*
1/2 *cup medium bulgur Beef broth*
1 *small onion*
2 - *inch piece cinnamon stick stick*

1. If using salted intestines, wash, and soak, in cold water several hours, changing water a few times. Cut casings into 3 feet lenghts. Place one end of casing over tip of a funnel. Rinse with water to flush out insides.

2. Pass meat and suet twice through meat grinder using coarse disk.

3. Place meat mixture in a large bowl. Add chopped onions, mint, pepper, salt, cinnamon, allspice. Rinse bulgur and drain. Add to bowl and mix completely.

4. Using sausage attachment on grinder, take one piece of casing at a time. Push casing onto nozzle and make a knot at end. Ease off casing as they fill. Leave about 1/2-inch empty space every 2-inches, for bulgur to expand while cooking. Or push meat filling through large funnel with spoon into casings if sausage attachment is not available.

5. Tie each strip into a coil pierce with a fork or skewer here and there. Place in a large saucepan. Cover with hot broth, add onion and cinnamon stick. Bring to a boil, reduce, cover and simmer for about 1 hour. Serve hot as is, or with mustard, bread and radishes.

SERVES 6

This is sometimes better known as bulgur pilaf and is quite good for you. The nutty flavor, goes very well with chicken, lamb and beef stews or roasts or barbecues, and a salad. Also good with a bowl of yogurt.

Cracked Wheat with Noodles
ARISHDAOV TZAVARI YEGHINTZ

PREPARATION TIME: 10 MINUTES
COOKING TIME: 30 MINUTES

1 cup large bulgur (cracked wheat)
4 tablespoons butter
1 teaspoon vegetable oil

1/2 cup thin egg noodles or vermicelli broken into 1-inch pieces
2 cups chicken broth
Salt to taste

1. Rinse bulgur. Drain in a colander. Set aside.

2. Heat butter and oil in a saucepan. Add noodles, stir to coat and saute stirring often for about 10 minutes over medium-heat. Butter will foam at this point. Stirring constantly is the secret to get evenly golden colored noodles. I use two wooden forks to separate noodles and toss them lightly while cooking. (it makes it easier to handle). When noodles are ready, immediately add bulgur. Stir and cook 1 minute.

3. Pour broth into saucepan, add salt to taste. Bring to a boil, reduce to medium-low, cover and cook about 15 minutes or till liquids are absorbed. Let stand 10 minutes stir gently to loosen and serve.

SERVES 4

VARIATION: Add 1 medium onion and 1 green pepper finely chopped to hot butter, saute till transparent, omit noodles and decrease broth to 1 3/4 cup continue as indicated. Extra flavorings such as: curry powder, basil or cumin, about 1/4 to 1/2 teaspoon may be added with broth. 1 or 2 peeled whole cloves garlic can be thrown into saucepan just before covering to cook. When serving, mash with a fork against the side of the pan, mix and serve. Or add 1 cup cooked chick peas to the 2 cups broth before covering and cooking. For a bulgur and meat dish see Ground Meat and Rice (page 167) under variation.

A health food salad from Lebanon and Syria. Somehow when this recipe flew over the Atlantic it lost its real flavors. Please remember a good Taboule has lots of parsley and tomatoes, not so much bulgur (cracked wheat). Do try this recipe below and then if you must, make your changes.

Parsley and Bulgur Salad
TABOULE

PREPARATION TIME: 30 MINUTES
COOKING TIME: 30 MINUTES

1/2 to 3/4 cup small bulgur
4 cups freshly chopped flat leaf parsley
1 cup chopped scallions with 2-inches of green tops
2 cups seeded and chopped ripe firm tomatoes
1/2 cup freshly chopped mint leaves or 3 tablespoons dried crushed mint

Salt and freshly ground pepper to taste
1/2 cup olive oil (preferably virgin)
1/2 cup fresh lemon juice or to taste
Tomato garnish
Romaine lettuce or cabbage leaves to serve

1. Rinse, and soak bulgur in water to cover for 25 minutes. Drain and squeeze out excess moisture as much as possible with your hands.

2. In a large bowl combine the parsley, scallions, tomatoes, mint, and bulgur. Toss together. Add salt, pepper, olive oil and lemon juice. Toss to mix thoroughly. taste and adjust if needed.

3. Serve in a platter surounded with extra chopped tomatoes or place a tomato rose in center, and hearts of romaine lettuce or inner small cabbage leaves to scoop up salad with.

SERVES 6

Parsley and Bulgur Salad

BULGUR (CRACKED WHEAT)

Stuffed Meatballs
MECHUGOV KUFTA

PREPARATION TIME: 45 MINUTES
COOKING TIME: 25 MINUTES

As the story is told, these stuffed Kuftas are said to be so tasty and light, that even on a full stomach you could eat 9 of them. The reputation of Armenian cooks depended on how well they prepared this dish. Also known as Harput Kufta.

FILLING:

2 tablespoons butter
1/2 pound ground lamb
1 large onion, chopped
1/2 green pepper finely chopped
2 tablespoons chopped parsley
1 teaspoon coriander
1 teaspoon basil
1/4 teaspoon cinnamon

Salt and freshly ground pepper to taste
1/4 cup pine nuts or walnuts broken up

SHELL:

1/2 recipe Kibbeh (page 194)

TO COOK:

8 cups lamb, beef or chicken broth
1 teaspoon sea salt

1. Heat butter in a skillet over medium-high heat. Add onions, saute till transparent. Add meat, and brown. Add green pepper, stir and cook 5 mintues. Stir in remainder of filling ingredients, taste and adjust. Cool completely. This can be made 1 day in advance.

2. Make kibbeh. Separate into 25 equal portions. Take one in hand, roll into a ball, then flatten in your palms, to make it as thin as possible, since bulgur will expand. Place about a tablespoon of filling in center and bring up sides to seal, (Kibbeh is the shell for the filling). Dip fingertips in water, and seal any cracks that occur by smoothing out surface. Place on a tray continue with remainder.

3. In a saucepan bring the broth to a boil. Add sea salt and few Kuftas at a time, do not crowd. Cook about 8 to 10 minutes or till Kuftas rise to the surface. Remove with a slotted spoon to individual bowls and serve with or without broth and a mixed salad, or without the broth and with Sour Eggplant (page 143).

MAKES 25

VARIATION: Add 2 or 3 tablespoons tomato paste to broth and 1 cup cooked chick peas.

Stuffed Swiss Chard Leaves
PANJAR PATOUK

PREPARATION TIME: 1 HOUR
COOKING TIME: 45 MINUTES

Stuffed Eggplants
(see variation in
Stuffed Swiss Chard Leaves)

3 1/2 *pounds swiss chard*
1 *pound ground lamb or beef*
1 *cup bulgur large*
1 *small green pepper, seeded and finely chopped*
1 *large tomato, finely chopped*
2 *tablespoons butter (room temperature)*
2 *tablespoons tomato paste*

1/4 *teaspoon sugar*
1/2 *teaspoon allspice*
1/8 *teaspoon nutmeg*
1/4 *teaspoon cayenne or to taste*
   Salt and freshly ground pepper to taste
3/4 *cup lemon juice*
   Lemon and tomato wedges to serve

1. Wash and cut ribs off of leaves, set aside. Boil water in large saucepan, blanch swiss chard leaves just till softened. Drain and set aside to cool.

2. Place meat, bulgur, green pepper, tomato, butter, tomato paste, sugar, allspice, nutmeg, cayenne, salt and pepper, and 3 tablespoons lemon juice, in a bowl, mix well.

3. Swiss chard leaves should be about 4-inches, if necessary cut in half. Spread 10 leaves, shinny side down on work surface. Place about 1 tablespoon of filling on bottom end of each leaf and roll up neatly. Line bottom of a 4-quart saucepan with extra torn ribs and leaves (so stuffed rolls won't burn), place rolls, seam side down, in row around edge of saucepan. Place remaining rows in center. Invert a dish over rolls to keep in place while cooking.

4. Pour just enough water to cover rolls in saucepan. Bring to a boil over high-heat. Reduce to medium low and cook, covered for 35 minutes. Add remaining lemon juice, cook 10 minutes, or until bulgur is tender.

5. Set aside for 5 minutes. Then hold inverted plate in place over rolls, carefully tip pan and drain liquids into a saucer. Remove plate. Invert large serving dish over pan (as for cakes). Invert quickly, but carefully, holding tightly not to slip. Lift pan off slowly to keep rolls in place. Serve with lemon wedges or tomato wedges.

SERVES 6

VARIATION: Beet leaves can be substituted for swiss chard leaves, discard stems, or substitute with 10 small 4-inch long eggplants, 4 tomatoes, and 3 green peppers. Cut off stem end 1/2-inch and reserve. Hollow out inside, salt and pepper, set aside. Saute 1 medium chopped onion in 2 tablespoons oil till transparent. Mix filling, as above, add onion and stuff vegetables. Cook with just enough water to cover for about 45 minutes, add lemon juice cook 10 minutes more.

CHAPTER ELEVEN

Breads
and
Savory Pastries

There is nothing that compares to the smell and taste of freshly baked bread and savory pastries. In the Middle East and Iran there are hundreds of varieties not seen anywhere else. They are creative and endless. You can not go wrong with a savory pastry when you have a workable dough and a tasty filling or topping.

The Bakers bake three times a day, usually there is a line outside waiting to buy it fresh from the oven. The dough is shaped into twists, flat loaves, puffy pitas (Khoubis Arabi), rings and regular loaves. One of the more unusual ones is a pita dough mixed with tahini creating a sweet peanut buttery tasting bread. An old world hint, the dough is just right when it feels like an ear lobe.

Bread with Tahini

Bread With Tahini
TAHINOV HATZ

PREPARATION TIME: 30 MINUTES, (plus time for dough)

COOKING TIME: 15 MINUTES

*1 recipe, Pita Bread dough
(page 216) except omit salt*
*1 1/4 cups tahini (sesame seed
paste)*

1 1/4 cups sugar
*2 teaspoons cinnamon
(optional)*

1. Make dough and let rise. About 2 1/2 hours.

2. Divide into 3 parts. Roll each part separately into a 12-inch circle.

3. Spread 1/3 of tahine over entire surface of each circle, sprinkle with 1/3 of sugar and 1/3 of cinnamon. Roll up jelly-roll style. Preheat oven to 400° F.

4. Squeeze and stretch each piece gently to make a smooth (rope like) length of 3 1/2 feet long. Cut into 6-inch pieces, shape each piece into a pinwheel. Roll each pinwheel into 4-inch disk with rolling pin.

5. As soon as each baking sheet is filled, bake immediately in preheated oven for 12 to 15 minutes or until lightly golden. Cool completely. Store in airtight container or freeze.

MAKES 21 SWEETBREADS

An Armenian version of Boereg that can be served as finger food with cocktails or as an accompaniment to soup.

Meat Pastries
MISSOV KHUMOREGHEN (BOEREGS)

PREPARATION TIME: 30 MINUTES (plus pastry)
COOKING TIME: 15 MINUTES

2 tablespoons butter
1 medium onion, finely chopped
3/4 pound lean ground beef or lamb
3 tablespoons pine nuts
1/3 cup freshly chopped dill or 2 heaping tablespoons dried dill

1/4 teaspoon cinnamon
Salt and freshly ground pepper to taste
1 recipe, pastry for Spinach in Pastry (page 160)
1 egg yolk, lightly beaten with dash, salt, for glaze

1. Make pastry as recipe indicates, set aside. Line 2 baking sheets with aluminum foil and set aside.

2. Melt butter in skillet. Add onion and saute until transparent, stirring often. Add meat cook, until browned. Add pine nuts, dill, cinnamon, salt and pepper. Set aside to cool.

3. Preheat oven to 375° F. Divide pastry in half. Roll out separately on lightly floured surface to about 1/8-inch thickness. Cut into 3-inch rounds or squares. Place about 1 tablespoon meat mixture on lower half of each round. Fold pastry over to make half moon and seal edges firmly with fingers or with prongs of fork. Brush with glaze and place on prepared baking sheets.

4. Bake in preheated oven 15 minutes or until tops are golden. Cool slightly on baking sheets and serve warm. Freezes well.

MAKES ABOUT 30 PASTRIES

VARIATION: Ham and cheese filling: combine 2 slices cooked, shredded ham, 3/4 pound diced or grated cheese, 1 egg, lightly beaten, and 1/2 teaspoon dried mint.

Meat Pastries

A specialty of Lebanon and Syria. These delicious open face pies can be prepared in advance. Take care not to dry out when reheating.

Yogurt Meat Pies

SFEHA / LAHM-BIL-AJIN

PREPARATION TIME: 30 MINUTES (plus dough)
COOKING TIME: 12 TO 15 MINUTES

**1 recipe Pita Bread
Dough (page 216)**

TOPPING:

**1 pound beef ground
1 large onion, chopped
1/2 cup pine nuts
3/4 cup yogurt
Salt and freshly ground
pepper to taste
1 teaspoon allspice
1/4 teaspoon cinnamon or
nutmeg**

1. Make dough, let rise once, punch down and divide into 35 equal parts. Roll into 3 1/2-inch rounds. Combine all of filling ingredients together. Place 1 to 2 tablespoons of filling in center of each round, shape into opened faced pies by folding then pressing together each of four corners with finger tips (you should have pie with pointed edges on each corner). Or shape into triangles as in Spinach Triangles (page 218).

2. Preheat oven to 400° F. Place on baking sheet covered with foil and bake in preheated oven 400° F. for 12 to 15 minutes until bottoms are lightly golden and tops start to brown. To freeze pastries layer with wax paper in sturdy container.

MAKES ABOUT 35

A Lebanese pizza with a topping called zaatar, made of sesame seeds and dried herbs that are bound together with olive oil. Served for breakfast or as a snack throughout the day.

Sesame Seed Herb Pie
MANAICH

PREPARATION TIME: 30 MINUTES (plus dough)
COOKING TIME: 8 TO 10 MINUTES

1 Recipe Pita Bread dough (page 216)

TOPPING:

1/4 cup sumac*
2 tablespoons sesame seeds
2 to 3 tablespoons roasted powdered baby chick-peas

1 tablespoon thyme
1 tablespoon oregano
1/8 teaspoon cayenne
Salt and freshly ground pepper to taste
1/4 cup olive oil
Tomatoes, feta cheese, mint and parsley leaves to serve

1. Make dough as directed up to step 1 and 2.

2. Punch center of dough down. Rest 5 minutes. Divide into 4 equal parts. With floured hands shape each part into a ball and rest on a lightly floured surface for 10 minutes.

3. Roll each ball to a rectangular shape, about 12 x 8-inches, rounding off edges on both ends. Place on heavy baking sheets. Preheat oven to 400° F.

4. Mix sumac, sesame seeds, chick-peas, thyme, oregano, cayenne, salt and pepper in a bowl. Add olive oil and stir till thoroughly blended. Spread 1/4 of mixture evenly over each rectangle of dough up to 1/2-inch from edges.

5. Bake in preheated oven for about 8 minutes. Check bottom of pie, it should be a very light golden color. Do not dry out. Remove from baking sheets. Cool on racks slightly, cut into 4 parts and serve warm, with sliced tomato, cheese and mint or parsley leaves placed in center and roll up or fold over to eat like a sandwich. Store in plastic bags. Freezes well, wrapped in aluminum foil. Topping is also served as a dip with bread and olives.

MAKES 4 12 x 8 PIECES

VARIATION: Shape into round pies. Spread mixture on puff pastry, cut into small squares, bake till puffed and lightly golden or spread on ready crescent dough roll and bake as directed.

* Sumac is available in Middle Eastern store.

Sesame Seed Herb Pie

In Iran Barbari bread is very popular for breakfast. It is carried home, as in France with the Baguette, in a paper wrapped around the center of the loaf. It is also cut up and used for french toast. Try this bread served warm with a piece of cheese and a cup of freshly brewed tea or with a slice of watermelon.

Persian Bread
NON-E-BARBARI

PREPARATION TIME: 20 MINUTES (plus dough)
COOKING TIME: 20 TO 25 MINUTES

1 recipe Pita Bread Dough (page 216)

1 egg white, slightly beaten together
Sesame seeds or poppy seeds (optional)

1. Make pita bread dough through step 1 to 2.

2. Punch center of dough down. Rest 5 minutes. Divide dough into 2 to 3 parts depending on how large a baking sheet you have, let rest 15 minutes.

3. On a lightly floured work surface, roll each piece into a rectangular shape about 1/2-inch thick. Round off edges. Place on baking sheets. Let rise for 30 minutes.

4. Position rack in the middle of oven and preheat to 400° F.

5. Brush tops of loaves with egg white. Make 3 to 4 parallel grooves 1-inch apart by raking fingers over surface up to 1 1/2 inches from edge. Or by pressing one finger into top of bread to make a groove. Sprinkle with seeds, bake in preheated oven for 20 to 25 minutes. This will depend on your oven. Check bottom of loaf it should be lightly golden colored. Do not dry out.

Cut into 3-inch squares and always serve this bread warm. The best way to reheat is sprinkle with water, wrap in foil and heat in oven. Store cooled bread in plastic bags or freeze in aluminum foil, heat directly from freezer to preheated oven 400° F. for about 15 minutes or till hot.

MAKES 2 FLAT BREADS

VARIATION: Bread rings, divide dough into 2 parts. Shape each into a log. Divide each log into 4 parts. Roll and make each part into a ring. Seal ends. Brush with egg white and sprinkle with seeds. Bake as above till lightly golden.

SUGGESTIONS: To make a sandwich, slit a piece of warm bread, butter if desired. Fill with feta cheese (Panir Sefid) and watercress, or sliced tomatoes, cucumbers and fresh mint leaves.

Armenian Meat Pies

![butterfly]

Armenian Meat Pies
MISSAHATZ

PREPARATION TIME: 30 MINUTES (plus dough)
COOKING TIME: 5-8 MINUTES EACH

ere is a pastry also known as Lahmajoon (in Arabic, Lahm Bil Ajin) and is to the Middle East what pizza is to the Western world.

1 recipe Pita Bread Dough (page 216)
TOPPING:
1 pound ground lamb or beef
1 large green pepper finely chopped
1 (16 ounce) can plum tomatoes, crushed
1 (6 ounce) can tomato paste
4 cloves garlic, crushed
1 large onion, finely chopped
1/2 cup freshly chopped parsley
2 tablespoons butter, room temperature
1 teaspoon cayenne or to taste
1 teaspoon allspice
1 teaspoon salt or to taste
1/2 teaspoon freshly ground pepper or to taste
Lemon wedges to serve (optional)

1. Make bread dough. When dough has doubled punch down, divide into 30 equal parts. Set aside lightly covered for 20 minutes.

2. Mix all of ingredients together in bowl. Cover, set aside. Preheat oven to 450° F. On a lightly floured work surface roll each part of dough into a 6-inch circle. Place on baking sheets. Spread with topping up to 1/4-inch around edges. Bake in preheated oven for 5 to 8 minutes. Serve hot or room temperature. Sprinkle lemon juice over pie, roll up and enjoy as a sandwich. Fresh fruits of the season for dessert.

MAKES ABOUT 25 PIES

VARIATION: SYRIAN VERSION:
TOPPING:
1 pound ground lamb or beef
6 medium onions, finely chopped
1/3 to 1/2 cup pomegranate molasses
1/3 cup pine nuts
1 tablespoon tomato paste
1 tablespoon sugar
1 teaspoon salt or to taste
1/2 teaspoon freshly ground pepper or to taste
1/2 teaspoon allspice
1/8 teaspoon cinnamon
Mix together, continue as for Meat Pies

ARMENIAN CHEESEPIE:
1 Pound cheese sliced or diced such as: monterey Jack, mozzarella, or Halloum
Salt and white pepper to taste
1 tablespoon dried crushed mint
4 tablespoons cold butter, diced

Mix cheese, salt and pepper together, spread over rolled out dough sprinkle with mint and dot with butter. Bake for 10 minutes or till slightly golden and cheese is softened. Serve hot with tomato slices, olives, and fresh mint sprigs.

HINT: Meat pies are perfect for picnics. Try cutting meat pies into wedges serve with drinks, or make in a large jelly roll pan, cut into squares and serve.

NOTE: Cool Meat Pies, stack meat side facing each other in pairs. Cover and refrigerate for several days, or freeze layered with waxed paper, wrapped in foil. Thaw out, remove waxed paper, and heat in hot oven in pairs turning once or twice, do not dry out.

My cousin bakes these cocktail rings specially for me whenever I visit her in Montreal. I find the small size of these flavorful rings very attractive. Many of my friends ask for them as a special treat. This is an old Armenian recipe and is still made throughout the Middle East in one form or another.

Miniature Rings
KAHKE

PREPARATION TIME: 30 MINUTES (plus dough)
COOKING TIME: 20 TO 25 MINUTES

8 ounces butter, (room temperature)
1/4 cup corn oil
1 large egg
1/2 cup milk
3 cups unbleached all-purpose flour
1/2 teaspoon baking powder

2 tablespoons mahlab*
1 egg yolk, beaten with 1 tablespoon water for glaze
1 tablespoon Nigella seeds (black sesame seeds) or 1 1/2 tablespoons sesame seeds

1. In large bowl add butter, oil, egg, milk, flour, baking powder, and mahlab, mix thoroughly. Cover and chill 1 hour.

2. Preheat oven to 350° F. Cover 2 baking sheets with aluminum foil and set aside.

3. Divide mixture into 16 equal-size pieces. Dip hands in extra flour and roll each piece of dough into pencil thin strip, 20-inches long. Cut strip into 2-inch lengths and shape each piece into ring. Pinch ends together.

4. Place rings close together on prepared baking sheets. Brush with egg glaze, sprinkle with seeds.

5. Bake in preheated oven 20 minutes or until lightly golden. Cool on baking sheets on wire racks. Store in airtight container up to 1 month. Or freeze. Seeds can be mixed into dough before shaping.

MAKES 160 PIECES

* Mahlab is available in Middle Eastern food stores. It is the inner pit of a sour black cherry.

Miniature Rings

Pita Bread
KHOUBIS ARABI

PREPARATION TIME: 30 MINUTES (plus dough)
COOKING TIME: 6 TO 8 MINUTES

A very versatile dough that can be used for many different kinds of stuffed savory pastries, as well as bread.

1 (1/4 ounce) package dry yeast
1 1/2 cups warm water
1 tablespoon sugar
3/4 teaspoon salt

3 tablespoons vegetable oil or melted butter
4 1/2 cups unbleached all-purpose flour or 1 cup whole wheat flour plus 3 1/2 cups all-purpose flour

1. Mix yeast, 1/2 cup of warm water and 1 teaspoon of the sugar thoroughly. Proof for 10 minutes till foamy on top.

2. Fit workbowl of food processor with plastic blade. Add flour, salt, remainder of sugar . Turn on-off twice. Add yeast mixture. With motor running, pour water, oil, through feed tube in a steady stream, mixing until liquids are absorbed and dough forms a ball around blade. Remove, knead several times and shape into a ball with floured hands, place in a lightly oiled large glass or porcelain bowl. Turn once to coat top with oil.
Cover with a kitchen towel or plastic wrap, set aside, in a draft-free area and let rise to double about 2 hours.
If using electric mixer. Proof yeast as above. With regular hook, mix in bowl. Change to dough hook and knead for about 10 minutes or until smooth. Continue as above.

3. Positioning rack on lower third of oven. Preheat oven 500 ° F. Punch dough down. Rest 5 minutes. Divide into 6 to 8 pieces. Taking one piece at a time, flatten and bring sides folding over toward center (like wrapping a package) seal together all sides. Turn sealed side down. Place on lightly floured surface and cover with flour dusted plastic wrap, rest for 10 minutes. Roll each ball into a flat circle. Place on ungreased baking sheets, bake until puffy and slightly golden colored about 6 to 8 minutes. Cool slightly on racks. Store in plastic bag while still warm or bread tends to dry out.

8 ROUNDS

VARIATION: To make a thinner bread (Lavash) roll rounds as thin as possible. Prick with fork and bake till dry. Serve crisp or sprinkle with water and cover till softened.

HINT: Brush the tops of bread as soon as they come out of the oven with water. This was done to remove extra flour and give shine to the bread by the bakers in Lebanon. Make bread dough above and have it on hand in the refrigerator. Cover bowl with a large plate and place a heavy object on top of plate so dough will not rise and ooze out over bowl. Use for Pizza, Manaich (page 210).

Pita Bread

Lavash

A opened faced sandwich that makes an interesting lunch.

Yogurt Meat and Pickle Sandwich
MEESOV HATZ

PREPARATION TIME: 15 MINUTES
COOKING TIME: 15 MINUTES

*Double recipe of Yogurt
Garlic Sauce (page 260)
room temperature*
2 tablespoons butter

*1 pound lean ground lamb
or beef
Salt and freshly ground
pepper to taste*
4 medium pita breads
3/4 cup diced dill pickles

1. Make Yogurt Garlic Sauce. Set aside.

2. Melt butter in skillet over medium-heat. Add meat and brown. Stirring frequently. Drain excess fat from skillet. Salt and pepper to taste. Keep warm.

3. Warm bread. Split apart, cut into 4 parts each side.

4. Place on serving dish. Spread with yogurt sauce. Top with meat, and sprinkle pickles over surface. Serve immediately.

SERVES 4 TO 6

When I lived in Beirut, I recall buying these delectable savory pastries and eating quite a few at one sitting. Unfortunately, I have not been able to find ready-made Fatayer in America. As a result, I make my own in large batches and keep them on hand in the freezer.

Spinach Triangles

Spinach Triangles
FATAYER SABANEGH

PREPARATION TIME: 1 1/2 HOUR
COOKING TIME: 25 MINUTES

DOUGH:
- 3 cups unbleached all-purpose flour
- 1 tablespoon salt or to taste
- 3/4 cup lukewarm water
- 1/4 cup olive oil

FILLING:
- 2 large onions, chopped
- 1 tablespoon salt
- 1/2 teaspoon cayenne or to taste
- 2 pounds spinach, cooked, squeezed dry and chopped
- 1/2 cup pine nuts
- 3/4 to 1 cup lemon juice
- 1/3 cup olive oil (preferably virgin)
- 1 teaspoon paprika
- 1 teaspoon freshly ground pepper
- Olive oil for brushing

1. To make dough, place flour and salt in container of food processor fitted with plastic blade. Cover, pour through feed tube 3/4 cup lukewarm water and oil with motor running. Stop motor when dough forms a ball around blade. Transfer to bowl, cover with plastic wrap, set aside 1 hour.

2. To make filling, mix onions with salt and cayenne. Cover and set aside 1 hour.

3. Cover 2 large baking sheets with aluminum foil and set aside.

4. Place chopped spinach in large bowl. Add pine nuts, lemon juice, oil, paprika, and pepper, toss well.

5. Drain onions, squeeze dry to remove bitter juice. Add to spinach mixture and blend well. Taste, adjust seasoning, if necessary (when pastry is baked it will loose some flavor).

6. Divide dough in thirds and let rest 5 minutes. Roll out each piece on lightly floured surface to 1/8-inch thick, large round. Cut into 4-inch rounds with lightly floured cookie cutter. Preheat oven to 400° F. Place about 1 1/2 tablespoons spinach mixture on center of each round. Bring sides up over filling from 3 points to center. Pinch ends firmly together to seal and shape into triangle (be carefull not to let any juice run out).

7. Dip bottoms of pastries in olive oil. Place on prepared baking sheets, about 1-inch apart. Bake 1 sheet at a time, in preheated oven 25 minutes or until lightly golden. Cool on baking sheets. Serve at room temperature. To freeze, cool completely. Stack, in sturdy container with plastic wrap between layers.

VARIATION: To prepare in the traditional way, use Pita Bread dough (page 216). Roll, as above, making 3-inch rounds (because pita dough will puff up). Fatayers can also be made with filling for Meat Filled Pastries (page 207). Cook as recipe directs, cool, and fill as above.

MAKES 38 PASTRIES

HINT: Both filling and pita dough can be made a day ahead. When using pita dough, prepare through step 1. Punch dough down, cover and place heavy object over bowl so dough will not rise. Refrigerate until ready to use. Remove from refrigerator and bring dough back to room temperature.

Armenian Brioche
CHORAK

PREPARATION TIME: 20 MINUTES (plus dough)
COOKING TIME: 20 MINUTES

2 (1/4 ounce) packages dry yeast
1/2 cup warm water
1 1/4 cups plus 1 teaspoon sugar
7 cups unbleached all-purpose flour
8 tablespoons, unsalted butter, room temperature
4 jumbo or 5 large eggs

3 tablespoons vegetable shortening
4 tablespoons vegetable oil
2 tablespoons powdered mahlab*
3/4 cup warm milk
2 egg yolks, whisked together, for glaze
Sesame seeds or poppy seeds

The aromatic smell of bread baking with mahlab is just wonderful throughout the house. Try this sweet bread with butter, marmalade and a cup of freshly brewed tea for breakfast. Made traditionally for Easter and Christmas.

1. Mix yeast, water, 1 teaspoon sugar and 2 tablespoons of flour together till smooth. Proof, about 10 minutes, till foamy on top.

2. Beat eggs together in a large bowl. Add sugar, butter, shortening, 3 tablespoons of vegetable oil and mix. Add mahlab, yeast-mixture and alternate with flour and milk. Mix together and knead with a dough hook of an electric mixer, or by hand on a floured work surface till dough is smooth and elastic and does not stick to your hands. If needed add 1/2 cup more flour.

3. With remaining 1 tablespoon oil, grease a large non-aluminium bowl. Place dough in bowl and turn once to coat top with oil. Cover with kitchen towel or plastic wrap and let double (about 2 hours), punch down center, cover let rise again 1 1/2 hours then punch down and let rest 10 minutes.

4. Divide dough into 2 equal parts. On a lightly floured work surface divide each part into 20 pieces. Make round balls of dough and place on foil covered baking sheets, let stand 30 minutes.

5. Preheat oven to 350° F. Brush with egg yolks and sprinkle with seeds. Bake for about 15 to 20 minutes. Check bottoms, if golden it is probably done. Make a note of the length of time it took to bake till perfectly done and use as a guide for the remaining dough.

MAKES 40 PIECES

VARIATION: Raisins or chocolate chips can be added to dough before baking.

DATE NUT FILLING :
1 pound (16 ounce pitted chopped dates)
1 cup chopped walnuts

2 teaspoons cinnamon
1 teaspoon cloves
2 to 3 tablespoons honey

Mix filling together. Flatten out each piece of dough fill centers of each piece, pinch seams together and place on sheet, seam side down, bake as above.

HINT: Chorak can be baked, cooled, wrapped in foil and frozen. To reheat, simply pop wrapped frozen chorak into a preheated oven 400° F. for about 15 to 20 minutes.

NOTE: Mahlab is available in Middle Eastern food stores. It is the inner pit of a sour black cherry.

Armenian Brioche

F ried cheese pastries are a favorite throughout the Arab world. They are particularly good when served hot as finger food.

Fried Cheese Pastries
SAMBOUSIC

PREPARATION TIME: 30 MINUTES (plus dough)
COOKING TIME: ABOUT 1 MINUTE EACH

DOUGH:

1 1/2 *cups unbleached all-purpose flour*
1/2 *teaspoon salt*
2 *teaspoons vegetable oil*

FILLING:

3 *cups grated or finely diced cheeses: feta cheese, mozzarella, jarlsburg, or any firm or semi-soft cheese*
1 *teaspoon freshly chopped dill (optional)*
Vegetable oil for frying
Parsley sprigs to garnish

1. Place flour and salt in container of food processor fitted with plastic blade. Pour in 3/4 cup water and oil with motor running. Stop motor when dough forms ball around blade. Place in bowl, cover with plastic wrap, and set aside 1 hour.

2. Mix cheese with dill.

3. Divide dough into 4 equal-size parts. Divide each part into 6 equal-size pieces. Roll each piece in palms to form 24 balls.

4. Roll out each ball on lightly floured surface to 4-inch round.

5. Place 1 heaping tablespoon cheese filling on center of each round. Moisten edges of dough and fold pastry over. Pinch edges together to seal. Flute with pronges of fork.

6. Heat oil in deep fryer to 375° F. Fry pastries a few at a time, until lightly golden (do not overcook or cheese will ooze out). Drain on paper towels and serve hot, garnished with parsley sprigs. Although these taste best when served immediately, they can be reheated a few minutes in a 450° F. oven.

MAKES 24 PASTRIES

VARIATION: Substitute meat or vegetable filling for cheese. Brush pastries with vegetable oil. Bake on foil lined baking sheets in preheated 400° F. oven, 10 minutes, or until golden.

CHAPTER TWELVE

Desserts

The most popular dessert served is fruits of the season. They are picked after ripening on the tree or vine in the warm sun. The difference between these fruits and ones from your local supermarket is amazing. You should see the expression on the face of a Lebanese when asked to describe a peach from Bikfaya or grapes from the Bekka, pure pleasure.

The prepared sweets from these areas are world renowned. Baklava is the most well known but there are many others including a fruit compote called Khosaf consisting of dried fruits, pine nuts and flavored with honey and spice. Cakes and pastries are sometimes made from farina and nuts. Many of the desserts have an orange blossom or rose water flavored syrup poured over them.

In this chapter you will find unusual combinations of ingredients turned into remarkable looking and tasting delicacies. There is a shredded dough stuffed with chopped nuts or ricotta cheese that looks and tastes delightful.

White Cookies
GURABIA

PREPARATION TIME: 30 MINUTES
COOKING TIME: 20 MINUTES

3/4 cup (6 ounces) unsalted
   clarified butter
1/2 cup vegetable shortening
1 1/4 cups sugar

1 teaspoon rose water
2 1/4 cups flour
Pistachios or almonds for
   decorating

1. Mix butter, shortening, sugar, and rose water till fluffy, in electric mixer. Add flour, mix thoroughly.

2. Preheat oven 275° F. Divide dough into 40 equal parts. Roll one part at a time into a smooth rope. Make a circle with rope and pinch seams together, top with shelled pistachio or almond on seam and press into cookie dough slightly. Place on foil lined baking sheets.

3. Bake in preheated oven for 20 to 25 minutes. Cookies should dry out but not brown. Only lightly golden on bottoms. Cool on rack completely and store in air-tight container or freeze in a sturdy container.

MAKES 40

K nafa, the Arabic word for this dough (similar to uncooked shredded wheat), is the main ingredient of this scrumptous pastry. When buying the dough it will be found under the Greek name Kadaif. Baked to a deep golden color, spread with cheese, and served with rose and orange blossom flavored syrup. Simple and your guests will never forget it.

Shredded Pastry with Cheese
OSMANLYA

PREPARATION TIME: 10 MINUTES
COOKING TIME: 20 TO 30 MINUTES

SYRUP:

2 cups sugar
1 tablespoon lemon juice
1 teaspoon rose water
1 teaspoon orange blossom
    water
1 pound thin Kadaif pastry

1/2 pound unsalted butter
3 tablespoons vegetable
    shortening
2 pounds ricotta cheese,
    room temperature
    Finely chopped blanched
    pistachios and rose petal
    jam to garnish.

1. Bring 1 cup water and sugar in saucepan to boil, stir often to dissolve. Boil 10 minutes. Remove, add lemon juice, rose and orange blossom water, stir. Set aside.

2. Preheat oven to 400° F. Grease two 10-inch round cake pans.

3. Divide pastry into two equal parts. Pull threads apart and place in prepared pans. Press down with your palms to compact. Melt butter with shortening. Pour evenly over both pans.

4. Bake in preheated oven till golden (about 20 to 25 minutes). Switch position of pans once during baking time.

5. Remove one part to large serving dish with spatula (not upside-down). Pour 1/2 cup of prepared syrup over entire surface evenly. (Reserve 6 tablespoons cheese). Spread cheese evenly over pastry. Top by inverting second pastry over cheese (you should have top layer upside down). Pour 1/2 cup syrup evenly over top pastry. Place reserved 6 tablespoons cheese around top edge, top each with some pistachios and rose petal jam. Serve remaining syrup on the side to suit individual tastes. Use sharp knife and cut into squares or wedges. This can be reheated in a 375° F. oven, covered till warm.

SERVES 8 TO 10

HINT: Syrup and pastry can be made one day ahead. Heat syrup and assemble when ready to serve.

DESSERTS

Pastry with Walnut Filling
KNAFA BIL JOWS

PREPARATION TIME: 15 MINUTES
COOKING TIME: 45 MINUTES

3 cups coarsely chopped walnuts	4 cloves
3 cups plus 3 tablespoons sugar	2 inch cinamon stick
1/2 tablespoon cinnamon	1 tablespoon lemon juice
1 tablespoon honey	1 pound thin shredded pastry (Kataif)
	3/4 pound unsalted butter

1. Mix nuts, 3 tablespoons of sugar, and cinnamon. Set aside.

2. Pour 2 1/2 cups of water in medium-size saucepan. Add remainder of sugar, honey, cloves, and cinnamon stick. Boil for 10 minutes. Add lemon juice. Strain, set aside.

3. Preheat oven to 400° F. Melt butter in saucepan.

4. Divide pastry into two equal parts. Take one part, pull apart to loosen strands of pastry over a large dish of tray to catch strands (you will need two identical baking dishes 13 x 9-inch or 10-inch round). Place shredded pastry in ungreased dish. Spread nut mixture evenly over pastry. Repeat pulling apart strands of remaining pastry, place over nuts evenly.

5. Place a piece of wax paper over surface, press down firmly and evenly (with your palms or small pan) remove wax paper. Pour melted butter evenly over surface. Bake in preheated oven for 45 minutes or until golden.

6. Remove from oven. Carefully invert into identical size pan. If desired, return pastry to oven and cook about 10 minutes longer to give a golden color on the top. Place on rack. Pour cooled syrup over hot pastry. Cool. Cut into squares and serve. Cover loosely and keep at room temperature.

SERVES 12

VARIATION: Substitute 2 pounds ricotta cheese mixed with 3 tablespoons sugar and 1/4 teaspoon cinnamon for nut filling, eliminate inverting to second pan. Serve warm with a teaspoon of rose petal jam on each portion. Store covered in refrigerator. Reheat wrapped in foil.

The pastry used for this dessert is readily available in Greek stores or speciality food stores. It looks like uncooked shredded wheat. A syrup is poured over the baked pastry making it wickedly rich.

Pastry with Walnut Filling

Powdered Rice Pudding
MUGLI

PREPARATION TIME: 10 MINUTES
COOKING TIME: 30 MINUTES

        5 cups warm water
    1/2 cup rice powder
        1 tablespoon powdered
            caraway seed
        1 tablespoon cinnamon

        1 tablespoon powdered
            aniseed
        1 cup sugar
            Coconut flakes, almonds,
            pistachios or walnuts to
            serve.

This is traditionally served to guests on the occasion of a birth in the family. If it's a boy there is always more topping.

1. Mix 1 cup water and rice powder in bowl. Set aside.

2. Mix 1/2 cup water in measuring cup with spices. Set aside.

3. Heat remaining 3 1/2 cups water in a medium-size non-stick saucepan. Add rice, stir constantly with wooden spoon till thickened (about 20 minutes) over medium heat.

4. Add sugar, spice, and mix. Stir constantly for 5 minutes. Pour into individual bowls. Cool, and sprinkle with desired topping or a little of each and serve. Keeps for 1 week covered in refrigerator.

SERVES 6

DESSERTS

Phyllo with Walnuts
BAKLAVA

PREPARATION TIME: 30 MINUTES
COOKING TIME: 40 TO 45 MINUTES

SYRUP:

1 1/2 cups sugar
1 teaspoon lemon juice

3 cups chopped walnuts
1 tablespoon cinnamon
1/8 teaspoon cloves
1/8 teaspoon allspice
1/2 pound unsalted butter
1/2 cup vegetable shortening
1 pound phyllo dough

1. Bring 1 1/4 cups of sugar and 1 cup water to a boil, stir often to dissolve. Boil for 10 minutes. Stir in lemon juice. Set aside to cool.

2. Mix nuts, remaining 1/4 cup sugar, cinnamon, cloves, and allspice together in a bowl. Set aside.

3. Melt butter and shortening together. Brush bottom of a 14 x 10 x 1-inch baking dish with butter-mixture. Unfold phyllo leaves and spread flat on work surface. Cover with a damp kitchen towel. Remove one leaf, place on baking dish and brush with butter. Repeat nine more times.

4. Position rack in middle of oven. Preheat oven to 325° F. Spread half of nut mixture over phyllo leaves in dish. Add 10 more leaves, brushing after each layer with butter-mixture. Spread remainder of nuts evenly on top. Continue with remaining leaves butter each layer. Cut into about 2-inch diamonds or squares with a sharp knife. Pour remainder of butter over top.

5. Bake in preheated oven for 35 to 45 minutes. Turn oven off. Leave baklava inside for 10 minutes longer. Remove, place on rack, and pour cooled syrup evenly over entire top. Cool about 2 hours. Run a knife between lines to loosen and serve. Store loosely covered at room temperature.

SERVES 15

HINT: To make the cutting of Baklava easier, freeze for ten minutes.

T his is a staple in the celebration of the Persian New Year (No Rooz). A variation of the Middle Eastern baklava.

Baklava Persian Style
BAQLAVA

PREPARATION TIME: 15 MINUTES
COOKING TIME: 25 TO 35 MINUTES

SYRUP:

2 cups sugar
1/4 cup rose water

2 cups finely chopped almonds with skins
2 cups coarsely chopped almonds with skins

3 tablespoons powdered cardamom
1/2 pound unsalted butter
15 leaves phyllo pastry

1. Bring sugar and 1 cup water to a boil, stirring often to dissolve. Boil for 10 minutes. Remove from heat, stir in rose water. set aside to cool.

2. Position rack in middle of oven. Preheat oven to 350° F. Mix nuts and cardamom together. Set aside.

3. Brush bottom of a 14 x 10 x 1-inch baking dish with melted butter. Unfold phyllo leaves and spread flat on work surface. Cover with damp kitchen towel. Place 3 leaves in baking dish, buttering each layer. Spread 1 cup of nut-mixture evenly over surface. Repeat with 3 phyllo leaves, butter, and spread 1 cup nut mixture, untill all used up.

4. Cut into diamond shapes with a sharp knife (about 1-inch long). Pour remainder of butter if any over pastry letting it run into cuts.

5. Bake for 40 to 50 minutes or until golden.

6. Remove from oven and cool 5 minutes. Pour cool syrup over hot baklava. Leave to cool on rack for 2 hours. Run knife between lines to loosen and serve. Store loosely covered at room temperature.

SERVES 18 TO 20

VARIATION: Substitute pistachios for almonds, or make half almond filling and half pistachio. Spread half a side of each 3 leaves when layering and bake. When serving you will have two kinds of Baklava.

HINT: To make the cutting of Baklava easier, freeze for 10 minutes.

Baklava Persian Style

W hile the bride dressed for the wedding these cookies were traditionally served to her and her attendants.

Tasters for the Bride
LOUKMET EL AROUS

PREPARATION TIME: 25 MINUTES
COOKING TIME: 20 MINUTES

1 cup walnuts coarsely chopped
2 tablespoons sugar
2 tablespoons rose water
2 tablespoons orange blossom water

14 tablespoons unsalted butter, room temperature
1 egg yolk
1/2 cup super fine sugar
3 cups unbleached all-purpose flour
1/2 powdered sugar

1. Mix walnuts and 2 tablespoon sugar. Add rose and orange blossom water. Mix together and set aside.

2. In large bowl of electric mixer, mix butter, egg yolk, super fine sugar, and flour together. Dough will be like oat meal at this point. Do not worry, it will pull together when walnut-mixture is added. Stir in walnut-mixture. Blend thoroughly.

3. Position rack in middle of oven. Preheat oven to 350° F. Divide dough into 3 equal parts. Divide each part into 14 parts. Roll each between your palms to make a smooth round ball. Place on foil lined baking sheets. Bake for 20 to 25 minutes or just till lightly golden.

4. Remove and roll each ball in powdered sugar to coat. Cool completely on racks. To serve, place each cookie in mini paper muffin cup on an attractive dish. Keep in airtight container for 3 weeks or freeze.

MAKES 42 COOKIES

Birds Nest
GLORE BURMA

PREPARATION TIME: 30 MINUTES
COOKING TIME: 25 MINUTES

This Armenian sweet is a variation of Baklava. It is made with phyllo dough shaped in a round accordion that looks like a bird's nest. Stuffed with walnuts, pistachios, or almonds and served with Middle Eastern coffee (Soorj). Bird's nests are often included on an elaborate buffet dessert table on holidays.

SYRUP:
- 2 1/2 cups sugar
- 2 tablespoons honey
- 4 strips of lemon peel
- 1 -inch cinnamon stick
- 2 whole cloves
- 1 tablespoon lemon juice

NEST:
- 1 package (16 ounce) phyllo leaves
- 1/2 pound unsalted butter

FILLING
- 1 cup coarsely chopped walnuts, pistachios, or almonds
- 2 tablespoons sugar
- 1/4 teaspoon cinnamon

1. Lightly grease 2 baking sheets with butter. Set aside.

2. To make syrup, place 2 1/2 cups sugar, 1 1/2 cups water, honey, lemon peel, cinnamon stick, and cloves in saucepan. Boil 10 minutes. Strain, add lemon juice, set aside.

3. Unfold phyllo leaves, spread flat on work surface. Cut in half and cover with damp kitchen towel. Remove 1 cut phyllo leaf and brush with butter.

4. Place small dowel at narrow end of pastry and roll loosely to within 1/2-inch of end.

5. Hold side of rolled pastry in hand. Gently but firmly push pastry forward with other hand to create accordion effect. You should have a piece 4-inches long.

6. Push dowel out. Push unrolled end of pastry inward to make bottom of nest. Gently bring ends of accordion together around bottom of nest and pinch seam. Place on prepared baking sheet. Repeat with remainder of cut pastry leaves, placing nests close together on baking sheets.

7. Preheat oven to 350° F. To make filling, mix 2 tablespoons sugar, nuts, and cinnamon. Spoon about 1 1/2 teaspoons of filling in center of each nest. Bake, 1 sheet at a time, in preheated oven 15 minutes or until golden.

8. Place baking sheets on wire racks. Pour cooled syrup over hot pastries. Cool completely. Remove from baking sheets with wide spatula.

34 PASTRIES

VARIATION: This variation is called Burma because the shape is straight not round as above. Glore means round in Armenian. Follow Steps 1, 2, and 3. Double amount of filling, but finely chop nuts. Mix well. Sprinkle 1 heaping tablespoon of filling over each half phyllo leaf. Leave accordion straight. Bake as directed above. If desired, use less syrup. Cut Burma into 2-inch strips.

HINT: If using pistachio nut filling for birds nest, bake pastries unfilled. Remove from oven and fill. Pour syrup over and cool as directed above. This will retain bright green color of nuts.

This recipe was given to me by a dear family friend, and is the most delicious plain cake I have ever tasted. It never fails to impress the fussiest critic and I know them all.

Butter Cake
GARGANTAG

PREPARATION TIME: 20 MINUTES
COOKING TIME: 55 TO 50 MINUTES

1/2 *pound unsalted butter, room temperature*
2 *cups sugar*
3 *jumbo or 4 large eggs*
2 1/2 *cups unbleached all-purpose flour*
1 *tablespoon pure vanilla extract*

1 *tablespoon baking powder*
1 *cup milk*
Grated zest of large lemon
Powdered sugar (optional)

1. Grease and flour 10-inch round cake pan. Position rack in middle of oven. Preheat oven to 350° F.

2. In large bowl of electric mixer, mix butter and sugar to blend. Add eggs and vanilla. Beat till light yellow and fluffy. Mix in alternating flour and milk. Stir in lemon zest. Scrap bottom and sides of bowl, if necessary, mix again.

3. Pour mixture into prepared pan. Bake in preheated oven for about 55 minutes, or till tooth pick inserted in center comes out clean. Cool, 5 minutes in pan, then turn onto cake rack to cool completely. Sprinkle with powdered sugar.

SERVES 10 TO 12

VARIATION: Stir grated zest of two lemons into batter. Mix 2 tablespoons flour with 1 cup seedless raisins and 1 cup chopped nuts (walnuts, almonds or hazel) into cake batter before cooking. Continue as above, or substitute 1 cup orange juice for milk. Add 2 tablespoons grated orange rind, 1 cup candied fruit chopped and mixed with 1 tablespoon of flour to batter before cooking. Decrease flour by 1/4 cup. Add 1/4 cup cocoa, and 1 cup chocolate chips.

HINT: Put extra dusting of flour on bottom of pan to insure easy removal.

Butter Cake

Stuffed Dates
TAMAR MEHSHI

10 whole, pitted dates   1/4 cup powdered sugar
10 whole blanched almonds   (optional)
    or blanched pistachios

1. Stuff each date with an almond or pistachio.

2. Roll in powdered sugar.

3. Place in small paper cups.

VARIATION: Fill dates with almond paste. Place on small silver dish and serve with coffee or tea after dinner.

Farina Cheese Roll
HALAWA TIL JUBIN

PREPARATION TIME: 1 HOUR
COOKING TIME: 1 HOUR

A sinfully rich Middle Eastern sweet. A shell of cream of wheat and cheese, stuffed with a custard type filling and rose water flavored syrup poured over it. Practice makes perfect.

FILLING:

- 1 cup milk
- 1 cup heavy cream
- 4 tablespoons sugar
- 4 heaping tablespoons cornstarch
- 1 tablespoon rose water
- 1 tablespoon orange blossom water

SYRUP:

- 1 1/2 cup sugar
- 1 teaspoon lemon juice
- 1 teaspoon rose water
- 1 teaspoon orange blossom water

SHELL:

- 1 1/2 cups sugar
- 16 ounces, mozzarella cheese, grated
- 1 cup farina (regular cream of wheat)
- 1 tablespoon rose water
- 1 tablespoon orange blossom water
- Blanched chopped pistachios for garnish

1. To make filling: Pour half of milk, cream and sugar into a non-stick saucepan. Heat over medium. Mix remaining 1/2 cup milk with cornstarch and gradually pour into saucepan, stirring constantly in one direction for 5 minutes. Reduce to medium-low, stirring constantly for another 15 minutes, till sauce thickens. Cool, stir in rose and orange blossom water. Set aside.

2. To make syrup: Bring 2 cups water and sugar to a boil. Boil for 10 minutes. Cool slightly, stir in lemon juice, rose and orange blossom water. Set aside.

3. To make shell: Mix 1 1/2 cups water and sugar to dissolve over high-heat in a large non-stick saucepan. Reduce to medium, add cheese, stir to melt in one direction (about 5 minutes). Reduce to medium-low heat. Add farina stir in one direction till consistancy of dough and pulls away from sides of pan.

4. Pour 1/2 cup of syrup into a 13 x 9 x 2-inch dish. Set aside. Cut 4 pieces of aluminum foil 12 x 12-inch. Take one piece, place shinny side down on work surface. Spread 1 1/2 tablespoons of syrup over entire surface.

5. Take one-fourth of shell-mix, spread over surface of prepared piece of foil evenly. Spread one-fourth of filling over shell up to 1/2-inch of edges.

6. Roll slowly and tightly with fingers peeling off foil as you roll. Stop as you get to last roll at the edge of foil. pick roll up carefully and turn it into dish with syrup. Continue with remainder of shell and filling, roll and place in dish. Cover and refrigerate 2 days. Spoon syrup from dish over rolls several times during refrigeration. Serve chilled, cut pieces into 1 1/2-inch lenghts. Place on a platter sprinkle over or dip sides into pistachios, serve syrup separately, to be spooned onto portions.

MAKES 25 PIECES

Farina Cheese Roll

Farina with Cheese
BANEEROV HALVA

PREPARATION TIME: 20 MINUTES
COOKING TIME: 20 MINUTES

A perfect cold winter breakfast or dessert.

  1 1/2 *cups milk*
   3/4 *cup sugar*
     4 *tablespoons unsalted*
         butter

  1 1/4 *cups farina (regular cream*
         of wheat)
     1 *cup grated mozzarella*
         cheese or imported
         Halloum cheese.

1. Bring 1 cup water, milk, and sugar to a boil, stir to dissolve. Boil 10 minutes, Set aside.

2. Melt butter in a medium-size saucepan over medium-heat. Stir in cream of wheat, lightly brown, stirring constantly.

3. Pour sugar-milk syrup into saucepan, stirring constantly till mixture boils, and liquids are absorbed. Remove from heat. Rest several minutes.

4. Quickly stir in cheese. Place in serving platter and sprinkle with cinnamon. Serve immediately. This may be reheated in a non-stick pan, covered, over low heat stirring occasionally.

SERVES 6 TO 8

VARIATION: 1/2 cup roasted pine nuts may be sprinkled over halva. Cheese may be omitted, decorate with halved walnuts all around edge of platter.

Walnut Pastry
ENGOUYZOV GARGANTAG

PREPARATION TIME: 30 MINUTES
COOKING TIME: 45 TO 55 MINUTES

DOUGH:

- 3 1/3 cups unbleached all-purpose flour
- 2 teaspoons baking powder
- 1/2 pound unsalted butter, room temperature
- 1 1/2 cups sugar
- 4 large egg yolks
  Grated zest of one large lemon
- 2 teaspoons pure vanilla extract

TOPPING:

- 4 large egg whites
- 2 1/2 cups ground walnuts
- 2/3 cup sugar
- 4 tablespoons unsalted butter, room temperature
- 3 tablespoons plain dry bread crumbs
- 1 tablespoon almond extract
- 1 tablespoon baking powder
- 1 teaspoon grated lemon zest

1. Position rack in middle of oven, preheat oven to 350° F. Grease and flour a 13 x 9-inch pan.

2. Sift flour and baking powder together, set aside.

3. Mix by hand or electric mixer, the butter and sugar. Add egg yolks, zest, and vanilla, mix thoroughly. Add flour gradually with 1/2 cup water, blend well.

Walnut Pastry

4. Reserve 1/3 of dough. Pat remainder of dough into prepared pan, evenly and smoothly. Bake in preheated oven for 20 minutes.

5. Meanwhile beat egg whites in medium-size bowl till foamy. Add remaining ingredients and mix thoroughly. Spread topping evenly over surface of hot pastry.

6. Divide 1/3 reserved dough into 4 parts. Dip hands in flour and roll each part into a thin rope. Decorated top of cake in criss-cross pattern. Sprinkle dough with some sugar. Bake for 20 to 25 minutes. Cool, cut into squares and serve with whipped cream.

SERVES 12

Caramelized Bread Puddi.

This truly marvelous dessert is bread coated with caramelized sugar, then layered with cheese and cream, and topped with pistachios.

Caramelized Bread Pudding
ASHSARAYA

PREPARATION TIME: 20 MINUTES
COOKING TIME: 50 MINUTES

3 cups sugar
3 cups boiling water
9 -inch round unsliced Armenian, Greek or Italian bread (see note)
1/4 cup rose water
1/4 cup orange blossom water
1 1/2 tablespoons lemon juice

FILLING:

1 pound ricotta cheese
1 (8 ounce) container frozen cool whip, thawed
1/4 cup chopped pistachios, garnish

1. In a 3 or 4-quart non-stick saucepan, add sugar and caramelize over medium-heat for 15 minutes, reduce to low, shake pan often to distribute sugar to a deep golden color (not too brown or it will have a burned flavor). Shake pan, do not stir, this will take about 30 to 40 minutes in all.

2. Place saucepan in sink, pour boiling water into caramelized sugar in saucepan, careful not to splash. If the sugar does not completely dissolve return to heat until liquified, stirring occasionally with a wooden spoon. Set aside.

3. Remove crust from bread with a sharp knife. Cut horizontally in half, about 1 1/2-inches thick. Place each 9-inch bread round into a 11-inch round cake pan or if using Italian loaf bread, piece enough slices to fill a 9-inch round in pan.

4. Preheat oven to 350° F. Mix rose, orange blossom water and lemon juice into caramelized sugar. Pour evenly over both bread rounds. Press down pushing bread with back of a spoon to coat bread evenly and fill pan. Bake in preheated oven for 10 minutes. Remove and cool completely.

5. Mix ricotta cheese and cool whip together (Reserve 1/2 cup cheese mix). Invert one caramelized bread onto a large serving platter, top with cheese-mix and spread evenly up to 1/2-inch of edge. Invert second bread over cheese. Place spoonfuls of reserved cheese-mixture around edge and one in center, top with chopped pistachios. Serve or refrigerate several hours.

SERVES 12

HINT: Bread can be prepared one day in advance, stored at room temperature, and assembled when ready.

NOTE: Sometimes sold as "Galin Ekmak" meaning brides bread in Turkish at middle Eastern stores.

Date Filled Cookies
SAMBOSAK HULOW

PREPARATION TIME: 30 MINUTES (plus dough)

COOKING TIME: 30 MINUTES

DOUGH:
- 1/2 *pound unsalted butter, room temperature*
- 3 *tablespoons vegetable oil*
- 3 *tablespoons sugar*
- 3 *cups flour*
- 1 *teaspoon baking powder*
- 1/2 *cup warm water*

FILLING:
- 2 *pounds pitted and chopped dates*

- 1 *cup hot water*
- 3 *tablespoons sugar*
- 1 *tablespoon unsalted butter, room temperature*
- 2 *teaspoons sesame seeds*
- 1 *teaspoon cinnamon*
- 1/2 *teaspoon cloves*

GLAZE:
- 1 *egg, slightly beaten*

Date Filled Cookies

1. Mix butter, oil, and sugar together using an electric mixer or by hand. Add flour, baking powder, and water. Mix until dough is smooth. Cover with plastic wrap, rest 30 minutes.

2. Place dates in bowl. Add remainder of ingredients, and mix very well, set aside.

3. Divide dough in two equal parts. On a lightly floured work surface roll out dough to a circle about 1/8-inch thick. Cut into 2-inch rounds with cookie cutter. Place 1 tablespoon filling in center of each round. Turn pastry over to make half moon shape. Press edges to seal. Brush with egg wash.

4. Preheat oven to 350° F. Place cookies on foil lined baking sheets, and bake till lightly golden (about 15 to 20 minutes). Remove from sheets and cool on racks. Store in airtight jar, or freeze, or divide dough in 3 parts. Roll each part into a rectangle and fill with 1/3 of filling. Fold dough over and seal ends well. Place on foil lined baking sheets seam side down. Bake for about 25 to 30 minutes. Cool slightly on sheet. Remove to rack. Cool completely. With very sharp knife, cut into diagonal pieces, 1 1/2-inches long. Sprinkle with powdered sugar and serve.

MAKES 30 TO 32

Walnut Cake

Walnut Cake
ENGOUYZOV GARGANTAG

PREPARATION TIME: 15 MINUTES
COOKING TIME: 45 MINUTES

6 *large eggs, room temperature, separated*	1 1/2 *teaspoons each: nutmeg, cardamon*
1 *cup sugar*	1 1/2 *cups ground walnuts*
1/2 *cup flour*	

1. Grease and flour 9-inch spring form pan. Preheat oven to 350° F.

2. Beat egg yolks and sugar until light in color. Add flour and spices, mix together, add walnuts.

3. Beat egg whites until stiff but not dry and fold into mix.

4. Transfer into prepared pan, bake for 40 to 45 minutes. Cool on rack. Serve with whipped cream and berries or dust with confectioners sugar and serve with tea. Keeps covered for 1 week, or freeze, wrapped in foil.

SERVES 8 TO 10

Armenian Sweetbread
NAZOUK

PREPARATION TIME: 30 MINUTES (plus dough)
COOKING TIME: 15 TO 20 MINUTES

>   1 (1/4 ounce) package dry
>   yeast
> 1/4 cup warm water
> 1/2 pound butter, room
>   temperature
> 2 3/4 cups sugar
>   2 eggs
>   1 teaspoon nutmeg
>   8 cups unbleached all-
>   purpose flour

GLAZE:

> 1/4 teaspoon saffron threads
>   steeped in 1 tablespoon
>   hot water
>   2 egg yolks

1. Mix yeast and water. Proof for about 10 minutes till foamy.

2. In bowl or electric mixer, beat together butter and sugar. Add eggs, nutmeg, yeast then flour. Knead until smooth, about 10 minutes. Cover and let rest for 6 hours or overnight. This dough will not rise like regular bread doughs because of the amount of sugar.

3. Divide dough into 8 equal parts. Roll each part into 7-inch round. Place on lightly greased baking sheets. Pinch edges to give fluted effect. Prick surface with pronges of a fork. Rest 1 hour.

4. Preheat oven 350° F. Mix saffron with slightly beaten yolks, and brush over pastries. After brushing with glaze, make decorative pattern with prongs of a fork and bake.

5. Bake in preheated oven 15 to 20 minutes. Keeps well, tightly covered in foil for 1 month or freeze. Can also be made into 24 smaller pastries.

MAKES 8 SEVEN-INCH ROUNDS

Armenian Sweetbread

Farina Diamonds

A Lebanese recipe to tempt your sweet tooth. Egyptians add eggs and call it Basbousa.

Farina Diamonds
NAMURA

PREPARATION TIME: 15 MINUTES (plus overnight)
COOKING TIME: 1 HOUR

SYRUP:
3 cups sugar
2 tablespoons lemon juice

3 cups farina (regular cream of wheat)
1 cup sugar
1 cup plain yogurt
4 tablespoons unsalted butter, melted and slightly cooled

3 tablespoons orange blossom water
1 tablespoon rose water
2 teaspoons baking powder
3 tablespoons tahini (sesame seed paste)
Pine nuts

1. Heat 3 cups of sugar and 1 1/2 cups water to boiling, stir often to dissolve. Boil 10 minutes. Remove, add lemon juice. Set aside to cool. Cover.

2. In a large mixing bowl. Mix cream of wheat, sugar, yogurt, butter, orange and rose water, and baking powder together. Grease 11-inch round or 13 x 9-inch pan with tahini. Spread mixture into pan and smooth out evenly. Cover with foil and refrigerate overnight.

3. Preheat oven to 350° F. Cut refrigerated mixture into diamond shapes or squares. Place one pine nut in center of each piece (Press well into mixture or when syrup is poured over it they will float off).

4. Bake in preheated oven for about 45 minutes or until golden colored. Remove to rack. Pour cool syrup over hot Namura and let stand to cool completely. Recut and remove to serving dish. Serve room temperature or chilled. Keeps for 10 days covered in refrigerator.

SERVES 18 TO 20

Dried Fruit Compote
KHOSHAF

PREPARATION TIME: 10 MINUTES
COOKING TIME: 25 MINUTES

1/2 cup sugar or honey
1/2 cup dried apricots
1/2 cup dried pitted prunes
1/2 cup seedless raisins, golden or dark or a mix of both

2 -inch cinnamon stick
2 tablespoons pine nuts
2 tablespoons skinned almonds
1 teaspoons lemon juice

1. Bring 3 cups water, and sugar or honey to a boil in medium-size saucepan, stirring often. Add remaining ingredients. Stir, bring back to a boil. Reduce, cover, and simmer for 15 minutes. Cool.

2. Transfer to glass bowl. Cover and refrigerate. Serve chilled or room temperature.

SERVES 4

SUGGESTIONS: Omit nuts while cooking. Refrigerate nuts in a bowl of water. Drain and spoon over center of compote when ready to serve. Spoon into large bowl for buffets with small bowls surrounding it, or in individual bowls with a crisp cookie.

A n Armenian stewed dish served mostly in winter when fresh fruits were not available. The flavor improves if made a day ahead.

Armenian Holiday Pudding
ANOUSHABOUR

PREPARATION TIME: 10 MINUTES
COOKING TIME: 1 1/2 TO 2 HOURS

1 cup skinless whole grain wheat
1 cup dried apricots, coarsely chopped
1 cup seedless golden raisins
3/4 to 1 cup sugar

2 tablespoons rose water
1 cup blanched almonds
1/4 cup coarsely chopped walnuts
Cinnamon, blanched walnuts and almonds for garnish

1. Wash and soak wheat grains in 4 cups cold water, covered with plastic wrap overnight.

2. Pour wheat with liquids into a heavy non-stick saucepan and cook over low-heat stirring often for 1 1/2 to 2 hours, or till soft. Cooking time will vary depending on freshness of wheat. If needed add some boiling water to pot and gently stir to mix (mixture tends to stick), should be a consistancy of porridge.

3. Add apricots, raisins and stir. Cook for 20 minutes stirring gently till soft.

4. Add sugar, mix, taste. Adjust. Add rose water, stir in with almonds and walnuts. Transfer to serving bowl and decorate with blanched nuts then sprinkle with cinnamon. Serve warm, chilled or room temperature.

SERVES 10 TO 12

A noushabour translated means sweet soup.

Dried Fruit Compote

S quares of this cake are sold by vendors on street corners throughout the Middle East.

Lebanese Peasant Cake
SEFFUF

PREPARATION TIME: 10 MINUTES
COOKING TIME: 35 TO 40 MINUTES

12 tablespoons unsalted butter, room temperature	2 tablespoons orange blossom water
1 1/4 cups sugar	1 tablespoon powdered aniseed
3 1/2 cups unbleached all-purpose flour	1 teaspoon baking powder
1/2 cup warm water	1/2 to 3/4 teaspoon turmeric
1/4 cup vegetable oil	1 cup hot water
2 tablespoons rose water	Whole blanched almonds (optional)

1. Generously grease and flour 11-inch round or 13 x 9-inch pan. Set aside. Position rack in middle of oven. Preheat oven to 350° F.

2. In bowl of electric mixer, mix butter and sugar. Add flour, 1/2 cup water, oil, rose and orange blossom water, aniseed, baking powder, and turmeric, mix well (batter will be quite thick).

3. Transfer into prepared pan and spread evenly with spatula. Dip knife into 1 cup hot water frequently to prevent sticking and cut into squares, press a whole almond in center of each square.

4. Bake in preheated oven for 35 to 40 minutes or till light golden. Cool in pan on rack. Serve with tea, coffee or lemonade.

24 PIECES

Sweet Rings
KAHKE

PREPARATION TIME: 30 MINUTES
COOKING TIME: 25 MINUTES

1/2 cup vegetable oil
8 tablespoons unsalted butter, room temperature
1 cup confectioners sugar
3 1/2 cups unbleached all-purpose flour

1 1/2 tablespoons aniseeds
1 tablespoon powdered aniseed
1/2 cup milk
1 egg, slightly beaten
Sesame seeds

1. Mix vegetable oil, butter and sugar. Add flour, aniseeds, powdered aniseed, and milk.

2. Preheat oven 350° F. Divide dough into 30 parts. Roll each separately into a smooth cylinder 5-inches long. Then make ring or circle pinch ends together.

3. Brush with egg. Dip egg brushed tops into sesame seeds to coat. Place on foil lined baking sheets. Bake in preheated oven for about 20 minutes or lightly golden on bottom. Cool on racks completely, store in air tight container. Keeps for 1 month or freeze.

MAKES 30 RINGS

Persian Rice Pudding
SHIR BERENJI

PREPARATION TIME: 5 MINUTES
COOKING TIME: 1 HOUR AND 20 MINUTES

1/3 cup rice, rinsed
3 cups milk
1/4 to 1/3 cup sugar
2 teaspoons rose water

1/2 teaspoon ground cardamom
Cinnamon or honey to serve

1. In a non-stick heavy medium-size saucepan bring 1 1/2 cups water and rice to a boil. Reduce to medium-low, cook till almost all of liquid is absorbed (about 20 minutes), stirring occasionally.

2. Add milk and sugar. Stirring occasionally, cook for about 45 minutes or till thick and almost all of milk is absorbed. Stir skin when forms back into pudding. Add rose water and cardamom, mix well.

3. Pour into individual bowls. Serve warm of chilled. Sprinkle with cinnamon or honey.

SERVES 4 TO 6

VARIATION: Add 1/3 cup raisins just before pouring into bowls. Substitute vanilla for rose water, and sprinkle with nutmeg instead of cinnamon, 1/4 teaspoon saffron may be added with milk and sugar.

This dough is wonderful to work with.

Sweet Rings

Stuffed Easter Pastries
MA'MOUL

PREPARATION TIME: 30 MINUTES (plus dough)
COOKING TIME: 20 TO 25 MINUTES

In the Lebanese mountain resort of Babdaat where we would pass our summers from the oppressive heat of Beirut, I discovered a small pastry shop making this traditional Easter Pastry. It was owned by a young man whose expert bakers in the back room consisted of his grandmother, mother and aunts. This recipe after much experimentation is the closest I could get to the texture and taste.

SHELL:

4 2/3 cups farina (regular cream
       of wheat)
3/4 cup sugar
1/2 tablespoon baking soda
1/2 pound unsalted butter,
     melted
1/4 cup rose water
1/4 cup orange blossom water
  1 cup hot milk

STUFFING:

2 1/4 cups coarsely chopped
       walnuts, or almonds
1/2 cup sugar
  1 teaspoon cinnamon
  3 to 4 tablespoons orange
     blossom water

TOPPING:

Powdered sugar

1. Mix farina, sugar, and soda to blend. Add butter, then milk, blend thoroughly. Sprinkled with rose and orange water, mix. Cover with plastic wrap, leave for 2 to 4 hours to rest.

2. Mix stuffing together and set aside. Preheat oven to 400° F.

3. Divide dough into 32 pieces. Flatten each piece into a circle and place 1 tablespoon filling in center and bring up sides to cover.

4. Place filled pastries in decorative wooden mold (see note) press down and smooth surface, tap mold on counter to remove. Place flat side of pastry on foil lined baking sheets. If mold is unavailable shape into a ball, and flatten slightly, press fork pronges criss-cross on top to make a pattern.

5. Bake in preheated oven for 20 minutes.

6. Dip immediately the bottoms in powdered sugar, and sprinkle very generously over entire tops. Cool on racks.

MAKES 32 PASTRIES

VARIATION: Use date filling for Sambusik (page 242) or pistachio filling for Karabich (page 254). Keeps in tins for up to 1 month or freeze. Sprinkle extra confectioners sugar over pastries after thawed out.

NOTE: Wooden molds are available in Middle Eastern speciality shops, and are called Tabi.

Pistachio Filled Pastries
KARABICH

PREPARATION TIME: 30 MINUTES (plus dough)

COOKING TIME: 20 MINUTES

1/2 recipe Stuffed Easter
Pastry Dough (page 252)

FILLING:

1 *cup finely ground*
pistachio nuts
1/4 *cup sugar*
2 *tablespoons orange*
blossom water

SAUCE:

2 *cups marshmallow fluff*
2 *teaspoons rose water*

Pistachio Filled Pastries

1. Make pastry dough and rest as in recipe. Divide dough into 35 equal parts.

2. Mix filling together set aside.

3. Preheat oven to 325° F. Flatten each part of dough in batches of 5 over work surface. Place 1 tablespoon filling in center of each and bring up sides to seal making an oval shaped pastry. Seal all cracks, making surface smooth. Place on foil lined baking sheet.

4. Bake in preheated oven for 20 minutes. Remove. Run pastries under broiler for golden colored tops if desired. Cool on racks.

5. Mix sauce together, serve in separate bowl. Spread over pastries as needed, or spoon 1 tablespoon sauce on dessert plate and place one pastry on top. Keep pastries in airtight container or freeze.

MAKES 35

Coconut Cake with Syrup
HUNTKENGOUYZOV GARGANTAG

PREPARATION TIME: 15 MINUTES
COOKING TIME: 50 TO 60 MINUTES

2 1/4 cups sugar
3 tablespoons pure vanilla extract
2 cups unbleached all-purpose flour
1 tablespoon baking powder
1/2 pound unsalted butter, room temperature
4 large eggs
1 cup milk
1 1/2 cups grated coconut

1. Bring 1/4 cup sugar and 1/2 cup water to boil, stir to dissolve. Boil 8 minutes. Add 2 tablespoons vanilla. Set aside to cool.

2. Position rack in middle of oven. Preheat to 350° F. Grease and generously flour a 10-inch round cake pan. Sift dry ingredients together.

3. In large bowl of electric mixer, beat butter and remainder of sugar together. Add eggs and remainder of vanilla, beat till light and fluffy. Mix in alternating flour and milk. Scrape bottom and sides of bowl, if necessary, mix again. Add 1 1/4 cup coconut, stir together. Bake for about 55 to 60 minutes.

4. Cool 5 minutes. Invert cake onto serving platter, place on rack. Spoon cooled syrup over hot cake evenly over surface. Cool completely. Dust with powdered sugar and sprinkle with remaining 1/4 cup coconut. Keeps well for 1 week or freeze.

SERVES 12

Coconut Cake with Syrup

Almonds or Walnuts in Water

**1 cup good quality almonds
or walnuts with skins**

1. Rinse nuts in glass bowl till water runs clear.

2. Add warm water to cover and refrigerate for 1 to 2 days.

3. Pop off skins and serve, or let guests peel them. Sprinkle with salt if desired. Keeps for 1 week in refrigerator.

Almonds or Walnuts in Water

In Teheran vendors, of freshly picked and shelled almonds and walnuts, would sit on small stools with kerosene lanterns all night selling their wares in cones of paper to passersby. The nuts were sold from large tins full of water and their taste was moist and crunchy. When in season they are sold throughout the Middle East. This method almost achieves the same taste.

Red Pepper Paste
GARMEER BUGHBEGHI PESDEGH

PREPARATION TIME: 10 MINUTES
COOKING TIME: 3 HOURS

**4 to 5 pounds sweet fresh
red pepper
Boiling water
1 tablespoon salt or to
taste**

**Juice of 2 lemons (about
1/2 cup)
3 tablespoons olive oil
1/8 teaspoon sour salt (citric
acid)**

Make this when red peppers are in season. Add a generous spoonful to soups and stews for taste and bright color. Also used in Mouhamara (page 14).

1. Preheat oven to 350° F. Wash peppers, seed and remove white membranes, cut into 1-inch pieces.

2. Place in a medium-size, non-stick saucepan, cover with 1-inch boiling water. Cover, cook 5 minutes over high-heat. Transfer to blender or food processor and puree completely. Pour into a baking dish. Cook in preheated oven. Scraping sides and stirring often for 2 1/2 to 3 hours or till it is the consistency of tomato paste.

3. Add salt, lemon juice, olive oil, and sour salt mix. Store in small glass jars, covered with a thin layer of olive oil over paste and replenish each time it is used. Once opened refregerate. For hot pepper paste add 2 chili peppers, slit and seeded to every 1 pound of red pepper used.
MAKES ABOUT 3 CUPS

This sauce is used as mayonnaise for Middle Eastern sandwiches like Shawerma (page 126), or Falafel (page 32), and also with fish. Use sparingly.

Sesame Seed Paste with Lemon Sauce
TARATOR

PREPARATION TIME: 10 MINUTES

3/4 *cup tahini*
1/2 *cup lemon juice*
1 *to 2 cloves garlic crushed*

Salt to taste
4 *tablespoons water*
(optional)

1. Mix tahini in its container to incorporate.

2. Pour tahini in a bowl, mix with lemon juice, salt, and garlic. Add water if sauce is too thick.

MAKES ABOUT 1 CUP

VARIATION: Add 1/4 cup finely chopped parsley, or a handful of crushed pine nuts, or hazelnuts and blend thoroughly.

Coffee is made in a long-handled pot called raqwi in Arabic. Traditionally made of brass and the inside lined with tin. It is served anytime and always accompanied with a glass of iced water. During a period of mourning the sugar is eliminated. Sometimes a small handmade silver container filled with rose water is passed on a tray for sprinkling into coffee, if desired. For a more exotic flavor add a pinch of ground cardamom. The ritual of coffee drinking is sometimes ended by the reading of the cup. This is usually done by an older woman who has learned the signs of the cup through the years. The reading can be very subtle and messages good or bad are revealed.

Middle Eastern Coffee
SOURJ, AKWEH, GAVEY

PREPARATION TIME: 3 MINUTES
COOKING TIME: 5 MINUTES

2 *demitasse cups water*
2 *teaspoons sugar or to taste*
2 *heaping teaspoons dark roasted pulverized coffee*

1. Mix water and sugar in a raqwi or small pot, stir to dissolve and bring to a boil.

2. Add coffee, stir very well, bring to a boil. Remove from heat, continue 3 times bringing back to a boil each time. Careful not to let coffee boil over.

3. Pour coffee into demitasses and distribute foamy topping equally. Do not drink the coffee grounds that settle to the bottom.

VARIATION: White coffee: Which is really not coffee at all.
This is used as a digestive and also if you are avoiding caffeine. Here are some guide lines. You may adjust to individual tastes. Few drops orange blossom water, 1/4 teaspoon sugar and 1 demitasse cup water. Boil water with sugar to dissolve. Add orange blossom water, mix and pour into cups. Rose water can be substituted for orange blossom water.

Yogurt Drink
AYRAN / DOOGH / TAN

PREPARATION TIME: 5 MINUTES

1 cup plain yogurt
1 cup water
Salt to tast

A wonderful beverage that takes some getting used to. Armenians call it Tan, Lebanese call it Ayran, and Iranians call a slightly different version Doogh.

Mix yogurt, water and salt in a pitcher of blender. Chill and serve with meals or in between.

VARIATION: Doogh is made by adding a little dried crushed mint and seltzer instead of water, mix. To have a lighter drink add more water or seltzer.

Parsley Butter Sauce
AZADKEGHI TAHTSAN

PREPARATION TIME: 5 MINUTES
COOKING TIME: 5 MINUTES

8 tablespoons butter
1 to 2 cloves garlic, crushed
1/3 cup freshly chopped flat
leafed parsley

1 teaspoon lemon juice
Salt and freshly ground
pepper to taste

1. Melt butter in small saucepan. Add garlic cook 1 minute. Add parsley, lemon juice, salt and pepper.

2. Mix, heat thoroughly, and serve immediately.

MAKES ABOUT 1 CUP

This sauce is used to give dishes more character.

For garlic lovers only! Delicious spread on bread with hot roasted chicken as a sandwich.

Potato Garlic Sauce
SALSAT EL TOUM

PREPARATION TIME: 10 MINUTES
COOKING TIME: 15 TO 20 MINUTES

1 large potato peeled and
cubed
3 to 5 medium cloves garlic,
peeled and hard tip cut
off
1/4 cup mayonnaise

1/4 cup vegetable oil (corn or
safflower)
Salt to taste
Dash sour salt (citric
acid)

1. Place potato in saucepan, cover with water and boil till tender. Drain, set aside.

2. With motor of food processor running, drop garlic one at a time through feed tube. Stop, remove top.

3. Add potato, mayonnaise, salt, sour salt, and turn on-off several times, just till smooth. With motor running, pour oil through feed tube just to blend. Serve a tablespoon or more of sauce to be spread over a piece of roast or barbecued chicken, and a tossed green salad. When I have a nice red skinned new potato, I don't peel it. The sauce will have pretty little specks of red.

MAKES ABOUT 1 CUP

A sauce that is used frequently as a topping for dolmas, fried vegetables, and some stews.

Yogurt Garlic Sauce
MADZOUNOV SUKHDOR

PREPARATION TIME: 5 MINUTES

     2 small cloves garlic, or to
        taste
        Salt to taste
 1 1/2 cups plain yogurt

1. Crush garlic with a little salt (about 1/4 teaspoon) in a mortar and pestle.

2. Mix with yogurt in a bowl. Serve or chill till ready, up to 2 days.

MAKES 1 1/2 CUPS

Index

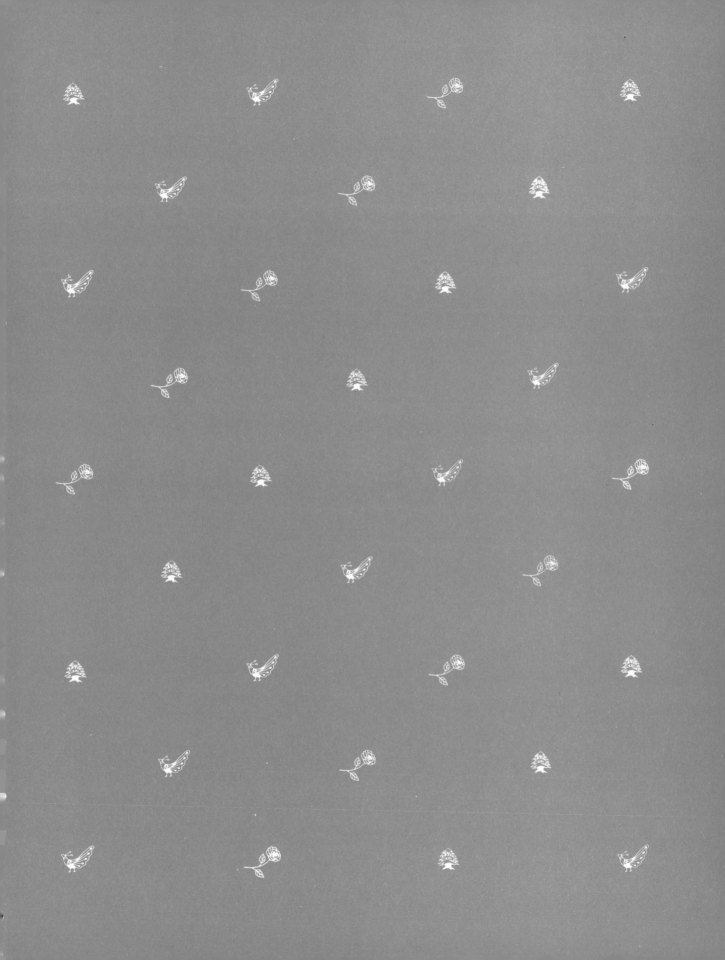